ROSAMOND:

OR, A

NARRATIVE

OF THE

CAPTIVITY AND SUFFERINGS

OF AN

AMERICAN FEMALE

UNDER THE POPISH PRIESTS, IN THE ISLAND OF CUBA,

WITH A FULL DISCLOSURE OF

THEIR MANNERS AND CUSTOMS,

WRITTEN BY HERSELF.

EMBELLISHED WITH NUMEROUS COPPERPLATE ENGRAVINGS.

WITH AN

INTRODUCTION AND NOTES,

BY SAMUEL B. SMITH,

LATE A PRIEST IN THE CHURCH OF ROME.

Read, blush, and weep;—the picture strikes with fear;—
The mask aside, what monsters now appear!—
And must the tale be told,—my bosom cries;—and ?—
It must :—for danger urges his command.
We blush to tell ;—but let the priest be warn'd, ...
Pop'ry expos'd, and our dear country sav'd.

NEW YORK:
LEAVITT, LORD, & CO.,
BOSTON: CROCKER & BREWSTER.
1836.

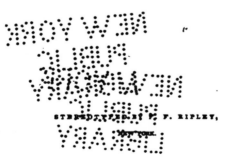

STEREOTYPED BY F. RIPLEY,
New York.

ROSAMOND CULPERTSON.

INTRODUCTION.

In the Narrative which is now to be laid before the public, the world will have a fair specimen of Popery reduced to practice. A sure criterion by which to judge of a religion, is to consider it in all its relations, and especially, in the influence it has over the moral conduct of those who live under its control.

It is vain to tell us, pointing to a book, "there is our religion; those are our principles; that is our doctrine." Religion is not an abstract good; not a mere painting to please the eye; neither does the essence of religion consist in ceremony, nor in a firm belief in creeds and doctrines. All this is, as it were, the mere bark; the substance and the pith lie in the heart. It is not through the bark that the sap is conveyed to the leaves, the flowers, and the fruit, but through the veins. Nothing is plainer, or more simple, than the Christian religion. It may be compared to a tree perpetually verdant, whose blossoms diffuse their fragrance all around, whose expansive branches extend a reviving shade to the wandering traveler, parched and panting with the heat of the day, and whose mellow fruit hangs in profusion, at once to assuage his thirst, and to nourish his body.

Every tree has bark, and the bark of religion is its exterior form. Every soul has a body, and it is through the senses of this body that impressions are conveyed upon the mind. Being, therefore, creatures of a compound nature, religion, although simple in its essence, is, to a certain degree, compounded for our use. It is necessary, therefore, that there should be some exterior form of worship, some bark around the trunk of this wide-spreading tree, to keep the sap to its direction, and to prevent its being dissipated by the winds. But it is not necessary that this bark should be so protuberant and complicated, as to afford shelter and concealment to vermin and corruption; much less necessary, that it should be overloaded with moss and fungus.

The religion of Christ has its forms, but like its divine original, these forms are comely, simple, necessary, few. In the whole system of the Christian dispensation, as it is delivered to us in the New Testament of our Lord and Saviour, the forms, or the exterior appendages of religion, are so simple and so few, that we are almost at a loss to point them out. They are all reduceable to these: the formation of a visible Church, who are commanded to worship the Father "*in spirit and in truth;*" the Sacraments of Baptism, and the Lord's Supper, and the preaching of the Gospel.

It cannot be supposed that our Lord and Saviour Jesus Christ, in instituting his Church, introduced any thing unnecessary ; nor can we think that any thing essentially necessary relative to the government, or to the prosperity of that Church, was forgotten, overlooked, or neglected by him.

In respect to his divine mission, Jesus Christ came to offer unto God his Father, a ransom for a lost world, to preach the glad tidings of salvation, and to point out the path which leads to glory. "*I have finished the work*," (said the Saviour,) *which thou gavest me to do.*" John xvii. 4. How, or where are we to find what were the works which Christ came to do, and which he tells us he has finished, except in his own *Word*, speaking of which the Psalmist exclaims : "*Thy Word is a lamp to my feet, and a light to my path.*" Ps. cxix. 105.

Since Christ came to save sinners, and since salvation was as attainable in the days when Christ dwelt visibly upon earth, as it is now, or ever, has been since his advent, all that was necessary for the salvation of man must have been accomplished by our Lord before he left the world. "*I have finished the work*," says he. The work was the salvation of sinners ;—"*The Son of Man is come,*" (said the Saviour,) "*to seek and to save that which was lost.*" Luke xix. 10.

Sinners cannot be saved without faith, for "*without faith,*" (says the Scripture,) "*it is impossible to please God ;*" Heb. xi. 6; neither can they be saved without works, since "*faith without works is dead ;*" James ii. 20; consequently, when Christ was upon earth, that faith which was necessary for salvation was both preached and believed; since "*faith cometh by hearing, and hearing by the Word of God.*" Rom. x. 17. The works, too, without which "*faith is dead,*" were, and must have been known and performed through faith and works, as the Scriptures declare, must go together. "*Now ye are clean,*" (said Christ,) "*through the Word which I have spoken unto you.*" John xv. 3.

It is true, that Christ said, addressing his disciples, "*I have yet many things to say unto you, but ye cannot bear them now.*" John xvi. 12. He did not tell them what those things were. It is probable he was alluding to what he would have to suffer, and also to what they would have to suffer for his sake. "*Howbeit,*" (continues he,) "*when he, the Spirit of truth, is come, he will guide you into all truth.*" John xvi. 13.

"*Ye now therefore have sorrow,*" (continues the Saviour, still addressing his disciples :) "*but I will see you again, and your heart shall rejoice.*" John xvi. 22. Christ, to comfort his disciples, who were afflicted at the thought of having to part with their divine Lord and Master, as to his visible presence, promises them the *Spirit of truth, the Comforter*, to lead and direct them in all their doubts, to strengthen them in their spiritual warfare, and to console them in their afflictions.

This was accomplished on the day of Pentecost, when "*they were all filled with the Holy Ghost.*" Acts ii. 4.

Being filled with the Holy Ghost, they were guided, as Christ had told them, "*into all truth.*" The sum and substance of the truth, which they preached, were committed by them to writing, in the Holy Scriptures. This is the Word of God, which the true followers of Christ now hold, and ever have held, as a sufficient, and their only rule of faith and conduct; for, as the Apostle says, "*All Scripture is given by inspiration of God, and is profitable for doctrine, for reproof, for correction, for instruction in righteousness; that the man of God may be perfect, thoroughly furnished unto all good works.*" 2 Tim. iii. 16, 17.

In order, therefore, that we might "*be thoroughly furnished unto all good works,*" the Sacred Scriptures, written by divine inspiration, have been transmitted to us from the days of the Apostles, down to the present time, and will continue to shine as "*a lamp to our feet, and a light to our path,*" through the dark vista of time, to the consummation of the world.

With such a light as this, we have no need of the tinsel trappings of Popery. We prefer to follow the meek and humble example of Christ and his Apostles, to the pomp, splendor, and pageantry of the church of Rome. The Apostles and disciples of Christ lived according to the maxims they inculcated. They were plain, and unostentatious in all their ways. They were never clad in purple or scarlet. No rings on their fingers, nor crowns, nor tiaras, nor mitres on their heads—No magnificent palaces had they for the residence of Popes, or Cardinals, or Bishops—No chariot and six, had Peter, Paul, or the rest of the Apostles—No high-sounding titles to flatter pride, such as the Right Reverend, the Most Reverend, Eminently Serene, His Holiness, My Lord, Our Lord, and Most Holy.* Their names were unadorned with any epithet soever to distinguish them from the poorest and lowest of their Christian friends and brethren.

They would not even suffer themselves to be saluted with the common title Master, or Mister, as we have it in English.

To an unbiassed mind, nothing more strikingly conclusive of

---

* Sismondi, the Italian historian, speaking of the influence that these pompous titles had on the people of Italy, says: "These decorations always descended still lower among the commonality. Since thirty years they no longer write even to a shoemaker, without calling him '*Molto illustre.*' But in multiplying titles, they only multiplied discontent and mortification. Each one, in place of what they granted him, only saw what they refused him: and there was no little gentleman, or dandy, and no petit officer, who did not look upon himself as mortally wounded, if, in mistake, he was saluted with the title of '*Most celebrated, or Most Excellent,*' ('CHIARISSIMO ed EX CELLENTISSIMO,') in place of that to which he aspired, '*Most Illustrious.*'" Sismondi Hist. Ital. T. xvi. p. 227.

1*

the apostacy of the Romish church could be exhibited, than the
contrast between the simplicity that every way characterized the
Apostolic and primitive Church, and the pomp, splendor, and
baubles, which encumber the Popish.

The glaring opposition, however, between the church of Rome
and the Church of Christ, is all glossed over by the defenders of
Popery, when they tell us that "the Apostles could not build
palaces, and live in pomp and splendor in those days; because
the Christian Church was yet in its infancy, the disciples few in
number, and their enemies powerful and intolerant. They would
have dressed in scarlet and purple, have lived in palaces, have
worn crowns, and tiaras, and mitres, &c. had they not been restrained by fear"!!

Such reasoning as this is quite sufficient to reconcile the minds
of Papists to the vast disparity between the pride and splendor of
their own church, and the primitive simplicity of the Church of
Christ.

If these were the reasons by which the Apostles were restrained, why, at least, we would ask, did they not assume some of the
glorious titles of the Right Reverend, the Eminently Serene,
His Holiness, My Lord, Most Holy, &c. ? These titles they
might have enjoyed with security. The reason, however, for the
whole, all Jesuitical subterfuge aside, is this :—The Apostles
trode in the footsteps of their divine Master, followed his pre-
cepts, and acted in conformity with the doctrines which they
themselves inculcated to others. But the Prelates of the Romish
church, on the contrary, have deviated from Apostolical simplicity, because they have wandered from the straight and narrow
path marked out by Christ, and have constituted themselves the
infallible judges of that, by which they are to be judged.

Having now shown, that the Bible, and not the church of Rome,
is the Christian's guide to salvation, we rejoice to have it in our
power to prove what we have advanced, not only from Scripture
and reason, as well as from the striking contrast and opposition
between the Romish church at large, and the simplicity of the
Church of Christ, but by showing the practical effects of the
erroneous and pernicious system of Popery as it works in its interior and more hidden recesses. The Narrative that is now laid
open before the public in this volume, is a disclosure made by
one who has had an opportunity of knowing, from sad experience,
what the influence and effects of Popery are, in circumstances
where it can have full sway.

The authoress of the Narrative was a poor, heart-broken widow,
who, by the death of her husband, was left destitute, and far
from her home, among strangers. Floating about, like a wreck,
on the stormy sea of life, the adversity of fortune drove her to
the island of Cuba. She landed at Havanna, the capital of that

island, and there fell into the hands, not of the desperate pirates whose depredations are confined to the highway ocean, but into the hands of those Spiritual Pirates who, under the cloak of religion, prowl, like the midnight wolf, to seize and satiate their appetites upon the poor and wandering sheep who happen to fall into their way.

Hardly had her foot touched the shore, before one of these prowling wolves in sheep's clothing scented her out. He was one of the Reverend Fathers; honored, revered, and worshiped, by his people, whose vices he Canonized, and upon whose credulity he lived. Disguised as a citizen, with the baldness of his head, shorn according to the discipline of his church, concealed and covered with a wig, he pays his addresses to the unfortunate stranger, gains her affections, conducts her to his house, and constitutes her, at once, Mistress of his domestic concerns. Had she known that the fond lover was a Popish Priest, never would she have yielded, as she declares, to his amorous solicitations. She knew it not, until she was his prisoner, and then the door of escape was closed.

With this fiend in human shape, (for such the sequel of this volume will clearly prove him to have been,) this forlorn and unfortunate woman lived five years.

Being Mistress of his house, and the Queen of his heart, all the domestic concerns were under her control. He poured out into her bosom the feelings that flowed through his polluted heart, and imparted to her, not only his own secrets, but those that were intrusted to him under the seal of Confession. She knew every thing; and she tells us what she knows. She was the witness of his character under all the various shapes which it assumed: at home, under the exterior of a Priest;—abroad, under that of a citizen. She was his companion at the ball-room, the masquerades, the gambling-tables, and the tea-parties. She accompanied him in the *Promenades ;* rode with him in his nightly excursions for dissipation; was introduced by him to his fellow Priests, who were as profligate as himself, and was conducted, dressed as a Monk, into the *sacred* (!) recesses of the Convents. In fine, he introduced her into all the scenes of dissipation and vice in which he was accustomed to be found. Even when he was sent by his Bishop, abroad, on a parochial visit to Puerto Principe, even thither she had to go to gratify his inclinations, and to witness his atrocities. Here, poor Rosamond, for this is the name of the authoress, poor Rosamond here saw what no one but a fiend would ever have thought of perpetrating, and what none but a beast would have had the immodesty to do. This was the seduction of the daughter of his friend, a girl, or child, in fact, of but fourteen years of age. Such was his beastly lust, such the mad phrensy of that lust, and such the

more than beastly, more than diabolical pleasure he took in the
exhibition of that lust, that, with a knife in his hand, he threatened death to Rosamond, if she should divulge what he was
going to do. He told her that she would have to be present in
the room while the deed was being done. Leaving her, then,
paralyzed with fear, he retires, for a short time. from her presence. and, having heard the Confession of the lamb whom he
was about to sacrifice to his lust, he returns, leading his victim,
the innocent Mariette, just blooming into her fourteenth year,
into the fatal slaughter-house of her virtue, and there, in the presence of the fainting Rosamond, perpetrates a deed, which, we
think we may say, is unparalleled in all the records of crime.

We regard these disclosures as the most important of any that
ever issued from the Press; and especially, the more so, at the
present juncture of events. Popery in Europe is evidently on
the wane, and the United States will probably be her cradle and
her throne. Europe, after being oppressed for ages, begins to
feel the weight of the "BEAST" upon her back. She now strug-
gles to be free. Her convulsive throes shake the mighty " *Babylon.*" The triple crown begins to totter on the head of the
" *Most Holy,*" (for this is the title of the *Roman Pontiff*,)* and,
rolling his eyes over the desolations of Europe, he has fixed
them upon this rising Republic, and has marked it as his own.
There are still in Europe, as the *Catholic Miscellany*, a Popish
Paper published in Charleston, states, no fewer than one hundred
and thirty million Roman Catholics now in the world, and the
concentration of that flood is now settling upon us.

When the influx ceases, and the dregs subside, be assured we
shall be buried in the filth, or shall have to fly from our native
soil. It is vain, futile, and demonstrative of ignorance too
gross, for any man, who calls himself a Protestant or friend to
liberty, to pretend that there is no danger from the Popish flood

---

* The celebrated Popish theologian, Peter Dens, treating on what is bordering
upon heresy, says, "A proposition *male sonans*,—a proposition that *sounds bad*, or
that is offensive to *pious ears!* is that, which, indeed, does not convey a meaning
that is openly contrary to faith, but which signifies, however, something that sounds
wrong, unbecoming, and unworthy: for instance,—if any one should say, that the
Roman Pontiff is not rightly called Most Holy, (Sanctissimum.") Dens' Theol. de
Virt. Fidei N. 55.

Here we see that it is bordering upon heresy. and sounds bad in Popish ears, to
say, that the Roman Pontiff is not rightly called " *Most Holy.*" Be he what he may.
—ever so wicked,—and that wicked, and abandoned some have been, Papists themselves cannot, and do not deny, still he must be called "*Most Holy.*" What can we
say to this? What can any rational man think about it? What a perversion of
language! What violation of truth! What execrable wickedness! to call a man
" *Most Holy,*" who is known to be *most unholy*. It is wicked enough in the Popish
church to Canonize and worship their Saints; but here their wickedness stretches
itself to so superlative a degree of blasphemy, that they blush not to Canonize, that
is, to beatify, and to declare " *Most Holy*" the very devil himself; or, what is the
same thing, his image, inasmuch as an abandoned sinner, is, at least, a figure of Satan,
whose image he bears. Well may we say, of those whose doctrine is such as this,
what John said of the Jews, " *Ye are of your father, the devil.*" John viii. 44.

that is pouring in upon us. *One hundred and thirty millions* of these restless devotees, all fixing their eyes on our smiling valleys of the West:—the Jesuits, that horde of spiritual highway-robbers, those restive arch-politicians, whose intrigues have convulsed the strongest monarchies of Europe, just suppressed, and *suppressed forever !* by the "*Royal Order*" of the kingdom of Spain, (as we read even in their own "*Irish Advocate,*" published in Montreal, September 1st, of the present year,) this horde of ruthless marauders, driven from their native Popish soil, whither can they fly, but to the wilds of our own dear country ?— Europe has again repudiated them, disfranchised them, spurns them, and confiscates their Monastic rendezvous to the public good. The Spaniards,—even the Spaniards,—the very name sounds Popish, and strikes a panic through the heart,—the Span iards themselves have drawn that sword, which they were taught to plunge in the heart, and to stain with the blood of heretics ; have drawn it at last, to defend their rights against the Jesuits, and against their Jesuitical influence.

Whither can they fly ?—I ask again—Whither, but to our own devoted country ?—Every thing here conspires to give them complete success. Our Constitution secures unto them, and theirs, the right of suffrage. One million and a half of their adherents are already here. Their colleges, and cathedrals, and churches, and Nunneries, are rising on every hill, and spreading through every vale. The soft persuasion of their eloquence drops like honey on the carnal heart, and many are the victims, especially in the West, who are caught in the snare of these arch-fowlers. All the rabble in the land is theirs, in preference to the pure and holy Gospel of our faith. And, for a handful of their Popish gold, many is the traitor that will sell the dearest interests of his country.

But our greatest danger lies in this—the apathy, the ignorance, and the indifference of our people in relation to this momentous subject. We see, or might see, would we but open our eyes, what the experience of Europe has taught the potentates there ; and yet we hear there is no danger. The chorus of this no-danger ditty, when two millions more of these Papists arrive among us, will, I fear, be the clashing of shillalahs,—down with the heretics. This tune has already tingled in our ears in Broadway-Hall ; and the star-spangled banner of our Republic, in St. Louis, has done obeisance to the *Consecrated Wafer*, and has been virtually pledged to espouse the cause of Popery.

No danger still,—and no danger will be the lullaby till the fangs of the Serpent clench the very vitals of our Republic, and his fiery tail sweep us from our shores.

If the horrid picture of Popery which is laid before the public in these disclosures, is not sufficient to convince our fellow-citizens that the diffusion of it through this country, is an evil to be deprecated by every philanthropist, I am at a loss how to conceive what will convince them.

The Narrative is the unadorned effusions of a soul that has been beguiled by Priestly solicitations; kept in captivity during five years; deluded,—lost,—bewildered,—and undone, by Priest-craft.

She represents, not the licentiousness of a single Priest, but the general depravity of a whole country. She presents us with the picture of Popery as it exists in Cuba; and the same, we have no reason to doubt, extends through all the West-India islands that are under the Priestly control of Rome. Many of the important statements that she makes, are confirmed by testimony that cannot be rejected. This we have introduced into the notes. Among other credentials, the thirty-two letters of the Rev. Father Pies, stand not the least conspicuous.

That these letters were written by the Reverend Father, whose signature they bear, we are ready to prove by *two witnesses* who are now in this city. We prove them too, by confronting them with his own handwriting, which it would be futile for him to deny.

We are sorry to have it to state, that the authoress, on her way in the steamboat from Philadelphia to New-York, had her trunk stolen, or carried away by mistake. In this were some important scrips, and several letters written by her Priest, the Rev. Father Canto, and by other Priests. These would have been an inestimable appendage to the work. They would have shown, as the authoress has observed, "the Rev. Father's heart."

While we are touching upon this unfortunate occurrence, we would take the opportunity of requesting any one soever, who may know any thing relative to where those papers and letters may be found, to inform us of it. The letters must be in the hands of some one; others may have seen them; and we may yet have the satisfaction of ascertaining where they may be found. Should they yet be recovered, they shall be spread before the public.

In regard to the truth of the statements contained in this Narrative, we can say we have not the least doubt. We are personally acquainted with the authoress, and we hesitate not to express our opinion that she is a sincere convert, and a devout Christian. She appears before the public with the best of recommendations; and we pray that her life may be spared; and that she may long continue to be a bright and shining light, and an ornament to the Church of which she is a member.

We can say that no pecuniary inducement led to the writing of this work. She was actuated by no other motive than the love of God, and the good of the world.

Her health is now so delicate and weak, that death seems already to have marked her as his own. She is wasting away under a complaint that seems bent on carrying her to the grave. She rejoices, however, at the prospect that lies before her; and feels willing to appear before her Judge. Her path of life has been strewed with thorns; her days have been few, and full of evil; or, rather, it may well be said, one continual night has spread its mantle over almost all her life.

Under all these circumstances, who can doubt the truth of what she has disclosed?

One of the most incredible of all her relations, is confirmed by the testimony of Dr. Ethan A. Ward of this city, a gentleman highly esteemed as a physician, and for the integrity of his moral character. This gentleman was in Havanna, and saw the wretches executed for the atrocious crime of stealing young negroes, for the purpose of cutting them up, and making them into sausages.

The Doctor returned to New-York about two years before the escape of Rosamond, and had frequently mentioned the fact of the men's being executed for the above mentioned deed, even before such a person as Rosamond's being in Havanna was known in this city; and Rosamond, the authoress of this Narrative, related the fact to her friends in this city, previous to her acquaintance with Doctor Ward, and without knowing that any one here had been informed of it.

We now leave the public to decide, whether the relation of our authoress is not confirmed in a manner that puts the truth of it beyond the shadow of a doubt.

Furthermore; we rejoice, for the sake of the triumph of the truth, that we have the means of exhibiting before the public, a presumptive evidence of the truth of the whole of the disclosures made in this interesting and important Narrative. I refer now, to the thirty-two letters, of which we have already spoken. These letters, written by the Rev. Father Pies, are in our possession; and the lady to whom they are written, is, also, actually present in this city. No further proof of the moral corruption of the Popish Clergy in the island of Cuba, need be exhibited, than these very letters. The superscription of two of them, of which we have given a *partial* fac-simile, shows that the Reverend writer had bid adieu to the last vestiges of modesty. His letters terminate with "*Fugo*," "*I fly.*" Well, indeed, may he have intimated, that his passions had taken the wings of audacity, and transported him into the blackest, foulest regions of libidinous excess!—A blank in the fac-simile, marks the absence of what, in the original, would raise a blush on immodesty herself. We have to suppress it. The indecency of the dotted thing, is so lasciviously abominable, that the exhibition of it before the public, would be an outrage upon modesty, that no motive, however pure or laudable, could sanction. Those, however, who are curious to see to what extreme pollution Priestly celibacy leads her captives, can be favored with the revolting sight, by calling at the office of the "Downfall of Babylon," No. 131 Nassau-st. New York.

Of the striking and frightful engravings which are interspersed throughout this Narrative, that of the *Purgatory-room*, at page 121, is one of the most terrific. It will doubtless appear to some, that the authoress, here, has really drawn a picture wholly of her own imagination. Devils are here seen dancing in the flames of Purgatory, with spectres the most hideous to behold. Some are playing on the violin, and others on the flute. Some have pitch-forks, to turn the poor roasting souls; others are armed with fiery serpents, to torment and sting them. Some have gaping mouths to swallow them up, and others seem ready to dart upon them, and, with their long iron claws, to tear them into pieces. One is seen, (strange figure, however, in Purgatory!) dressed like a Monk, standing in the middle of the devilish place, over a pot of burning sulphur, with a snake coiled round his feet, and with a fire-brand waving in his hand. A horrible grin spreads his mouth from ear to ear. He stands, and looks, commander-in-chief of the infernal group. All this is to be seen.

The thought occurs,—"if, indeed, there is a Purgatory after death, we doubt not that Monks and Priests are, verily, and indeed, commanders-in-chief;"—for, of all men, as this Narrative proves, they stand the most in need of *purging*.

Poor Rosamond was introduced into this sulphureous abode, this Purgatorial bug-bear in the Convent, to show her how much more the wicked heretics would have to suffer when they go to hell.

Purgatory, with all its hissing serpents, and sulphureous flames; with all its pitch-forks, devils, and voracious mouths, is only meant for pious Catholics, whose venial sins have not been expiated while on earth. This is their prison "*till they have paid the last farthing;*" and this farthing must be paid by them, or by their friends, to the Holy Priests for *Masses.* Those that have no money, have to roast until the Day of Judgment.

Incredible as this Purgatory account may appear to the people of these United States, I will inform them, that in Popish countries, it is a common appendage to almost every *Religious Order !* both of Monks and Nuns. There is one of these Purgatorial scare-crows, even now, in Kentucky. I myself, when a Priest, frequently visited it. I have done penance in it, and have seen the Nuns on penance in it. This one is in the Convent of Loretto, about twelve miles from Bardstown, in the state of Kentucky. The Nuns in this establishment are, or, at least, were, in the year 1829, under the direction of the Reverend Father Chabrat. The Purgatory-room in this Nunnery is, indeed, different from that in Cuba; but, still, it is frightful and horrible enough to terrify, not only Nuns, but even Priests themselves, as I know from my own personal experience. Here there is no pot of burning sulphur; but, they have the devils, and serpents, and pitch-forks, and a variety of other horrible figures, to terrify and keep the poor deluded Nuns in subjection to their Ghostly Masters. Instead of sulphur, the punishment in this Purgatory-room, is cold. The Nuns are confined here, doing penance on their knees, in the coldest days of winter, without a spark of fire to warm them. They remain in this painful attitude, shivering with cold, until they are almost ready to expire. I myself have done penance in that room until my body sunk exhausted to the floor.

I speak of this Purgatory-room as being at Loretto now. It was there, at least, in the year 1829, and during all the time of my residence at Bardstown college, previous to that time, which was, I think, about nine years. If any of the Protestants have children being educated in that Nunnery, as they generally have, they can ascertain from them the truth of what I state. They also, at times, are admitted into the Purgatory-room, accompanied by one of the Holy Nuns, to explain to them the nature of the thing; and, by their sophistry, to proselyte them *to the faith!*

In all the disclosures which are made by our authoress, and in the "*Downfall of Babylon*," nothing is advanced, incredible as it may appear to some, but what is strictly true; and what can be proved by Protestants, or by Papists, if the latter could be induced to give their testimony.

Every circumstance taken into consideration, the truth of this Narrative cannot be doubted. The authoress is a sincere, humble, and pious convert, declining in health, and, apparently, sinking into the grave. She appears to have a well-grounded hope beyond the declining shadow of the present life. She looks upon death, not as a king of terrors, but as a friend. She speaks of the world as if it were a mere transitory dream. She remembers what she has suffered; is conscious that it is to God alone she owes her deliverance; and she longs to be with her deliverer. She seems to feel, and to know, with St. Paul, "*that if her earthly house of this tabernacle were dissolved, she has a building of God, a house not made with hands, eternal in the heavens.*"

The testimonials of her character, which are given by her pastor, the Rev. N. E. Johnson, and by others, we think, are sufficiently recommendatory to remove any doubt that might arise in the public mind relative to the sincerity and veracity of the authoress.

2

Two of the most incredible facts related in the Narrative, have been proved by the testimony of others,—by testimony, too, that can be substantiated beyond a doubt. I allude to the negro sausages, and the Purgatory-room.

Then, again, she has the testimony of the Rev. Father Pies himself, in the thirty-two letters written by his own hand, and signed with his own signature.

The substance of all the facts which she relates, is also confirmed, in the notes, by authority which Papists, at least, cannot dispute; that is, by the authority of their own Councils, Popes, Saints, and historians.

With all this mass of positive, circumstantial, and presumptive evidence, there is not a jury in the world who would not pass the verdict, *guilty*, against the Reverend culprits, who, in this Narrative, are brought before the bar of public opinion.

The picture which is drawn, is not of a solitary individual, but of the whole confraternity, from Bishop, down to the lowest Priest that earns his bread *by telling fortunes*. From Bishops, whose hoary locks have been bleached with a century of crimes, to Priests whose faces are disfigured with licentiousness, and whose tottering limbs no more can bear them to the masquerades, balls, or cock-fights.

The picture which is drawn, is not a portrait, but the *tout ensemble* of what Popery is, where Popery bears the sway. It is principle and doctrine put to practice. It is the "*work working*," as they call it, "*ex opere operato*." It is the demonstration that the system was framed in hell;—that hoods, and veils, and cloaks, are masks to screen the vast deformity from view;—that incense, bells, and beads,—Breviaries,—Pater's,—Aves, are but fumigated sounds, a kind of lullaby for superstition.

Let them not tell us, that it is in Cuba alone, that *the work* thus works. The same scene is presented to the view in France, Spain, Portugal, and Italy. The curtain there, has been raised by their own Popes, Saints, and historians; and the tragic scene has been handed down from age to age, polluted on every leaf, in every page.

There is not a corner of the earth where this insidious Serpent has coiled his way, but the slime of his pollutions has defiled the land, or the venom of his sting has paralyzed the heart. Cast the eye over the distant walls of China, and there we see this " *Queen of heaven*" rolling, Juggernaut-like, upon a car with the goddess of the Pagans. Turn again the eye to India's burning plains, and peep into Goa's loathsome dungeon of the Inquisition, and there behold the ghastly victims of intolerance, panting and suffocating for the air of heaven, because they are guilty of the crime of thinking for themselves. Look upon the verdant fields of Ireland, that land of native genius—the sight draws tears into one's eye;—the Priestly pedagogues, with whip in hand, drive the poor submissive sons of Erin, as a teemsman drives his cattle. See them buried in ignorance and superstition, deprived of the Word of God,* and believing that a prayer-book is the Bible.

Let the eye wander again to the North, and spread itself over the vast domains of Canada. There may we count ninety and nine of a hundred, so illiterate as not to distinguish one letter from another. They can count their Beads or Rosaries, but have not learned to lisp their A, B, C.†

Go where we will, if Popery has long been there, we see a desert, and we breathe on death.

We present this Narrative before the public, plain and simple, as it flowed from the pen of the authoress. The only corrections which we have made, are in the orthography and punctuation. Beauty, when unadorned, is said to be adorned the most. The beauty of originality, and the artless expressiveness of truth, which run through every line of this important Narrative, would have been lost, had it been retouched. We, therefore, present it as the genuine production of a heart bleeding at the recollection of her past misconduct; bruised and crushed under the iron hand of despotism: stained and polluted by the Spiritual Guardians by whom she was decoyed.

A tale she has told to the world, that ought to be wafted upon every wind that blows around the globe. Pictures she has drawn which have been etched on copper, and which, we trust, will be engraved on the memory of every patriot who loves his country, and of every Christian who fears his God.

I have this day, and having thus far advanced in the Introduction, been sent for by the authoress. I found her dangerously ill. Her physician, Doctor Ethan A. Ward, was standing by her bed-side, expecting every moment to see her breathe her last. The faculties of her mind were unimpaired, but her body was exhausted. She tried to speak, but was unable. After a short interval, however, she recovered the use of speech; the Doctor, then, at my suggestion, asked her if what she had written in her Narrative was true: she replied, "*Yes, the truth, and nothing but the truth.*"

A death-bed is a detecter of the heart,

> " Where thr'd dissimulation drops her mask,
> That mistress of the scene, through life's grimace:
> Here, real and apparent are the same."
>
> YOUNG's NIGHT THOUGHTS.

Who could doubt her word?—Death, with his stern visage, seems to stand before her.—The Christian fears him not. I ask-

---

ed her, "Rosamond, are you happy in the Lord?"—"I am happy," she replied; "my trust is in the Lord Jesus Christ."—Her countenance stamped the approbation of truth on what she said; and resignation sat smiling on her lips. Testimony such as this, even incredulity itself could not resist. Is it to be supposed, that a person, apparently in the very arms of death, and exulting in the glorious hopes of immortality, would breathe her last in confirmation of a lie? The strongest motives now were present to induce her to speak the truth: the world receding from her view; death standing at the door; and eternity opening before her. The truth of her Narrative cannot be doubted. The pious convert has again, through the blessing of the Lord, recovered; but the testimony which she gave, was, to all appearance, the last; therefore, it may be said, that her Narrative is confirmed by the seal of death itself.

Admitted:—the Narrative is true.—Where does Popery now stand?—or, rather, where will it fly to hide itself?—the picture is drawn:—truth has confirmed it.

It is vain for the Papist to tell us, that these are abuses unsanctioned and condemned by the church. If they are abuses, they are universal wherever Popery prevails. They are, moreover, sanctioned by their church;—or what do they mean by Church? —If it be asked, "what is the established religion in Cuba?"— Will not the answer be, "it is the Roman catholic religion?"— By whom is the church there governed?—Is it not by Romish Archbishops, Bishops, and Priests?—What is the doctrine taught there?—Is it not the same as that which is taught in Rome?— Are they not under the jurisdiction and authority of the Pope of Rome?—And why does he not, in the plenitude of his Apostolical power, correct the abuses?—"An error," (as Augustine remarks,) "which is not condemned, is approved." Neither let it be said, that these abominations are unknown to the Pope. If they are unknown, it is because he does not wish to know them; and what sort of a universal Shepherd, then, is he?—Is there a foot of territory in the United States upon which this Spirited Hawk has not fixed his eye?—When his *authority* is resisted, the fact soon reaches his ears; witness the case of Hogan, the refractory Priest in Philadelphia; and of Fearnon, the schismatic Priest in Brooklyn. His eyes are keen enough to see, when danger, however distant, threatens his own royal throne; and his voice is loud enough to thunder his anathemas from pole to pole. But, alas! when his own wolves are tearing the sheep to pieces, and the honor of the King of kings is trampled in the dust, he can neither hear nor see.

Where, too, is the Infallible Church all this while?—Where are the Infallible Pastors, who pretend, that he who hears them, hears Christ; and he who despises them, despises Christ?

Strange paradox! the Holy Roman Catholic Church *is* in Cuba, and it *is not* in Cuba.—If it *is* in Cuba, then it witnesses the desolations of which we speak; and, not correcting them, it stands amenable for all the crimes it sanctions.—If it is not in Cuba, then it is nowhere on the globe; because the Bishops in Cuba, as well as those in every other country, are not consecrated until the Pope's Bull arrives to sanction and confirm it.

The authoress informs us, indeed, that *some* of the criminal Priests are recalled to Rome; but then, the rest are left to desolate the country.—Where is the Church of Christ, we ask, all this time?—According to Popery, the people have no other guide than their Pastors, the Popish Priests. To these they are bound to Confess their sins, to submit their conscience.—If these err, then, if the doctrine of Popery be true, the people must err with them; for, as the Scripture declares, "*If the blind lead the blind, both shall fall into the ditch.*" Matt. xv. 14. Where, then, we inquire again, is the Church of Christ?—If Popery be true, Christ has not a Church upon the earth; for Christ declares that "*the Son of man is come to seek and to save that which was lost,*" Luke xix. 10; but the Popish Priests, as we see, go to *seek and to destroy those over whom they preside.*

The effect of Popery, as we see, and which is confirmed by every page of history, is to subjugate the understanding to the dictates of Priestly authority, to keep the people in ignorance, to encourage superstition, and to work upon their fears with threats and tortures. Had they the Word of God, instead of interested and wicked Priests, to direct them, all these *abuses*, as they call them, would cease. Looking into that Sacred Mirror, they could not but see the moral deformity of their own character; and, if a spark of conscience glowed in their bosoms, they would be stimulated to correct their lives. But under the Popish system, the Word of God is closed forever. The Confessional is the dark recess whence emanates the instructions by which the people are to regulate their lives. The keys of "*Peter*" debar from heaven, all who do not enter by that door. How deplorable is the necessity which excludes from the kingdom of heaven, all who do not pour their thoughts into the polluted hearts of Romish Priests, and submit their conscience to their dictates!—Ever to be pitied is the virtuous female who has no other path to heaven, than by passing through the door of the Confessional, and bending at the feet of Ghostly Fathers burning with lust.

Christ never instituted a system fraught with so much danger; subject to such inevitable evils. He never could have been so unreasonable as to make it obligatory upon sinners to Confess to sinners, for obtaining from himself the pardon of their sins.—Never could he have bound us to submit our conscience, and regulate

2*

our lives, by the dictates of men, sinful and fallible as ourselves. What a contradiction, and what a chasm in the Popish doctrine! "The Church," (say they, meaning their own church,) "is infallible, and we are bound to obey the Church."—If we ask them what constitutes the Church, they tell us that it is "the Congregation of all those who profess the faith and doctrine of Christ, and who are governed, on earth, by one Sovereign Head and Pastor, *after* Christ." Dens' Theol. de Eccle. No. 70. This Sovereign Head and Pastor, is the Pope; who (mark the expression) governs *after* Christ;—not *under* Christ.

But now, for the Infallibility.—The Church, the say, is infallible. This infallibility they distinguish in a twofold sense. The one, they denominate an active and authoritative infallibility; that is, an infallibility in teaching and defining; the other, they call a passive infallibility, by which they mean an infallibility in learning and believing. (Id. ib. No. 80.)

Infallibility, considered in its active and authoritative sense, belongs to the Church in respect to its Head, the Sovereign Pontiff, and to its Prelates; that is, to its Bishops. This infallibility does not belong to the Church in respect to its lay members, or inferior pastors; that is, the Priests. (Id. ib.) Thus a man is said to see, although this seeing does not belong to him in respect to any of the other members of the body, except the eyes; so, in regard to the Church, infallibility belongs to it only in respect to the Pope, and to the Bishops of the Church. (Id. ib.)

The Priests are not infallible; they can err, and yet we are bound to submit our conscience and the regulation of our lives to their dictates!—The blind are bound to follow the blind!—Where is the Infallible Church all this while?—Of what practical utility is the Infallible Church, if we have to follow fallible Guides?

It is in vain, and a mere gratuitous assertion, for them to tell us that the Priests, although fallible, cannot long *preach* a doctrine contrary to that of the Romish Church, without the knowledge of it reaching the Bishop's ear: this, in the first place, we take the liberty to deny; because they can preach, and often do preach, just what they choose. Even granting, that in their public instructions to the people, they should not preach any thing in direct opposition to their leading and cardinal doctrines, or dogmas of faith; yet, they often, nay, I can say, always, preach in such a manner as to wind into their discourses a certain system of morality, the tendency of which is to lull the consciences of their people into security; instead of preaching to them in such a manner as to awaken them to a sense of their danger.

Moreover, although what they preach should reach the

Bishop's ear, the objection does not end there. It may reach his ear, and there it may stop. Who is the Bishop?—a fallible man, (as they admit,) like the Priests themselves. Even if it should be admitted that they were all infallible, in the Popish sense of the word, their infallibility does not render them impeccable. The prerogative of impeccability they have not yet had the audacity to claim, and that for reasons too obvious to need an explanation.

If the Priest and his Bishop, therefore, are not truly spiritual and holy men, but directly the contrary, it is foolishness, and inconsistent, to suppose that they will conscientiously discharge their duty in relation to the spiritual necessities of their people; because "*the carnal mind is enmity against God; and. to be carnally minded is death!*" Rom. viii. 6, 7.

Is it not, therefore, as repugnant to reason and common sense, as it is to the Word of God, to suppose that the mind that is " *enmity against God,*" will endeavor to promote his honor and glory in the salvation of souls? And, as the being carnally minded is death, spiritual death, can those, who are spiritually dead, give life to those who are spiritually dead ? To establish the claim of infallibility upon a foundation such as this, is an insult to the world.

But it is not in the pulpit, however, where the poor deluded people drink their deadliest draught. It is in the Confessional, that secret tribunal, where the deadly whisper never reaches his Lordship's ear; in that tribunal which is closed with what they call the Seal of Confession, and locked with the keys of Peter's authority. It is in that dark labyrinth where those Spiritual Guides lead the blindfolded victims to the chambers of death. There they are hid from the view of all; and it is there that they can chisel out the rough and passive block into whatever shape they choose, into the very " *image of the Beast.*" Here, then, the Priest, who (even according to their own admission) is a fallible man, leads his victim secretly along a path where no eye can reach him, and no ear can hear; and, O! well do I know the path they tread, since I, one of their anointed, had to tread it.

Even supposing these spiritual guides were all converted and spiritual men, still, in the Tribunal of Confession, they are, (as is not denied,) fallible, and liable to err; consequently the advice and instructions they give, must vary according as their judgments vary; and the variability of their judgment depends on a thousand fortuitous circumstances; such, for instance, as the natural frame and constitution of the mind, education, prejudice, ignorance, and many other *et ceteras,* which might be named.

But to suppose that all these spiritual guides, or even a

majority of them, are converted and spiritual men, is a stretch of credulity which cannot be sanctioned by the Word of God, by probability, or by common experience; and living facts prove that they are any thing else than spiritual, or any thing like spiritual and converted men. How great, therefore, must be the havoc which they make of those souls who are thus blindly and secretly led by their instruction! Where now is the bubble of infallibility?—It all disappears in the dark recesses of the Confessional; and, like a stone dropped into the water, its multiplied undulations are lost in the wide ocean of uncertainty; and not a line or ripple is left to mark its limits, or to show where it can be found.*

Having now introduced the reader to the interesting and important disclosures which this volume unfolds, we commend the work to our fellow-citizens, with the prayer, that God may make it subservient to his honor and glory.

Of all scourges with which a country can be afflicted, Popery, confessedly, is the worst.

May the watchmen, who stand upon the walls of Zion, re-echo the alarm. May every Christian church be now united in resisting the insidious foe whose standard is already erected on every hill, in every dale, of our wide extended country. Christians, statesmen, philanthropists, Jews, infidels, and savages, all are interested in the result, whether Popery shall rise or fall.—Christians, first, will feel the sting of the Serpent under the crackling fagot:—statesmen next, when the banners of liberty shall be furled in obeisance to the triple crown, who owns no head on earth, nor head in heaven.—Philanthropists, kind and indulgent as their hearts may be, must also bend before the despot, or be crushed beneath his power.—Jews know, from the past, what their future lot would be,—exile, slavery, or death.—Infidelity might amalgamate awhile, and lend their arms and forces to "*the Beast*;" but, in the end, would share the common fate; for Popery must be Lord of all.—The savage, whose heel is like the deer, would fly, in vain, before the blood-hounds that have fattened on the carcasses of the defenceless aborigines of Peru and Mexico.—The country would be a desolated waste.—One temple would be seen, the temple of "*the Beast*,"—one throne erected, church and state combined.—Liberty of conscience, liberty of the Press, liberty of speech, would be driven, hand in hand, over the precipice of infallible supremacy; and the "*Most Holy*," and Spiritual Despot of the world, would seat himself in the temple of God, "*showing himself that he is God.*" 2 Thes. ii. 4.

NE FIAT, DEUM DEPRECEMUR.

---

* See "DOWNFALL OF BABYLON," on Infallibility, Vol. I. No. 94—95.

Gonia Books

If undeliverable, return to: Fulfillment Center 1030 Mission Acres Road Pleasant View, TN - Tennessee 37146 UNITED STATES	Ship To: **Keith Campbell** **401 N SEMINOLE AVE** **CLAREMORE, Oklahoma 74017**

Order No.: Biblio.com - B5324867

Ship Method: Standard

Qty	SKU	Item Name	Condition	Notes	Price Each
1	HB-5221	Rosamond: Or A Narrative Of The Captivity And Sufferings Of An American Female Under The Popish Priests, In The Island Of Cuba (1836) by Culbertson, Rosamond		Ships Next Business DayCOVID-19 Precautions are taken.	$12.35

Customers: Please retain this packing list for your records.

If you have any questions about this order, please contact the bookseller directly at raybubbaflatt@gmail.com.

P. S. In order to distinguish the notes of my own introducing, from those of a respected friend who has lent me his assistance, I have distinguished them, at the end of each, with the syllable Ed.—For the accuracy of these, I hold myself responsible; and my coadjutor, who writes the Appendix, will be responsible for his.

We here subjoin an abstract of the thirty-two letters spoken of in the Narrative and Introduction. They have been translated by a native of Spain, a gentleman of high respectability, and a master of the language.

We present a fac-simile of one of them in its original dress, with the signature of the Reverend writer. It is signed "*Besa tus Pies*," "I KISS THY FEET."—This is a Priestly witticism. The Rev. Father's name is Pies: this signifies feet. From this circumstance, the playful and Reverend lover takes occasion to play upon the word; and, therefore, runs the amorous conclusion into his own name.

In order that the public may have a further specimen of the playfulness of the Rev. Father's love, we present them also with fac-similes of three of the superscriptions of his letters, or, rather, to speak more properly, of his *billets-doux*. A part of two of them, however, owing to their shocking immodesty, we are under the necessity of suppressing.

INTRODUCTORY TO THE LETTERS

WRITTEN BY THE REV. FATHER PIES TO DIFFERENT FEMALES.

IN the following letters, we have a specimen of the moral depravity of the Romish Priesthood, drawn by their own pen. Can they now tell us, "it is a Protestant calumny?"—A *Holy Capuchin Friar*, a venerated Priest, in the full exercise of his Ecclesiastical functions, is the writer of them. Who, on reading these amorous and licentious effusions, would suppose that they were penned by a man sixty years of age!—This, however, was the age of the *venerated* Priest who wrote them. How must not the fires of concupiscence have burned in his polluted heart in the vigor of youth, when the flames thereof still rage, with such ungovernable fury, under the ashes of his declining years!—How many innocent victims must not have been sacrificed at his *Sacred feet* in the dark recesses of the Confessional, where all that transpires is closed, forever, under the *Sacred Seal* which binds the "Spiritual Father," and his *fair penitent*, to perpetual secrecy!*

How passing strange, that mothers can be found so destitute of common prudence, so infatuated with delusion, as to expose their daughters to danger so imminent as that of being subjected to the vile solicitations of men burning with lust! subjected to it, too, under circumstances so every how calculated to excite the most criminal of passions, screened from detection by the obligation of inviolable secrecy!—And Americans, too, of whose conversion to Popery, we sometimes hear the tale,—Americans, and Popery!—strange amalgamation! even they are found, fascinated by the imposing outside show of the pretended *only Church* of Christ.—They drink the draught of the intoxicating doctrine; reason reels on her throne; and, in the delirium of fanaticism, they throw themselves, their daughters, and their immortal souls, into the jaws of the ravenous "*Dragon*."—The reflection harrows up every feeling of the soul.—We drop a tear as we record the fact; and if tears would erase it, a flood of them would not be spared.—The evil spreads, like a flood, over our land; and what will be the limits of its desolation, remains for posterity to tell.

We draw aside the Priestly mask, the Monkish hood, and, in the sequel, present the Reverend and Infallible Ones in their undisguised deformity, as the best of antidotes for the evil which we deprecate. We show them as they are, and they show them-

* See CATECHISM OF THE COUNCIL OF TRENT, revised and corrected by John Hughes, Priest of St. John's church, Philadelphia, p. 195.

selves; and would that the picture could be spread on one wide canvass, that the world might see it.

Some of the expressions of the Reverend letters are so obscene that we are under the necessity of presenting them to the public under the original cloak of Spanish; others are of a nature too foul to appear in any dress soever;—these, we entirely suppress. For the sake of those unacquainted with the Spanish, we have translated what we dare to present in that language, into Latin.

I would observe, before closing these remarks, that these letters furnish us with further evidence of the truth and accuracy of the Narrative. The authoress has stated, (as will be seen in the perusal of her disclosures,) that the Rev. Father who wrote these letters was sixty years of age. The autograph of the letters is so evidently written by a hand tremulous with age, that they are almost illegible. So difficult was it to decipher the hand-writing, that several persons to whom I applied, and persons, too, well acquainted with the language, were unable to do it. Every one of them observed that "the letters must have been written with a trembling hand, or by a decrepit old man."— The Reverend lover, truly, as the letters show, and as the authoress has stated, must have been, at least, *"sixty years of age."*

Seventeen, and some of the most important, disclosures in this Narrative, are confirmed by the Rev. Father Pies himself. Here, then, we have the very testimony of the *party concerned,* to prove the truth and accuracy of the statements made by the authoress.

They are as follows:

1. Rosamond, in the Narrative, states, that the Rev. Father Pies belongs to the Order of the Capuchins :—The Rev. Father, in his letters, writes, "I have told you, my dear wife, that I live with the Capuchins." (Letter XV.)

2. Rosamond tells us, that there are many rogues in Havanna :— "There are many rogues here," (in Havanna,) says the Rev. Father. (Letter II.)

3. From Rosamond we learn that, in Havanna, to be pious, signifies to be wealthy :—"No one," (says Father Pies,) "would give a shilling for you if you are sick." (Letter III.)

4. Rosamond tells us, that many of the Priests would emigrate to the Valley of the Mississippi, could they be assured of the means of gaining a living:—The Rev. Father, writing to his beloved, says, "If I had the means of gaining a livelihood," (in New-York,) "believe me, my dear, I would go and live with you." (Letter III.)

5. Rosamond assures us that the licentious Priests are revered by all, so long as their faces are not disfigured *by disease:*— Father Pies, profligate as he was, was honored and caressed by the Prelacy ;—"I had the unspeakable pleasure," (says he,) "of

seeing your lovely, graceful, and rosy face, passing by, on my way to pay a visit to the *Prior of St. Domingo Cathedral.* To-morrow I am invited to the Archbishop's." (Letter IV. and II.)

6. Rosamond speaks of their enormous beards, and tells us how they contrived to conceal them :—The Holy Capuchin talks of his beard in the following strain ;—"You remember, I told you, once, that my beard would bother you a great deal ; and it has proved to be troublesome, since you always resisted my approaches." (Letter III.)

7. Rosamond tells us it is a common thing for Priests to have their Mistresses:—The love-sick Father, addressing the wife of a Spanish nobleman, salutes her with the epithets,—" My dear Margaret!—My loving wife !" (Letter V.)

8. Rosamond, speaking of the Priests, and those with whom they were enamoured, says, " they would be *contemplating* which was the youngest and the handsomest :"—The loving Priest exclaims, almost in despondency, " I have been incessant in complimenting and *contemplating* you, and you have not shown any regard." (Letter V.)

9. Rosamond, throughout her Narrative, speaks of the frequent assignations of the Reverend lovers:—"My own dear wife !" (exclaims the Rev. Father, under the vow of celibacy,) "and my most beautiful and desirable pink ! should nothing occur to you or to me, to-morrow, between 9 and 10, we shall meet." (Letter XVIII.)

10. Rosamond mentions that the Priests prefer the prettiest females :—" Let me know," (says the Rev. Father,) " whether you love me or not ; for if you don't, I must get another girl, even prettier, if possible, than yourself." (Letter XIV.)

11. Rosamond speaks of the frequency of the Rev. Fathers' faces being *"disfigured with disease:"*—The Rev. Father seems bent on gratifying his passions, even although he should run the risk of " —— disease." (Letter XIV.)

12. Rosamond relates that the Priests change their dress, that they may not be detected in their licentious conduct :—" I would not, for the world," (exclaims the Rev. Priest,) "that any one should know what I am about." (Letter X.)

13. Rosamond describes how addicted they are to cursing and swearing ; and how they confirm it with the *"hoorie :"*—" I swore, and cursed that ——", cries the Rev. Father. (Letter X.)

14. Rosamond writes, at large, upon the subject of the Priestly Mistresses ; *"believing that what she writes here, will also be written in heaven:"*—"His mother is a kept Mistress of *Friar Pedro Alcantara*," writes the Rev. Father Pies. (Letter XV.)

15. Rosamond describes the nicety of the Priests, when about to pay their addresses to the ladies ; and the use they make of perfumes and Cologne :—" Now, my dear wife !" (exclaims the

Reverend Celibate,) "since I am determined to come and see you, I shall appear nice, shaved, and clean." (Letter XV.)

16. Rosamond points out the presents of the Priests; and tells us something about the Nuns:—"Accept of these presents," (writes the Reverend and generous lover,) "which I got of my *dearest Nuns.*" (Letter XVIII.)

17. Rosamond says that the Priests are possessed of a *jealous* disposition:—The Rev. Father, after having tried every means to seduce the lady to whom he writes, "Regrets to find that the *torments of jealousy* are also added to his accumulated disappointments." (Letter XIX.)

> "Roma locuta est : causa finita est.
> Rome has spoken : the case is decided."
> *The favorite axiom of Popery.*

On the following page, we present the fac-similes of the superscription of three of the Rev. Father Pies' letters. They mark the frivolity of his mind.

On the next page is to be seen a fac-simile of one of his letters, the translation of which is given on the page immediately following, marked, No. II.

The following numbers exhibit an exact translation of some of the letters written by the Rev. Father Pies to different females. There are thirty-two of the original letters now in our hand. The following we deem will be a sufficient specimen to show the depravity of his heart. Some of the letters are so excessively obscene, that we are under the necessity of suppressing them altogether.

We present as much of them as we dare; and in presenting them, we have to beg the indulgence of the reader. The importance of unfolding them before the world, in order to show the deep depravity of the Romish Clergy, will, we hope, be a sufficient apology for what we do.

SUPERSCRIPTION TO THE FOLLOWING LETTER.

" *To one whose beauty I adore, who am anxious to kiss those hands which I hope will soon be mine, since I am thine.*"

LETTER II.

A TRANSLATION OF THE FAC-SIMILE.—"SOPHIA."

" My pretty girl!—My lovely dear!—Beauty of the world!— Your dear soul I did not see. But I threw into your window a

3

billet-doux.—Tell me if you got it.—Because in it many things are expressed: and I expected from your good, dear little heart, some consolation in answer thereto. May I yet live for you, since I already know you, and without you I cannot live!—To-day, I am engaged to pay a visit to your neighbour opposite.—Be on the look-out;—and to-morrow, I am invited to the Archbishop's. But I assure you that the remembrance of you alone is my consolation.—A-propos!—tell me, for your own safety, whether you understand the coins of this country; lest you might be deceived or cheated by any one.—Be careful, my dear child, with whom you have any dealings: because *there are many rogues here.*

(Signed,)

"BESO TUS PIES.

"I kiss your feet; or, Place me at your feet."

LETTER III.

" My dear loving soul! nothing serious has occurred. Something was due to me, and you have paid me.—You, my dear love, were not in fault, because you evinced a readiness to resist. The fault was entirely mine; for I had such a desire to be with you, that I lost all patience; and, (in the hurry,) I *porque tenia tantas ganas de estar con tigo que no pude esperar y manche tus carnecites tan bonitas y gorditas,* (omnem pellem tuam delicatam formosissimamque; tamque venustam, atque voluptuosam, ego inquinavi.)

Whenever you will, just tell me, my dear soul, as I hear you want to return to your native country; and you leave me here alone. Yet I advise you, you would be doing well. They are ruining your health; and mine, too, suffers; and no one would give a shilling for you if you are sick. Indeed, if I had the means of gaining a livelihood, believe me, my dear, I would go and live with you. The folks here are great cheats. Again, I repeat, take care of your health; for if you fall sick-a-bed, then will begin your great troubles; and my cares will commence with them; as I cannot, by any means, allow you to perish without assistance. To Spain I could not take you, although I might wish to do it; nor am I going for five or six months yet: and even then, much depends on *all the money* that is due me. To go to Spain by the way of New York, would be attended with difficulties; but, nevertheless, I will come and see you, and talk over the thing, and enjoy the pleasure of being with you. You remember, I told you, once, that my beard would bother you a great deal; and it has proved to be troublesome, since you always resisted my approaches whenever I attempted to kiss you.—Perhaps you did not love me: but whether you love me or not, you will always remember me, wherever you may be, as he will remember you, who kisses your feet.

"BESO TUS PIES."

SUPERSCRIPTION TO THE FOLLOWING LETTER.

" *To my dear little pet.*"

LETTER IV.

"My dear beloved!—My adorable beauty!—O, I would kiss you to death if I could. My desire would be always to be gazing upon your beauty; but, lovely as you are, my difficulties to your embraces daily increase. Yet probably, unknown to you, I had the unspeakable pleasure of seeing your lovely, graceful, and rosy face passing by, on my way to pay a visit to the Prior of St. Domingo Cathedral, and on my return from his house, I passed by yours, in hope of seeing you again, to have a little talk with you, and hand you that little paper, to remove from your mind any anxiety. I saw you, even then, but I kept aloof, because I perceived two persons standing opposite to your door; one I knew to be your servant in attendance, who, if he had seen me speak to you, would have reputed you as a woman of ill-fame, and would have said that you show me many attentions; but if I show any to you, it is, my dear, because I am yours."

LETTER V.

"My dear Margaret!—My loving wife!—Yesterday, (Monday,) neither could I see you, nor hear from you; which leaves me very unhappy. For neither seeing you, nor hearing from you by note, does not suit me at all.—Surely, what affection does this show towards me?—Certainly, none at all.—And that I should continue to love one that does not love me, can never do. I have been incessant in complimenting, and *contemplating* you, and you have not shown any regard.—Are we not in a fine country, where every thing is abundant, but never mind;—adieu, till to-morrow.—If you will, think about it."

LETTER VI.

." My dear life!—It is a common saying with those of our nation, that when one has agreed to perform any thing with another individual, and on the question being put, no answer is given, the inference is, that silence gives consent: or, in other words, that all is right, and we both agree in sentiment. Now, then, my dear! how comes it, that so much as I have said to you, and written to you, you have neither deigned to write me an answer, or advance any thing satisfactory to me?—From this I must infer, that you have no intrinsic regard or wish for the person you thus treat.—Perchance it may be your sickness occasions all this:—yet I repeat, I am yours.

"N. B. Believe me, that I feel it most grievously, to be constrained to speak to you so clearly, and pointedly; but it is because I love you.—I love you extremely; and always shall; and I hope you consider me before any one else."

LETTER VII.

(This letter is of so indelicate a nature, that we have to suppress it. His deeply laid scheme required her utmost ingenuity to baffle it, in order to save her reputation.)

SUPERSCRIPTION TO THE FOLLOWING LETTER.

" *Addressed to the most precious, lovely, and dearest girls, my eyes ever beheld.*
" *You, whose names I do not know, but am anxious to learn.*"

LETTER VIII.

"My dear, loving sisters!—Lovely girls!—And pretty dears!—I have already informed you that I have been at the brink of the grave. No one would believe it, or would believe that I could recover; and I still remain very unwell and feeble, distressed with intermittent fever; so that I am now fit for nothing, my dears.—My health still continues very much on the decline;

and although you have invited me to your house, (a compliment more than I deserve,) yet I have not accepted your invitation. Only let me recover, and I will seek for you, without giving you further trouble."—(The letter continues in an amorous strain, and bids them "Adieu, for the present.")

LETTER IX.

"Delight of my eyes!—Lovely beauty of the world!—Thou queen of the fair!"—(This letter continues with amorous expressions so profusely dealt out, that it absorbs the whole letter, and is unimportant, and he concludes by observing, that his *religious duties* prevent his seeing her whom he only lives *to adore*.)

LETTER X.

"My soul!—My heaven thou art!—Now, I must be very cautious when I am acting indiscreetly. *I would not, for the world, that any one should know what I am about.* Dona Andrea, who lives opposite to your dwelling, wishes you to pay her a visit. Her son, who spoke to me at the door, and whom you saw standing there, wanted, forcibly, to enter to see what I was about; but I opposed this strenuously; and, although you may have noticed, in this dilemma, that I nodded to you, I am certain he did not notice me. I am, now, not suffering under any *enfermedad pagasosa mis carnes limpias y blancas como un marfil.* (Nulla, lues, aut mala contagio me invasit: corpus meum purum est; marmoreoque nitore nunc splendet.) However, I am anxious to recover from my attack of the *liver,* which is the *true illness* that has brought me so near the gates of death; and under which I am still suffering.—To-day, my dear, you appear to be dissatisfied about something.—Adieu."—

LETTER XI.

(The purport of this letter is, "that if she should continue sick, she would know where to send her servant-girl to find him; namely, at the Convent of the Capuchins.")

3*

LETTER XII.

(*To the same.*)

(He writes her another letter ; and states that he cannot see her that day, as " he has been commissioned to attend the prison chapel, to hear, as usual, the Confessions of the prisoners."— He concludes the letter in these words :) "Adieu! my heavenly creature !—Believe me, I remain in great anxiety concerning your health.—Tell me, beautiful damsel ! what ails you.—Do tell me.—Don't deceive me.—I shall never abandon you.—I s***r to love you, whether well or ill.'

LETTER XIII.

(*To the same.*)

"My beautiful and adored *esposa!*—My sweet little woman ! To me you are the prettiest of your sex.—You cannot think, my dear, how I am disgusted with your neighbors opposite, who are always gazing, and noticing every one that speaks to you, every one that looks at you, and every one that loves you ; and talking, and grumbling at all they see ; which, to my disposition, is so disgusting, as I have a decided aversion that any one should see what I do. Nothing but those creatures over the way has prevented my coming oftener, as their curiosity is always alive when they see me.—Now, my dear, I have to request that you will correspond to my feelings, and I will reciprocate with yours.—I hail your recovery.—But take care that I don't fall sick, as we should lose all if you were to give me any *contagion.* As to me, you may examine *mi cuerpo limpio y sin ninguna muncha sospechosa.**—I shall, therefore, be really happy to find your dear self exempt from any thing, but all as lovely as your face.

LETTER XIV.

"My loving dear !—dearest of my heart !—you saw what an awful and stormy day yesterday (Friday) was ;—so unpleasant that I could not go out.—So that I have no pleasure of any thing in this world, since I am deprived of the pleasure of being with you.—Well, now, do tell me candidly, and don't let me suffer

---

* Corpus meum perscruteris, si tibi placeat ; et nunquam investigando illic invenies maculam ullam quæ tibi suspicionem vel minimam excitet.

any longer. Let me know whether you love me or not; for if you don't, I must get another girl, even prettier, if possible, than yourself, *mas que no tonga las piernas tan gorditas como las tuyas,*" (the preceding too shocking to be translated.) "But all this would give me much displeasure; and, besides, it is important for me to know in what relation we stand to each other; for it seems strange, after so much, that you should still refuse my amours.—I often think you must be laboring under some contagious disease, that you would save me catching from you, and it is that which makes me anxious to learn the real fact; for, surely, if you were hale and hearty, you would, before this, have evinced some desire to see me.—Well, now, to clear up the doubt, you have only one course to take; and be aware, that in these hot climates, women easily get sick."

LETTER XV.

"I have told you, my dear wife, and my most beautiful creature, that I live with the Capuchins, but I do not take my meals with them.—I have my dinner brought to me at noon, every day. Yesterday afternoon, I had some special visits to make, which kept me out till half past five.—I swore and cursed against that son of a *puta*, who seemed to stand in my way, on the opposite side of the way, whom I did not like to trouble myself with, his mother being of a very turbulent character, and *a kept-mistress of Friar Pedro Alcantara.* Well, on account of these fellows, I could not have the pleasure of being with you. And, indeed, was it not that you had made up your mind to leave this soon, I would advise you to remove from where you are; for I could not come and see you while those d***ls opposite are always gazing at us.—Now, my dear wife, since I am determined to come and see you, I shall appear nice, shaved, and clean; so as not to be at all unpleasant to you.—But if I should then be disappointed, I shall despair, not knowing what to do, my beautiful creature."

LETTER XVI.

(It would appear that our worthy Capuchin, after encountering so many obstacles, from the object of his unwarrantable love, begins to think that the low state of his funds, at that moment, might be considered as the obstacle to the fulfilment of his wish; but begs to remind his dear, that her pledges were more than mere words, and as an evidence of this, he would "refer her to the two notes that had *those figures* on them."—He alludes here to the two letters, of the superscriptions of which we have given the fac-similes. The figures they had on them, of which mention is here made, we suppress, nor can we give the most distant allusion to what they were.)

LETTER XVII.

" My beautiful creature, and all that is lovely to me!—you cannot think what a desire I have to see you, and" (what flows out here, along a line or two, must be suppressed,) "I begin to despair, for I don't know ———. I have even shaved my beard to please you, that it might not incommode; but that would not do.—And now that your stay here is so short, I don't know what to think."—(He continues by expatiating on his misery and disappointment; and concludes, by wishing rather that a dagger should be plunged into his breast, than suffer the imputation of the "*enfermedad Galico.*")

LETTER XVIII.

"My own dear wife!—and my most beautiful and desirable pink!—should nothing occur to you or me, to-morrow, between 9 and 10, we shall meet. This is my particular wish; I hope it is also yours.—I give you this notice that you may be prepared, and not be taken unawares by my visit.—I shall add nothing further in this note; but shall express myself more fully when I see you.—Accept of these presents, which I get from my *dearest Nuns.*—Do not forget that we are to meet to-morrow.—I will off with my beard, that your soft delicate face may not be incommoded by its roughness."

LETTER XIX.

(In this letter, the Reverend lover soars into the highest ecstasies of amorous expressions towards "the object of all his cares and anxieties;" and he regrets to find, that "the *torments of jealousy* are also added to his accumulated disappointments.")

From the above specimens, we see what Popish celibacy leads to. If we could have the letters of all the Priests thus unfolded, what a picture would be presented to the view!

As corroborative of the licentious character of the Romish Priesthood, as depicted by the authoress of this Narrative, we will introduce the following communication, just put into our hands by the Rev. David Gillmer. The facts which he states, were related to him by his uncle, Joseph Ray, Esq., late American Consul to the Brazils.

He states as follows:—"It gives me pleasure to learn, that you are about publishing another work on the subject of Popery, in which the iniquity of the "*Man of Sin*," and particularly the licentiousness of the Romish Priesthood, is to be exposed. I believe such a volume is much needed, in order that the citizens of our country may know to what lengths the Popish Clergy go in iniquity, where they have the reins of the civil government under their control. The licentiousness of the Priests in South America is almost unparalleled. Under the garb of sanctity, they practise the most enormous acts of wickedness. In a Convent, in the Brazils, for the purpose of entering into the apartment of the nuns, they have made a kind of '*wheel*,'* into which the Priest gets, and covers himself with a cloth, that he may not be seen; the 'wheel' is then turned by one of the Monks. (for each takes his turn.) and thus he is introduced into the Convent. The late American Consul to the Brazils, Joseph Ray, Esq., resided in South America about ten years: from him I have received these facts. He informed me, that there was an aged Monk, named 'Joachim,' in the Monastery of that place; he wore a gown resembling the cassock of the Episcopal Clergy; the sleeves were very long, and the back and breast were made full. Every week he would come to the counting-house for wine, with which Mr. Ray supplied him gratuitously. The manner in which he carried it into the Monastery, may illustrate the hypocrisy and deception of the Monks.—He would put three bottles into each sleeve, and two into his breast and back, and walk into the Convent with as great an air of sanctimony, as though he had been the greatest saint on earth. The common people held 'Father Joachim' in great veneration, and considered him worthy of Canonization. The other Monks were as debauched and depraved a set of men as could be found. Dr. M——, who is a native of South America, and born a Roman Catholic, but has embraced Deism, through the corruption of the Clergy, informed me, that the Bishops and Priests were

---

* Mention is made of the "*wheel*," and the wheel-turner, by the great St. Ligori. See "DOWNFALL OF BABYLON," Vol. 2d, No. XI.

guilty of the blackest deeds of iniquity. They are infinitely worse, as it respects licentiousness and crime, than any other class of men. These things ought to be known to every citizen of the United States. But it is said that 'the Priests in North America are moral men, that they are not guilty of open wickedness, more than the Clergy of other denominations.'—This is denied. They *are* guilty of more crime than the Clergy of other denominations. And the reason why they are not detected more than they are, is owing to the fact that the Bishops conceal their crimes, 'because of the jealousy of Protestants;' and because they employ none in their service who are not Roman Catholics. Instances are known where Priests have been detected, in North America, of crimes of an aggravated nature. But let Popery once be established in the United States, and we shall then see exhibited their crimes. They will have no restraint, and no motive to influence them to conceal their wickedness. Our country will be like South America and Spain. The crimes of Priests will then stalk forth as they do in Popish countries.

"Romanism is the same the world over. This is acknowledged by Papists themselves. It is the same in America as it is in Rome. And were it the established religion of this country, the very same enormities would be committed, and the deep depravity which is manifested in civil governments, where the Pope exercises authority, would be committed and manifested in the United States of America.

DAVID GILLMER."

CERTIFICATES

RESPECTING THE CHARACTER OF THE AUTHORESS.

This certifies, that Rosamond Culbertson is a member of the Third Free Presbyterian Church in this city, in good and regular standing; that she possesses the confidence of her brethren and sisters in this church, and is cheerfully commended to the confidence of the Christian public in general.

By order of the Session,

N. E. JOHNSON, Mod.

New York, 16th Dec. 1835.

I have been acquainted with Rosamond Culbertson about two years; almost from the commencement of her religious experience. I have the fullest confidence in her integrity and Christian character; and knowing, also, the circumstances under which the accompanying Narrative has been written, (the writer herself being brought several times to the brink of the grave,) I can cheerfully commend her statements to the public, believing that they contain nothing but the truth.

ISAAC N. SPRAGUE,

Pastor of the Fourth Free Pres. Church, N. Y.

New York, Dec. 15, 1835.

I have been acquainted with Rosamond Culbertson for six months past; during which time I have been her physician. I believe her to be a devoted Christian. I think there can be no question as to the truth of the Narration she has written.

In December, 1835, she was very sick, and not expected to live from one hour to another: in fact, for several hours, she was speechless; and I could but just discern that she breathed. When she revived, so as to speak, I asked her if what she had written in her Narrative was true: she replied, " Yes,—the truth, and nothing but the truth."

J. A. WARD, M. D.

241 Spring St., N. Y.

New York, Dec. 18, 1835.

DEAR SIR—Rosamond Culbertson united with the Third Free Church of this City, on the 20th of June, 1834. Since that time, her walk and conversation, as far as I know, or can learn, has been very exemplary, and worthy of her high vocation. I have seen her more or less frequently since she united with the church, both in seasons of health and sickness. At all times she has seemed to maintain the same unshaken confidence in the Saviour, and the same determination to live, as far as her influence might extend, for the promotion of truth and righteousness in the earth. In my opinion, the most implicit confidence may be placed in her character for veracity and truth.

J. F. ROBINSON, Clerk of the Session of the Third Free Church.

REV. MR. SMITH.

New York, Jan. 7, 1836.

Auburn, January 2, 1836.

To J. F. ROBINSON, Esq.

DEAR SIR,—You will not be surprised, that I take a deep interest in the forth coming work of Mrs. Culbertson, when you learn that it was undertaken at my particular suggestion. She had given many facts, relative to her past life, in conversations held at different times, with my wife. These were reported to me, and so deeply impressed my mind, that I communicated a wish to have them committed to paper, fully impressed with the conviction, that the time was not far distant when the public good would be promoted by having them published. The papers were accordingly prepared, and committed to the care of my wife. We read them with interest, and were astonished and afflicted at the "mystery of iniquity" which they revealed. Several months elapsed, before my mind became settled as to the course which duty dictated in the case. At length I concluded to publish the Narrative, in successive numbers, in a newspaper, edited by the Rev. Mr. Smith, and entitled "THE DOWNFALL OF BABYLON." But before arrangements for presenting them to the public, through this medium, were completed, the design of publishing them in the form of a neat little volume, suggested itself to my mind. Accordingly the subject was proposed to the Rev. Mr. Smith, and also to H. D. Ward, Esq. To the latter gentleman the papers were committed for his perusal, and with a view to their being prepared for the press. After this I saw them no more. But I am happy to learn through your letter to me, that the work is soon to be presented to the public.

My sole desire, next to the public good, in wishing this Narrative to take the volume course to the eye of the community, was, that the unhappy, and yet happy, because, in my judgment, redeemed Rosamond, might derive from it something to support her in the midst of those infirmities, which, though self-induced, yet because *penitently wept* over, have awakened our tenderest sympathy. I hope, Dear Sir, that as professed Christians have had the charge of this matter, the individual most deeply interested, will, under no pretence of the claims of services rendered, or charity, be deprived of the entire avails of the book, after reasonable and even liberal charges are paid.

It is true, that, so far as my own impressions of facts, in regard to the subject of this Narrative, are concerned, there was little that I had not long before fully believed to be true. Indeed, such are the views given by writers in her own communion, of the abominations of the Romish church, that those who do not see and acknowledge them, must blush to complain against the charge of *voluntary* blindness. The circumstance of the authoress living amongst us enhances the subject of her own story, the more so as she has experienced in her own person, and seen with her own eyes, the enormities and abomination of which she speaks. She names persons—gives dates and localities—speaks of circumstances and events of public notoriety, and all in a way of such honest and undisguised simplicity, as to force conviction upon the mind of the reader, all but in despite of the strongest prejudice.

D. C. LANSING,
Pastor of the Presbyterian Church.

CONTENTS.

4

38   CONTENTS.

NARRATIVE.

CHAPTER I.

"So live, that when thy summons comes, to join
The innumerable caravan that moves
To that mysterious realm, where each shall take
His chamber in the silent halls of death,
Thou go not, like the quarry-slave at night,
Scourged to his dungeon; but, sustained and sooth'd
By an unfaltering trust, approach thy grave,
Like one who wraps the drapery of his couch
About him, and lies down to pleasant dreams."
BRYANT.

The author's introduction.—A brief sketch of her family.—Her marriage with Lieutenant C——.—Her departure from home with her husband.—They proceed to the West.—Her husband dies in New Orleans.—Goes to Covington to escape the yellow-fever.—Becomes acquainted with Mr. M——.—Marries Mr. W——, of Kentucky.—Removes to Louisville.—Flies from Mr. W——.—Is set on shore on the west bank of the Mississippi.—Is delivered from her forlorn situation by the captain of a steam-boat, on his way to Nashville.—Attempts to commit suicide.—Returns to New Orleans.

I HAVE had a great desire, for some time past, to let the world know of a poor wanderer, who has been living in the southern countries for the last fifteen years, in Mississippi, Missouri, New Orleans, and Kentucky; and for the five years from 1828 to 1833, on the Island of Cuba. On the 28th of July, 1833, through the mercies of the Lord, I was brought again to this Christian country; and when I look back on the last fourteen years, and on how many thousands and thousands of individuals I have seen, who are led and kept in darkness, as to seeking the salvation of their poor immortal souls, by the Roman Catholic Priests, my heart aches within; and I feel it my duty to let the world know what I know about them.

O! I pray that I may not dictate my pen!—that I may be guided in all I write by the help of the Lord, believing what I write here, will also be written in heaven!

I was born in Lebanon, in the state of New Hampshire,

4*

in the year 1803. My father removed to Charlestown, on Connecticut river, earlier in life than I can recollect.

I am at a loss how to bring my past life to view. Since I was eight years old, I have been, as I may term it, a wandering traveler. My father was a farmer in good circumstances. My parents were good and kind to all their children, who were eight in number, six sisters and two brothers. We were all brought up with as good opportunities for education as that country afforded.

Being a troublesome child at home, I was sent to live with my eldest sister at Concord, Vermont. I continued to be so mischievous and froward, that my sister was glad to get rid of me, and I was sent about, first to one, and then to another of the family, still remaining headstrong and unmindful of advice. My attention was fixed more upon dress and amusements, than it was either upon work or upon my book.

Some time after this I was sent with my youngest sister, to a school at Windsor, Vermont. We were placed under the care of a family by the name of I. P——. They kept a boarding-house for married and single ladies, and gentlemen. At this house there were several officers of the United States' army, who were recruiting, or enlisting soldiers for the public service. My affections here were soon won by an officer who was boarding in the same house with us. He was a lieutenant, and being a gay and fashionable person, he soon gained my affections. His attentions to me were noticed by the family, whose protection I was under. Mrs. P—— would sometimes tell me it was not prudent to be so intimate with him, and that she knew my mother would not approve of it. This, however, only seemed to increase my affections.

Some time after this I returned home to my parents in Charlestown. Lieut. C—— soon followed me, and although my father and mother were entirely opposed to his visiting me, he succeeded in introducing himself into the house. My father was an old revolutionary soldier, and was fond of talking about war affairs. Lieut. C—— had been in the battle of Bridgewater, and was wounded there. This was a good deal in his favor in respect to my father, who now seemed to take a delight in conversing with him.

The next day Lieut. C—— wrote a letter to my father, asking his consent for our marriage, but he remained as much opposed to it as ever.

During Lieut. C——'s stay at this place, which was but a few days, as he was going to be stationed at Boston, he wrote me several letters full of professions of his love. I answered his letters, and consented to marry him. All this was done without the knowledge or consent of my parents.

We then took a private opportunity of passing over into the state of Vermont, just on the opposite side of the Connecticut river; this was in the month of December, 1818, and were married by Squire M——.

Lieut. C——'s time being now expired, he had to proceed on to Boston. We sat out together, and I left home without bidding my dear parents farewell, because they would not be reconciled to us, or forgive us.

O! how well do I remember what were my feelings at that time! I knew that I had done wrong, and had left a poor heart-broken mother, with one brother and sister, who were all of the family that was with her at that time.

We boarded, while in Boston, at a Mrs. Lincoln's, in Hanover Street, where a number of officers and their families were also staying. We remained here six weeks, and then he received orders for Albany, where he was stationed at Greenbush. From this place he was ordered to Detroit, Michigan territory, and then to Greenbay. From Greenbay he was sent to New York, where he was stationed for a short time on Ellis' Island.

While we were in New York, I remained in Dr. ——'s family, in James Street. It was at this time that the large whale was to be seen at Brooklyn. I think it was in the year 1819.

Before my husband left New York, he was promoted to be Captain, and had the command of a company.

From this place we went to Pittsburgh, and, descending the Mississippi river, arrived at Baton-rouge, where Captain C—— was stationed.

After we were settled, I wrote to my dear friends. It was then one year since they had heard from me, and I was upwards of a thousand miles from them. In three months I received an answer from them, saying they had forgiven me, and had buried me, or that they would feel more happy if I were dead, and buried in a grave in my own country.

I lived with my husband between four and five years, and we had three children, but none are living. He was always a kind and affectionate husband to me.

From Baton-Rouge he was ordered to Black-Rock, which is situated in the interior of Arkansas Territory, and which is inhabited principally by Indians. Soon after this, we went to New Orleans, and there happened my death-blow. My husband caught the yellow-fever and died, being sick only twelve hours.

This, I think, was in the summer of the year 1822. I was left in a strange country, without friends, and with very little to live upon; and where they mourn but little, when they lose any of their friends, being principally Catholics, who think it a sin to mourn. Here I wrote to my parents of the death of my husband, and that I should come to them as soon as I could get a conveyance; and that I should probably leave the country before I could receive an answer from them. This was in August, and the yellow fever was raging, and every person leaving the city, who had the means to do it, going to different places. I was then boarding in a French family, who could speak no English; and was advised by some friends to leave town.

I left this place with some others, with whom I had a slight acquaintance, and went to Covington, across the Lake Ponchartrain. Here I remained but a few weeks, during which time the fever abated. While I was at this place, I became acquainted with a gentleman from New Orleans, who treated me with kindness and politeness.

He was a wealthy and respectable merchant of the name of M. M——, formerly of Baltimore. While he showed polite attention to me there, I had not the least idea he had any bad or evil motives. How easily innocence can be deceived! After my return to New Orleans, I remained in a French family, and was making inquiries for a passage to Boston, but there was no vessel going at that time, for the fever had not long abated, and commercial intercourse was not yet restored. It is customary, after being absent from the city, for your acquaintances to make calls, when you return; and M. M—— called on me. He had a slight acquaintance with the family where I resided. The French manners are very free. He made calls after calls, at the time the money I had was nearly gone, expenses being very high in that place. He, of course, knew my circumstances were low, as to money; and knew how to treat me and to train me to his wishes.

In the winter, the masquerades came on; and, as I mentioned how little they mourn for their friends, I was not long before I forgot the death and loss of my husband; and, being left in a strange country without friends, or wherewith to help myself, I soon forgot my troubles, and consented to go to the masquerades, balls, and theatres, gallanted by M. M——. These are places where all go: married and single, virtuous and others: all mix together. One imprudent step after another, with my money all gone, and M. M—— lavishing presents upon me, step by step, I consented to become mistress of his house without the rites of matrimony. He furnished me a house, and bought me a servant girl. By this time I had almost forgotten the death of my husband, and my dear father and mother, brothers and sisters: all my fine feelings were banished, and new ones commenced. I am sure I did not realize the loss of my character, as I should have done, if I had been in some other place; for it makes but very little difference among the French of New Orleans whether you are living with a gentleman married, or not, if you are living in good style.

Shortly after this, I received a letter from my parents,

begging me to come home without delay, and stating that my father had been to Boston, and made arrangements with the captain of a ship to bring me ; and if I wanted money he would remit it to me. At this time my circumstances were such I could not go ; it was now too late. When the captain called at my house, I told him I was married to M. M——, and could not go till another year. This he believed, as that country is very different from this. They do not take much pains to learn each other's character. I wrote to my friends by him, telling them I was married, and could not go for another year.

At that time I was twenty-one years of age. M. M—— always treated me kindly, and indulged me in every thing. He was wealthy, and in extensive mercantile business. With him I lived three years, wanting for nothing. In this time he had given me four servants, and I had some money in the bank. I had almost forgotten that I had any parents, or any friends grieving and mourning after me. I had become perfectly reconciled to my situation, being always indulged in going to parties, masquerades, balls, and theatres ; and every summer, during the sickly time, leaving the city for different places. I received another letter from my dear mother, informing me that all the family were pleading with me to return home. I answered her letter, and told her I would return next year.

By this time I became acquainted with a gentleman from Kentucky, who had received an education for a lawyer. He was of one of the first families in that state, by name W——. I became acquainted with him at the masquerades ; and meeting together at different places of amusement, he, at length, made me an offer of marriage, to which I immediately consented, for the sake of changing my life to a respectable one, knowing that he was of a good family, and that I should not go to his friends poor ; for, at that time, I had in the bank three thousand dollars, besides four slaves and my furniture. I had no reason to grieve for leaving M. M——, because I knew he never would marry me; and I wished to recover my lost reputation. When he knew I was going to marry Mr. W——, he had no wish to take any thing that he had given me; but gave all that I had up to me. Soon after I was married to Mr. W——, we went on to Louisville, in Kentucky, where his friends lived.

When we arrived in Kentucky, we were not received by Mr. W——'s friends. A certain friend of his, who advised and helped me to marry him, and who was with us at the time, wrote to his friends, that their son had married a person of a bad character; and the letter arrived a few days before us. Here I was again in a strange country, with money, but without character. O, what wretched feelings I had! We boarded at the principal hotel in the place. Mr. W—— had no money, and it was natural that he should flourish away on mine, as fast as possible. The eyes of every individual were on me, as I thought, to see if they could find any thing wrong in my conduct. Mr. W—— knew I was dejected, and felt lost to the world; and instead of trying to get into some business with what money I had, he was for dashing, sporting, and drinking. At length, he could give me a pleasant word, only when he came to ask for money.

All this time I kept within, and began seriously to think of my situation, and dear parents, brothers, and sisters; and most of all, that my character was gone. I felt lost to every thing. My money going, and Mr. W——'s cruel treatment, laid me on a sick bed, with no one to comfort or sympathize with me. They did not refuse to take us in to board, even in the first houses, for they knew we were married, and had money. Often did I reflect, when I was there, and all alone, "What have I done, that I should be so lost to all the world!—no kind friend to speak to, and a cruel husband to add to my sorrow."

When I recovered from my sickness, my money was almost all spent. Then I began to think on my distressed situation;—all my hopes blasted of ever Mr. W——'s providing a living for me; and my character gone:—for Kentucky, in this respect, is very different from New Or-

leans.   Mr. W—— had become very dissipated, and
knowing that he had spent almost all my money, trouble
on every side now stared me in the face.   When my money was all gone, we had no other resource for paying
our board, but selling some jewelry, which lasted but a
little while, and then all was gone—friends, character,
and means, to obtain money.   Such was my situation in
Kentucky.   I did not know how to work, and had a cruel
and unkind husband.   I could get no friends to tell my
troubles to, and my husband did not sympathize with me.
I had to act and advise for myself.   How I thought of
my dear mother! I could hear and see her mourn for her
lost child.   Then I could see how wrong I had been; but
it was too late.   I knew, for the first time, and was sensible that I was lost—lost for ever.   You may imagine
how wretched my feelings were.   I shortly after made up
my mind to leave him; but I knew not where to go, or
how to defray my expenses.   I made a confidant of my
chambermaid, to assist me in leaving him, as we were
then owing considerable for board.

    In my situation, it was easiest, and I thought it was
best, to go to New Orleans, as I had friends there, and
there were steamboats leaving Louisville every day for
that place.   I dressed myself in travelling apparel, and left
our lodgings, unknown to any one, except the chambermaid, to whom I gave all my clothes, except what I had
on, which were of value.   She made arrangements with
the captain of a steamboat, who was going to New Orleans the next morning, to take me on board.   Here I was
obliged to intrust myself to the charge of a strange captain, with no money, for a passage of a thousand miles.
I told him I had no money, and would pay him when we
arrived at New Orleans; on which he took me on board;
and as the cabin-berths were all taken up, he gave me
his stateroom, which was a little room opening from the
cabin, where he kept his books and clothes.   This I was
obliged to consent to; and he would often come into my
apartment, and question me, "why I was alone, unprotected, and without money in that country."   I did not

think myself obliged to tell him.   The steamboat was de-
layed by running on a sawyer, near a place in the Ohio
river, called Devil's Point.

A few days after leaving Louisville, when we were
about a hundred miles below the mouth of the Ohio, he
came to my room, heated with strong drink, and insulted
me.   I told him before I would consent to his liberties, I
would go on shore.   Although I was far astray, I still had
some respect for my person.   The noise which he made,
was heard in the cabin, and the next morning some of the
passengers made inquiries of the captain about it.   He
said, he suspected I was a person of no character; and
that it must have been one of the passengers who was
there at my room; and if he found that to be the case,
he would put me ashore.   This excited some of the passengers to try to get a glimpse at me, and I received books
to read, and notes were handed me by the steward, which
I did not understand; but I knew all was not right.   I
again reflected on my lost situation, and then, on my past
imprudent conduct.

The next night, about 10 o'clock, the captain entered
my room again.   He was much intoxicated, and told me,
he would put me ashore in that wilderness country, where
the houses are often forty or fifty miles from each other.
We came to plain words; and he then ordered a boat,
and put me ashore in the night, on the west bank of the
Mississippi river, by a wood-pile, far from any house, except the old man's who kept the wood-pile, who came to
me, and asked what I was put on shore for.   I could n~
tell him, but said I had no more money to pay any mir-
ther.   Upon this, he took me home with him to a little
village of about ten or fifteen houses, all made of logs,
very poor, and each containing only one room.   He told
his wife he had picked up a poor girl, who had been put
ashore, for having no money to pay her passage.   She
got me the best she had for supper, and was very kind to
me; she had six children.   I was put in bed with four of
them, the other two slept with their parents.   After I went

to bed, reflecting on my lost situation, I imagined I was among robbers, and that they would kill me before morning. I spent the night under these feelings. The next morning she got up early, and appeared to do every thing that laid in her power to provide me a good breakfast. I remained here a number of days, before I could decide what to do. My mind was fully made up that I was lost for this world; the next did not come into my mind. I did not see how I could get away from this place. Every day the old gentleman used to go to his wood-pile, to sell wood to the steamboats; and one day, I asked him, if he would beg some captain to take me. He used to tell me no captain would take me without money, and that I must stay with them. All the little village became jealous at my remaining with them, they all wanted me to come and spend a day with them; but I did not leave the old gentleman.

Here I was destitute of clothes, for I had nothing besides what I had on. One day, while I was reflecting about what would become of me, I saw the old man and a gentleman coming towards the house. He was captain of a steamboat; and had heard, from some of the passengers who arrived at Natches by the boat I left Kentucky in, that Captain B—— had left a poor female in a wilderness country on the Mississippi river. The captain knew him and his character, which was one of the worst sort. He had done the same thing before, and was taken up for it; but the boat, or part of it, being his own, they could do nothing with him. The captain who relieved me, was bound to Nashville, in Tennessee, where he belonged. He made the poor people a present of five dollars, and some provisions from the boat. He took me on board, and treated me with the kindness of a brother.

In nine days we reached Nashville; but not without meeting some more trouble. The steamboat ran on a snag in a dark night; and every one of us thought we should be lost; but only the boat was damaged, and that was soon repaired.

When I arrived at Nashville, I again found myself in a strange country, without friends, character, clothes, or money; and I was brought to reflect on my lost situation for ever. How I could seem to hear and see my dear mother grieving and mourning for her lost child! The captain took me to an acquaintance of his, who was of a respectable family, and told them a favourable story concerning me, which I had told him. He was a married man, and had a family living not far from Nashville. Here, again, I asked myself what I should do; for, although I had gone so far astray, I was now determined to respect my person. I was alone, unprotected, poor, and in a disguised character, as to the family I was with. The captain gave me money for one week's board, out of pity for my situation, before he went home to his family. I knew the week would soon come to a close, and then what should I do for the next! I had no clothes, except what were on me; and I was sick.

Here I reflected upon all my past life, from the time I was at Montreal with my sisters. Since then I had always been imprudent, deceiving my dear mother, and I had no one else to blame but myself. I felt lost to the whole world, and I had rather die than live. I was not brought up with religious instructions, and neither knew nor thought what would become of my soul, nor whether I had a soul. I made up my mind to make away with myself. I bought seventy-five cents worth of laudanum, which I got by selling a lace veil that I had on my hat. I bought it at different apothecaries, and came home, and told them I had been to see a French family, with whom I had become acquainted in New Orleans. I had it in six vials, and put it all in a tumbler in my room ready. I then went and sat down with the family. The lady was the mother of five children, two daughters and three sons. This was about 8 o'clock in the evening. I reflected on my dear home, and my dear mother, seeing all her dear family around her. I thought,

Oh, mother, mother! where am I!* I got up immediately and went to my room, and swallowed the laudanum.

Immediately after I had taken it, I felt a pleasant sensation, which lasted but a short time; I was then sorry I had not written to my dear mother, but it was too late: I soon fell on my bed. One of the daughters slept with me, and by the time she came to bed, I was past speaking. She gave an alarm, and a doctor was soon sent for. He immediately knew what ailed me, and said, that by taking such a large quantity I had saved my life. When I was brought to my senses, I knew what a wicked deed I had done, and that I had brought myself into a more distressed situation than before. I was covered with blisters, and not only suffering bodily pain, but was confined to my bed, and required the strict attention of a doctor, besides the burden I was to the family. The captain also was blamed for taking me there; and it was said all was not right; but the doctor, being a feeling man, said I should not be removed, till I was better; and that he would pay my expenses. He said he knew my friends in New Orleans, as he did my first husband by reputation. Through his kindness, I was here three weeks, on a sick bed. He paid me strict attention, and all the family were very kind. A great many persons called to know what was the cause of my rashness; but they could get no other information, than that I was tired of living, and wished to die.

When I was recovered, the doctor advised me to go out into the country a little way, as it would be better for my health; and I went to a hotel about six miles from Nash-

---

* "My mother's voice! How often creeps
   Its cadence o'er my lonely hours,
Like healing sent on wings of sleep,
   Or dew to the unconscious flowers!
I can't forget her melting prayer,
   E'en while my pulses madly fly;
And in the still, unbroken air,
   Her gentle tones come stealing by.
And years, and sin, and manhood flee,
   And leave me at my mother's knee."
                  A New England poet.

ville, near the president's residence. There I found a young lady with whom I had a little acquaintance formerly at New Orleans. She was boarding there, and I found some relief in telling her my troubles. I looked pale, like death. She was a person of my size, and well supplied with clothes. She gave me leave to make free, and take what I wanted, the same as a sister, and would not consent to my leaving for New Orleans, until she was ready to go. In a little time I recovered my health; but never thought it was through the kind mercy of God that friends had been raised up to minister to my wants among strangers, and that I had not gone to an everlasting hell.

I revealed all my troubles to my friend, as I esteemed her. She was a person who had seen a great deal of the world, and never took any trouble to heart. I soon thought very little of my past situation : but a few days ago I was so near another world and lost for ever! O, I cannot now help saying, Lord, I was not deserving thy kind mercies! But I had not these feelings at that time; I knew not the value of my soul, and I felt lost to the whole world. I left for New Orleans with my friend, who defrayed my expenses on the journey. Here I found myself again in the place where my troubles commenced. Only eighteen months ago, I was living a thoughtless life, in splendour and in wealth ; and now I had nothing but what my friend gave me. I could not bear the idea of going to see Mr. M——, the gentleman I had been living with. I knew I had brought all my troubles on myself; for I married Mr. W—— more to reclaim my character, than any other motive. I had no desire to see any of my acquaintances, partly through mortification at my low circumstances, and partly because many of my friends had told me I should be sorry if I trusted to Mr. W——. I had known a lady, when previously living in New Orleans, who, at this time, lived in Havana, but was on a visit at New Orleans. As I had no desire to live in New Orleans, I consented to go with her to Havana. She was in good circumstances, but not married to the gentleman she lived with, which was thought little of in that country.

CHAPTER II.

ON THE CELIBACY OF THE POPISH CLERGY.

"Proh dolor ! hos tolerare potest Ecclesia Porcos
Duntaxat ventri, veneri, somnoque, vacantes ?"

PRELIMINARY REMARKS.

Such is the dark picture of the moral corruptions of the Romish Priesthood, that is about to be laid open before the public in the following Narrative, that we have thought it expedient to introduce this chapter, which is principally taken from " EDGAR's VARIATIONS," by way of introduction to it.

Our object in this, is to prepare the public mind for believing the disclosures that are to be laid before them, by exhibiting to them a mere glimpse, as it were, of the pernicious effects of Priestly celibacy, as it has been portrayed by their own writers, theologians, Saints, Popes, and Councils.

The disclosures made by the authoress of this Narrative, astonishingly wonderful and black as they are, do not, however, make the picture of Priestly licentiousness more atrocious than the character given of them by their own writers.

The picture which is drawn by the pious authoress of this Narrative, although not darker than that traced out by the pen of Popish writers themselves, is, however, more interesting, from the circumstance, that the events which she describes are of recent date, and most of the personages of whom she speaks, are now actually living, and are still implicated in the crimes and abominations which form the subject of the Narrative.

We, therefore, earnestly beg the public to give this 2d chapter a reading previous to entering upon the 3d, which is the commencement of the captivity and sufferings of the authoress on the island of Cuba, and of the horrid disclosures which she makes.

The origin of Popish Celibacy.—Its immediate and pernicious effects.— Pope Gregory VII, who was promoted to the Popedom, A. D. 1074, enacts severe laws to restrain the profligacy of the Clergy.—The effects of his severity.—Councils convened for the same purpose.—Character of the Popish Clergy previous to the Reformation.—The Prelates of the General Councils of Lyons, Constance, and Basil, as criminal as the Clergy whom they pretend they wish to reform.—Character of the Popish Clergy since the Reformation.

THE Decretal of Pope Syricius, addressed, in the year 385, to Himerius, contains the first general interdiction of

Clerical matrimony. Its priority, as a general prohibition, is acknowledged by Clithou as well as by Bruys, Espensaeus, Cassander, and many other patrons of Popery. No authority of an earlier date can be produced for the enactment. Clithou, c. 4. in Bell. I. Bruy. I. 142.

The consequence of this Decree was, that the Romish Clergy, from that day, became the most licentious of men. Many of them absolutely refused to obey it. Various plans were resorted to in order to evade its severity; one of which was the introduction of SUNISACTANISM or DOMESTICISM. A second party engaged in open or concealed concubinage; while a third party, in bold, honest, and honorable violation of unjust, unnatural, and unscriptural Canons, married and lived, not indeed in abstinence, but in chastity with their lawful wives.

Many of the Clergy had recourse, in this extremity, to Domesticism. This consisted in keeping female inmates in their dwellings. These women were devoted in profession, though not by vow, to virginity. (Now-a-days, these Priestly coadjutresses are styled *Nieces*, or Nuns.) Their ostensible duty was to superintend the domestic concerns of the house. Cyprian, Jerom, and Chrysostom, have depicted the cohabitation of these holy domestics with a bold, but faithful pencil. These holy Priests and their domestics, if the statement of the Saints may be credited, occupied the same house, the same chamber, and the same every thing else;—" Eadem domo, uno cubiculo saepe uno tenentur et lectulo." Jerom ad Eust. 4. 33. Cyprian ad Pom.—Edgar.

The Clergy, after that memorable and fatal epoch, were converted into mere gallants and coxcombs. Their whole attention, says their St. Jerom, was engaged on dress and perfumery. Their fingers shone with rings, their hair was frizzled by the curling-tongs, and they walked on tiptoe, lest their shoes or feet should get besmeared with dirt. Jerom, 4. 40.

Chrysostom also gives an animated description of the society of the Romish Priests and their housekeepers. He portrays in glowing colors, " their smiles, their laughs, their free conversation, their soft words, their communications at table during the day, their supping together at night, and other things which we deem it proper to omit." Chysos. de Subin. I. 231.

A second variety of evasion of these Canons, consisted in concubinage. This was a native result of the unnatural regulations against wedlock. The accounts on this subject, transmitted by the historians of those times, are appalling. Profligacy, says Giannon, prevailed among the Clergy, who practised all kinds of lewdness. Ratherius, Bishop of Verona, represents the Clergy as guilty of bigamy, drunkenness, and fornication. The Italian Priesthood, in particular, says he, fomented their passions by excess of food and wine. Gian. V. 6. Dach. I. 354. Bruy. 2. 268.

Atto's language on this topic is equally striking. He says that the Priests lived in a public manner with their consecrated paramours. Fascinated with their wanton allurements, the abandoned Clergy conferred on the partners of their guilt, the superintendence of their family and all their domestic concerns. Their courtezans, during the life of their companions in iniquity, managed their household; and at their death, heired their property. The Ecclesiastical alms and revenues, in this manner, descended to the accomplices of vile pollution. Atto, Ep. 9. Dach. I. 439. The hirelings of prostitution were adorned, the Church wasted, and the poor oppressed by men, who professed to be the patrons of purity, the guardians of truth, and the protectors of the wretched and the needy.

Damian represents the guilty Mistress as Confessing to the guilty Priest. Dam. in Bruy. 2. 356. Gian. X. §. 1. This presented another absurdity, and an aggravation of the crime. The formality of Confessing what the Father Confessor knew, and receiving forgiveness from a partner in sin, was an insult on common sense, and presented one of the many ridiculous scenes which have been exhibited on the theatre of the world.

The adultery and fornication of the Clergy degenerated, in many instances, into incest and other abominations of the grossest kind. Some Priests, according to the Council of Mentz, in the year 888, "had sons by their own sisters." Bin. 7. 137. Labb. 11. 586.

The Council of Nice and some others of a later date, through fear of scandal, deprived the Clergy of all female company, except a mother, a sister, or an aunt, who, it was reckoned, were beyond all suspicion. But the means intended for prevention, was the occasion of more accumulated scandal and more heinous criminality. The interdiction was the introduction to incestuous and unnatural prostitution. The Council of Mentz, therefore, in its 10th Canon, as well as other cotemporary and late Synods, had to forbid the Clergy the society of even their nearest female relations. .

A third variety for the evasion, or rather for the infraction of these Canonical interdictions, was clandestine or avowed matrimony. Some of the Priests who still had some remains of conscience, shuddered at the commission of fornication, adultery, or incest ; and had recourse, therefore, to the honorable institution of marriage. The number of these continued to increase in opposition to the Decretals of Popes, the Canons of Councils, and the prepossessions of the people. Epiph. H. 59. Jerom adv. Vig. · Thom. I. 43.

Such was the state of Clerical matrimony, at the accession of Hildebrand or Gregory VII. to the Popedom, in the year 1074. The reign of this hierarch commenced a new era in the annals of Sacerdotal celibacy. Gregory enforced celibacy with a high hand among the Latin Ecclesiastics; and was supported in the undertaking by many of the laity. The attempt, however, was long opposed by the Priesthood : and its success terminated in the general concubinage and debauchery of the Western Clergy.

Gregory succeeded, to a great extent, in the suppression of Priestly marriage. Several of his predecessors had made a similar attempt, but in vain. Stephen, Nicholas, and Alexander, had labored for this purpose, and failed. But Gregory proceeded in this, as in every other design, with superior ability, perseverance, and resolution ; and his efforts were crowned, in the end, with wonderful success. He summoned a Council, and issued Canons, separating the married Clergy from their partners, and forbidding the ordination of any who would not vow perpetual continence. He prohibited the laity from hearing Mass, when celebrated by a married Priest. Bin. 7. 473. Bruy. 2. 388. 418. Labb. 12. 547. Du Pin, 2. 244.

Such swelling innovations, and such severe enactments against marriage in the Clergy, caused all Popish Christendom to be polluted with Sacerdotal profligacy of the deepest dye, as is evident from the relations of Bernard, Agrippa, Henry, Clemangis, and Mezeray. Bernard the Saint of Clairvaux, in the 12th century, admitted and lamented the licentiousness of the Prelacy and Priesthood, " who committed, in secret, such acts of turpitude as would be shameful to express." Bernard, 1725—1728.

Clemangis reckoned the adultery, impurity, and obscenity of the Clergy, beyond all description. They frequented the stews and taverns, and spent their whole time in eating, drinking, reveling, gaming, and dancing. Surfeited and drunk, these Sacerdotal sensualists fought, shouted, roared, rioted, and blasphemed God and the Saints ; and passed, shortly after, from the embrace of the harlot, to the altar of God. Clemangis, through shame, drew the curtain over the abominations that the Nuns practised in their Convents, which he called brothels of licentiousness. To veil a woman was, in that age, to prostitute her.

For further details relative to the shocking depravity of the Popish Clergy during the succeeding centuries, and up to the time of the Reformation, for brevity sake, I refer the reader to Henry, Clemangis, Mezeray, and other historians of those days, whose annals are stained with the universal depravity of the Romish hierarchy ; Popes, Cardinals, Bishops, Priests, Monks, and Nuns, are all included.

Lest the weight of the above testimonies should be considered by the Papists as insufficient, we will add to it that of their venerable Councils. The Council of Valladolid, in the year 1322, in its 7th Canon, confirms all that is stated above. "The Clergy," (according to this Council,) "prodigal of character and salvation, led lives of enormity and profligacy in public concubinage." The Canon of Valladolid was renewed in the year 1473, in the Council of Toledo. This Council represented the clergy as living in the filthiest atrocity, which rendered them contemptible to the people. Labb. 15. 247. Several other Councils, which for brevity sake have to be omitted, also thundered out their Bulls and Decrees against the licentiousness of the Priestly marauders.

The Italian and Roman Clergy appear, of all others, to have been the most licentious. Dachery, I. 354.

A select Council of Cardinals and Bishops assembled by Paul 3d, in the year 1538, have drawn a picture of the Roman courtezans, and the attention paid them by the Roman Clergy. These courtezans lived in splendid palaces, walked or rode as matrons through the city, and were attended at noonday by a train of the Clergy and the nobility, the friends of the Cardinals. Crabb, 3. 823. Coss. 5. 547.

To put the climax to all these abominations, we find that even the very Prelates themselves assembled in *General Councils* were as licentious, abandoned, and guilty as the Priests in their dispersed capacity. This was exemplified in the General Councils of Lyons, Constance, and Basil. The Council of Lyons demoralized the city in which it was convened. Cardinal Hugo, in a speech to the citizens, immediately after the dissolution of the Sacred Synod, boasted that Lyons, at the meeting of the assembly, contained two or three stews; but, at its departure, comprehended only one ; which, however, extended without interruption, from the Eastern to the Western Gate. Labb. 16. 1436. Bruy. 4. 39. Labb. 16. 1435. Edgar.

We shall now turn to the Decrees of Pope Benedict XIV. as recorded by the great St. Ligori ; either of which authorities, no Papist will dare to call in question. By these documents we shall see that the Popish Clergy are still what they ever have been, men of morals the most corrupt; and men too, of all others, who are not to be trusted alone with females.

The Decrees to which I allude, of the Sovereign Pontiff Benedict XIV. are recorded by the great St. Ligori, in his Theological Treatise, Tom. ix. De Rom. Pont. Decr. cap. 2. The Decrees are headed thus : "CONTRA SOLLICITANTES," &c. et "CONTRA EXQUIRENTES," &c. "*Against those Priests who entice others to sin, and who abuse the sacrifice of the Mass,*" &c.

In respect to one of the Decrees, the Saint, speaking of the Sovereign Pontiff Benedict XIV. says, "Our Most Holy Lord," (the Pope.) "seeing how great is the sin of those lost men," (alluding to the Priests,) "who abuse the Holy Sacrifice of the Mass, and the Sacrament of Confession, which was instituted for the salvation of the faithful, but which they make use of for their destruction and damnation"—"Decrees, that hereafter all Priests, both secular and regular, of whatever Order, Institution, Congregation, or Society soever they may be, who solicit those whose Confessions they hear, to filthy and criminal actions, shall, besides the penalties already threatened by the Canon Law, the Apostolical Constitutions, and especially by the Constitutions of Sixtus V. and Gregory XV. of happy memory, shall, we decree, incur the perpetual inability of celebrating the aforesaid Holy Sacrifice of the Mass."

The other Decree was issued by the Pope, in order to put a check to a custom that was common among the Priests in Spain, of compelling their penitents, in the tribunal of Confession, to tell them who were their accomplices in sin. It is stated in the Decree that the Ghostly Fathers were so pertinaciously bent on ascertaining the names and the residence of those with whom their penitents were in the habit of committing sin, that, not content with merely soliciting them to tell them where their accomplices lived, they were compelled to do it, by not granting them the absolution of their sins. "Which intolerable IMPUDENCE !" (says the Pope,) "they color over, under the pretext that they wish to visit them *merely to give them good advice!*" "IAM VERO !" exclaims the

Holy Father, the Pope, " *experience has taught us* what evils have followed from such a course as this !" [Ligori Theol. T. ix. De Rom. Pont. Decr. c. 2.]

Ligori has also presented us with another Decree of this same Pontiff, entitled " SUPER CLAUSURA MONIALIUM."

By this Decree, all Clergymen, of whatsoever dignity they may be, are strictly prohibited from entering into Nunneries, or from having any communication with the Nuns, under any pretext whatever.

It appears, from what the Saint writes, that this Decree of Benedict XIV. is no more than a renewed promulgation of Decrees which had already frequently been made, relative to the same subject, by many of his predecessors, and especially by the Holy Council of Trent.

" *Exceptis dumtaxat.*" The only exception that is made to this interdiction, is respecting the Superiors of those Establishments, that is, those Clergymen under whose immediate jurisdiction the Nuns are placed ; and even in regard to these, the Decree is as follows : " in cassibus tamen necessariis, et servatis de jure servandis, et non aliter omnino," they, the superiors, are to have no intercourse with the Nuns, " except in cases of necessity, observing, at the same time, the Rules laid down by the Canons, but otherwise, they are by no means whatsoever to have any intercourse together." (Id. ib.)

The rules laid down by the Canons, which are here spoken of, are, that Priests shall never hear the Confessions of Nuns in a private or clandestine manner, but openly, in the Confessional-boxes, in the Chapel.

So much importance was attached to the observance of these mandates, that those Priests who dared to infringe them, incurred, " *ipso facto*," the Censures of the church, from which no one could absolve them but the Sovereign Pontiff himself, except at the hour of death. (Id. ib. D. vi.)

The aforesaid Decrees were given, " SUB ANNULO PISCATORIS," "*under the ring of the Fisherman*," the one, on the 4th of the Nones of June, A. D. 1746, the other, on the 3d of January, 1742.

The great St. Basil, it seems, knew as much about the

6

Priests, as St. Ligori, and Pope Benedict XIV., and Sixtus
V., and Gregory XV., and the compilers of the Canon
Law, and of the Apostolical Constitutions, and the Holy
Council of Trent ; for all of these were perfectly well acquainted with the character of the Priesthood, and took
every precaution in their power to keep them within
bounds.   The great St. Basil, we say, knew as much
about the thing as any of the rest.   " It is more proper,"
(says this great Saint,) " for the Lady Superieure to be
present while a Nun is Confessing to a Priest, *for the sake
of decency and safety.*" Basil, Reg. Brev. Int. 110.   We,
the wicked heretics, generally consider that a child is perfectly safe with its father ; but we see from the above,
that the Popes and the Saints had reason to think that the
spiritual children of the Priests, are not altogether safe
with their Spiritual Fathers.

Thoroughly assured, indeed, must we be, that the dis-
orders which reign amongst the Priests, must be of a character of the deepest dye, to force even their own - - -tiffs
thus publicly, and plainly, and severely, to reprimand
them, and to threaten them with the Censures and the
penalties of the church, unless they reform, and restrain
their passions.

I am fully aware that the Romish Priests, although they
cannot deny the truth of the statements made by their
own Saints, will endeavor to cloak the thing over by saying, that there are bad men to be found in every state and
condition of life, that there was a Judas even among the
Apostles.   This is all true, but, unfortunately, it appears
that the number of the guilty is not few, but many.
"*Many Priests,*" (says Saint Ligori,) " who before," (they
began to hear the Confession of the spiritual women,)
" were innocent, afterwards, on account of their attractions, lost both God and their soul !" Ligori, Prax. Conf.
T. VIII. C. 8. N. 119, 120.

Poor, fragile Spiritual Fathers indeed must they be !
that, in order to preserve their Spiritual Children from falling a prey to their unruly passions, it was found necessary,
as St. Basil states, that " the Superieure or Abbess of the

Monastery should be present to watch them while hearing the Confession of the Nuns !" or that it should be found expedient, as St. Ligori states, "that the doors should be kept open while the Priests are hearing the Confession of the women, and that they should sit where they could be seen !" Ligori, Prax. Conf. T. VIII. C. 8. N. 119.

" Experience has taught us," (says the Pope, Benedict XIV.) " what evils have followed from such a course as this !" that is, as has been related above, from the Priests' " visiting females *under pretence of giving them good advice.*"

We now see what precautions are absolutely necessary, in order to protect female innocence from the dangers to which they are exposed by Confessing to their Ghostly Fathers.

Now, if it be found that none of these prudent precautions are observed, but, on the contrary, the very opposite extreme is adopted, these two conclusions irresistibly rush upon the mind ; the one, that there must be something radically wrong in the Priests. Certain things are peremptorily forbidden them, by their Saints, by their Popes, and even by the Infallible Council of Trent; and they disobey. And the consequent conclusion; which presses with the weight of demonstration, is, that they must have some ulterior design in view, for the accomplishing of which, they are willing to sacrifice their conscience in the sacrifice of obedience ; and when conscience is gone, the depravity of nature under the influence of the passions, usurps her place.

Now, when we reflect upon what Bellarmine, Ricci, Petrarch, and others, have told us respecting Nuns, those spiritual women, as Ligori calls them, that is, "that MANY of them enter into the Monasteries who are NOT CALLED OF GOD ; enter through motives PROMPTED BY FLESH AND BLOOD," (Bellarm. Gem. Colom. 3 Opusc. L. 11. C. 5.) and compare it with what Ligori, Pope Benedict XIV., and others, tell us respecting the Priests, that is, " *that many of them,* who before were innocent, have, ON AC-COUNT OF THE ATTRACTIONS of those spiritual women, (the Nuns,) lost both God and their soul;" I say, when we reflect on all this, we are demonstratively convinced, that the Monastic Institutions, the Tribunal of Confession, and the Celibacy of the Priesthood, are very far indeed from being of Divine institution, as is pretended. Nor were these Institutions ever introduced into the world under the influence of the Spirit of God. For, certainly, the Spirit of God, is a Spirit of wisdom, a Spirit of counsel, and a Spirit of love. But where would be the wisdom, in unnecessarily placing his creatures in the midst of danger, when he tells us, "*that he who loveth danger shall perish in it?*" Where would be his counsel, in subjecting the infirmities of the flesh to excitements, which his Holy Word throughout commands us to shun? And where would be his love, in placing his creatures in that situation of life which will be their ruin? No—God wishes us, and commands us, to shun danger; to avoid the occasions of criminal excitements; and to pursue a course of life that will ultimately lead to happiness.

Before we close this chapter on the baneful consequences which emanate from a Popish system of Clerical celibacy, we will unfold a leaf or two of the writings of the celebrated St. Ligori, who was Canonized by Pope Pius VII., on the 15th September, A. D. 1816. His system of Theology, from which I quote, is received and taught in all the Popish schools. That it stands on the highest pinnacle of esteem and commendation in the church of Rome, I prove by the eulogiums passed upon it by the same Sovereign Pontiff, by whom he was Canonized, as well as by the exalted praises lavished upon it by the " SACRED CONGREGATION OF RITES," and by his " SUPREME EMINENCE THE CARDINAL OF CASTILE." The two former of these, that is, Pope Pius VII., and the " SACRED CONGREGATION OF RITES," have declared, that " *in ea nihil censura dignum repertum fuisse,*"— " THAT THEY HAVE FOUND IN THE MORAL THEOLOGY OF ST. LIGORI, NOTHING WORTHY OF CENSURE." The latter, that is, his " SUPREME EMINENCE THE CARDINAL OF CASTILE," says, that " St. Ligori is the ornament of

our age, and the splendor of the Episcopal Order," and
that "there is nothing in what he teaches, that is not
sound, wholesome, and according to God,"—" *Sana ac
secundum Deum*." Ligor. Theol. Prefatio VI.

Now, according to this same Saint Ligori, I am going
to show, that the church of Rome propagates a doctrine,
under which all their Clergy can find a cloak to screen
the vices to which they are addicted in consequence of
their forced and unnatural state of celibacy. The doctrine to which I allude is, that the devil has the power of
assuming a human shape, and that he actually exercises
this power for the purpose of indulging his lustful appetite. Theol. Ligor., Prox. Conf. T. VIII. C. VII. S. 7.

In the exercise of this power, the church of Rome
teaches, that the devil " potest etiam verum semen afferre
aliunde acceptum, naturalemque ejus emissionem imitari,
et quod ex hujusmodi concubitu vera proles possit nasci,
puta a viro in somno pollutionem patiente, et prolificum
calorem conservando, illico in matricem infundere; quo
casu proles illa non erit quidem filia dæmonis, sed illius
cujus est semen, ut ait D. Thomas." Id. ib.

Hence it is, that in Popish countries, the Priests have
nothing more to do than to lay the fruits of their illicit
intercourse to the charge of the devil, who, according to
the doctrine of the Popish church, has to father all the
progeny of Priestly propagation.

Let a Priest act in regard to this matter as he will, he
can exculpate himself with ease, by merely insisting that
it was not he who committed the deed, but the devil who
assumed his person. In vain is it then, for a Nun, or any
other Miss soever, to pretend to identify the Priest in her
accusation of his criminality. He will tell her, (and she
is bound to believe him,) that it was the devil who as
sumed his shape, imitated his voice, and deceived her in
disguise.

So firmly persuaded is the church of Rome of the truth
of what is spoken of above, that the very last victim that
was publicly burned by the Inquisition at Seville in Spain,
on the 7th November, in the year 1781, was burned ex-

6*

pressly on account of her being supposed guilty of the thing above stated. Llorente* in his History of the Inquisition of Spain, speaking of this woman, who, he says, was a supposed Saint, tells us that she was burned to death by the Inquisition, for having made a covenant with the devil, and for having had illicit intercourse with him under the disguise of a man. Had she not remained "*negatively impenitent*," to use the Inquisitorial technicality, i. e. had she acknowledged that she was guilty, says he, she might have escaped death. Lorente T. iv. C. 66.

This fact proves at once, independent of other proofs, that the above stated horrors accord both with the doctrine of the Romish Divines, and with that of the Romish church.

Thus we see to what satanic stratagems these men resort, in order to satiate their lust with impunity. O! the horrors of their pretended purity! Such are the results of their boasted celibacy!—and the execrable doctrine they affirm is found in Scripture, "*verissima Scriptura testatur*," says Ligori. Ibid.

Are men who can invent such a doctrine as this, to be trusted with virtuous females? Nuns, if they had a spark of virtue, should spurn such "*Holy Fathers*." Were they innocent, and not destitute of common sense, they might see the object of a doctrine so foul, and so fraught with every danger.

Enough has now been said. Let the world pass its sentence.†

* Llorente was a Popish historian, and wrote with truth and candor.
† For further details respecting Popish celibacy, see "DOWNFALL OF BABYLON," a weekly Periodical, published in New York, Vol. 1, No. 21, 22.

CHAPTER III.

"Fear God!" the thunders said; "Fear God!" the waves;
"Fear God!" the lightning of the storm replied;
"Fear God!" deep loudly answered back to deep.

                 POLLOCK. -

Voyage to Havanna.—Engages with Father Manuel Canto, a Romish Priest.—Learns the Champara Spanish.—Has the Stranger's Fever.— Attempt to make her a Roman Catholic.—Manuel's habits of Gambling. — The dress of the Priests.—Second attack of the Fever, and attempt to make her a Roman Catholic.—Dress of the Capuchins.—Reasons with the Priest on their wicked course of life.— On their power to forgive sins. — The Confession of Criminals who had committed robbery, in order to get money to fee the Priests for saying Masses to save their souls.— Manuel's Supper Parties, and Friends, at Rosamond's House.— The Priests sell different sorts of Candles for various Superstitious Purposes.

WE left New Orleans for Matanzas, there being no vessel direct for Havanna, and had a rough and dangerous passage of ten days. Once we were in a severe storm, and every one on board expected to perish. This was the first time I ever was afraid to die. Oh! I well remember what my feelings were at the time; when I thought, if I died, I should go to everlasting torments. Now I reflected on my cruel treatment to my dear mother, and what I had done while at Nashville, which I had never thought or felt the wickedness of till then. I prayed, and said, if God would spare my life, and let me get on land again, I would go home to my dear parents. One of the sailors was washed overboard, and lost in the storm. When we got to Matanzas, I soon forgot the serious promise I had made; and how could I expect to prosper! We remained here but a few days, and then went to Havanna.

Here I found myself in another world, as I thought, in a Spanish country; I did not understand their language, nor they mine. The people are more easy and free in their manners, than in New Orleans; but, as to character, it does not make much difference who, or what stranger you are, so long as you dress, and make a good appearance. Several American ladies were living on the

island, who were all wealthy. and appeared happy in their
private relations.   I had been there but a few days, before I became acquainted. through one of my female
friends, with a Spanish Priest. named Manuel Canto, and
commonly called Father Canto, who belonged to St.
Francisco Convent.   Through an interpreter, he made
me an offer to take me under his protection : and I consented to live with him. not knowing, at the time. that he
was a Priest. He immediately hired a house for me, at three
ounces. or fifty dollars a month, and he furnished me five
hundred dollars to commence with. and I put myself
under his protection wholly.   Then it was too late to re-
consider the step : for if once you put yourself under their
protection, it is dangerous to leave a Roman Catholic
Priest in that country.   I remained with him there on the
island about five years.   In that time I was put in the
way to learn and see a great deal of their wickedness, and
the way they lead their people in darkness.   At the time
I went first to live with him, I could not understand one
word of his language, nor he of mine.

He was always desirous to learn the English ; but he
preferred that I should learn to speak and read the *Champara* language, which is a sort of Creole Spanish, half
Spanish and half African.   In this language he always
conversed and corresponded with me : and in it I shall
write the names and Spanish words found here.

He got me a teacher, and I soon learned his language ;
and when I left him he could write and understand my
own language.   During that five years I lived a gloomy
and a wretched life with him.   I suffered every thing but
death, in body and in mind ; I was as ignorant as any
heathen in the right view of eternity, although I was
born here in America ; but I was young when I first
went to live in those countries.   I still knew and felt that
their religion was not right.[*]

> [*] " For both prophet and priest are profane ; yea, in my house have
> I found their wickedness, saith the Lord.   And I have seen folly in the
> prophets—a horrible thing : they commit adultery and walk in lies :
> they strengthen also the hands of the evil doers, that none doth return
> from his wickedness."—Jer. 23 : 11. 14.

When I had learned sufficient of the language to understand what he said, I soon forgot my past troubles, the value of a character, and the promises I had made while crossing the ocean.

I had lived here but a short time with him, before I took the creole, or stranger's fever, which they call the black vomit. I laid very sick three weeks, and was not expected to recover by any one, even by the doctor, who belonged to one of the Convents. I was visited by several of Manuel's friends, and treated kindly by all. I was again afraid to die, and they wanted me to be christened, and said I was a Protestant, and if I died I must go to hell. I never can forget, when I lay very low one day, my Priest came to my bed, and told me he was afraid I was going to die, and it was his desire I should be christened, as I was a Protestant. I did not know what he meant by a Protestant, as I had been always brought up in darkness. I cannot help saying, Lord! why was I kept so long in darkness, without knowing I had such a kind and merciful God? Yes, dear Saviour, I can never do too much to serve thee here, should I live ten thousand years; for I now know, and can see, what a merciful and forgiving God I have! When I knew thee not, I used to think, in trouble, what an unjust God! but I adore the righteous God, and pray, O Lord! that from this very day, this very hour I am writing this, I may serve thee henceforth with sincerity, since thou hast opened my blind eyes!

They soon after lighted up candles in my room, and a Capuchin Priest came, with three or four Priests in habits, and death-candles were lighted. I asked Manuel what the candles were burning for? He said, to get me through Purgatory.* I did not know the meaning of it,

* The Popish Divines place Purgatory in the bowels of the earth. The vast cavity in the central regions of the world, is, according to these theologians, divided into four apartments, which form Hell, Purgatory, and the Limbo of infants, and of the Fathers. The two former, according to them, are in the same neighborhood. The prison of the children is raised above Purgatory, say the Schoolmen and Innocent III., so that the flames of the latter come not near the establishment of

but it appeared to me, I was in a worse place, and every one of the priests, devils, with the old Capuchin at the head of them.   At this time, one of my American friends came in, who could speak their language.   It was not the former. Alex. 9, 352. Bell. II. 6. Aquin. III. 69. VII. Rosaccio, an Italian Doctor, in the year 1620, determined with mathematical precision, the exact situation of Purgatory. According to this celebrated Doctor, Purgatory is precisely 15,750 miles above the sphere of hell, and 2,550 1-2 miles from the inhabitants of the world. Bell. II. 6. Rosaccio, C. 4. Edgar.

In regard to what specific punishment they undergo in Purgatory, the Papist Divines have always been at variance. Some think they suffer by hot and cold water, others by fire. The water of Purgatory, according to the most authentic accounts, is both hot and cold; and the wretched sufferers are perpetually driven by the current, first, among icy glaciers, where the soul becomes congealed into lumps of ice, and then again are driven back into the sulphureous regions, where they boil. Alex. 9, 393. Greg. IV. 40. Bellarmine II. 6.

Drithelm, whose story is related by Beda and Bellarmine, was led on his journey by an angel in shining raiment; and proceeded, in the company of his guide, towards the rising of the sun. The travelers, at length, arrived in a valley of vast dimensions. This region, to the left, was covered with roasting furnaces, and to the right, with icy cold, hail, and snow. The whole valley was filled with human souls, which a tempest seemed to toss in all directions. The unhappy spirits, unable in the one part, to bear the violent heat, leaped into the shivering cold, which again drove them into the scorching flames, which cannot be extinguished. A numberless multitude of deformed souls, were, in this manner, whirled about, and tormented without intermission, in the extremes of alternate heat and cold. This, according to the Purgatorial conductor who piloted Drithelm, is the place of chastisement for such as defer Confession and amendment till the hour of death. All these, however, will, at the last day, be admitted into heaven; while many, through alms, vigils, prayers, and especially the Mass, will be liberated even before the General Judgment. Beda, V. 12. Bell. L. 7. M. Paris, 83, 180, 207. Edgar.

These, and a thousand other such fictions, are believed in Popish countries, and are recorded, for the edification of the people, by the gravest Popish writers.

Papists must acknowledge, if their doctrine is consistent, and the Word of God is true, that there is no such place as Purgatory to be found, except in the brains of the Popish Clergy, who conceive and bring forth the monstrous doctrine for no other end than to fill their coffers, and impose upon the ignorance of their devotees. The Romish church acknowledges, that those who die in a state of sanctifying grace, that is, the righteous, do not go to hell. This being admitted, Purgatory must disappear like a shadow before the sun, when the Word of God shines forth upon it; for the Scriptures expressly declare, " *Blessed are the dead who die in the Lord from henceforth: Yea, saith the Spirit, that they may rest from their labors.*" Rev. xiv. 13. To this, we take the liberty of adding a text from the Popish Canon of the Scriptures, which reads as

her wish that I should be christened, and she interfered, and told them, that if they did not put out the lights, it would make me crazy. Upon this it was done in a little time; and the old Capuchin said, the Americans were like dumb beasts, and were Satan's children. I soon after recovered, but did not think it was God's kind mercies that restored me to health again. I then entered again upon a thoughtless life, during which, I seldom gave a thought to my dear, dear mother, brothers, or sisters; but felt happy in indulging in the customs of the place, where they have every thing rich and splendid, horrid and wicked.*

follows, " *The souls of the righteous are in the hand of God, and there shall no torment touch them.*" Wisdom. Consequently there can be no Purgatory after death; for, according to the Popish doctrine, that is not a place of *rest*, but torment.—ED.

* It is wonderful that men living in open and gross violation of the Gospel law, should be anxious to confer an ordinance of the Gospel on a poor sinner for the saving of her soul. The strong delusion of Popery, is seen in this very thing, that its ministers thought by the imposition of their hands in baptism, they could cleanse the heart of Rosamond, and give her entrance into heaven. No repentance was required; but only a willingness on her part, or, in failure of her power to express that willingness, the consent of her American friends for her to receive the ordinance. These friends abhorred the Priests from the very heart. Knowing both the sanctified airs, and the secret works of darkness of the Romish Priests, they refused to consent to the prostitution of the holy rite in the case of Rosamond.

The doctrine of Rome teaches, that by baptism a person is made free, not only from the guilt of original sin, but also, from the guilt of all actual transgression, however enormous; so that the desire of Manuel to baptize Rosamond, was by no means frivolous. He believed the doctrine of his traditions, that all guilt is washed away in the laver of baptism, and he desired to make her happy, by opening to her the portals of heaven. He believed that without baptism she would die a heretic, and that she could not possibly escape the damnation of hell. How reasonable then, that he should make some effort, to procure so great an improvement of her eternal condition? A small ceremony, an outward rite, was not too much to perform, to produce so wonderful a change.

The ceremonies of the Romish baptism are numerous. The person is first catechised. The sponsors may answer, when the person cannot. He is then exorcised, by words of sacred import, and prayers, used to expel the devil from him. Next, salt is put into his mouth, with much signification. The forehead, eyes, ears, breast, and shoulders, are signed with the sign of the cross. The nostrils and ears are touched with spittle. He is then taken to the font, anointed with oil, on the breast and on the shoulders. After all this, with many questions interspersed, he is baptized either by immersion, or pouring, or sprinkling

During the time that I was with Manuel, he took me to the theatres, masquerades, and gambling-houses, as it is customary for fashionable ladies there to visit all those places, and he gave me money to gamble with.

He often gambled himself, but was not fortunate, except in the Convents. He would often tell me on coming from the gambling-table in the Convent, how he had lost money, or how he had won ; and how this Priest was angry, and another Priest had tried to cheat him ; and I have often heard one and another of the Priests speak of their success in gambling.

In the day time, they are dressed in their Priestly habits ; their head is shaved upon the crown, and round about the ears, by which, they have a ring of hair around their heads, and they disfigure their countenances much. At night, they put on a citizen's dress, and wear a wig.

They look deathly pale in their habits ; and when they put on a citizen's dress, they generally paint with *rouge*. Manuel Canto always painted, when he went to the theatre, or where the light was bright ; but when he rode, or walked in the citizen's dress, he did not paint. I could always see their countenance change to a solemn and ghostly expression, whenever they put on their habits. In a citizen's dress, that the change is so great, you would hardly know them. In this dress they can mix in places of iniquity, among the same persons, who go to them to hear Masses and to give in their Confessions. In the day time, to look upon them, you would take them to be Saints, by their dress and by their countenances.

I had been living with him about a year, when I was taken again sick with the black vomit, and was thought by myself and others to be near to death. Now, for the first time, I was brought to see and feel my lost

the water. The crown of his head is then anointed with oil of chrism, a white garment is put on him ; a burning candle is placed in his hand, and, lastly, his name is given, which ought to be that of some Saint, able to be the guardian of his life. So, Patrick is name enough for the Irish,. but the Spaniards take the names of many Saints to protect a single child.—Cramp's Text Book of Popery, p. 133.

situation, so sensibly, that I knew, if I died, I should be lost.

Manuel would never allow any, but the Convent physicians, to attend me in my illness. Several physicians are attached to each Convent, and habited like the Priests. My Priest then tried to persuade me to be christened, and to become a Christian ; for he told me, if I died as I was, I should surely go to hell. He brought several Priests to see me, and to persuade me, that if I would only consent to be anointed, and to become one of their persuasion, I should then be a Christian and die happy. In all this, he appeared to be moved solely by a desire for my spiritual and everlasting good.

They sent for a Capuchin Priest, who belongs to St. Philip's Convent, whom they look upon to be more holy than any other. Those Priests, by their looks and dress, appear to be something more than natural beings of earth. Their heads are shorn in such a form, that you can perceive but very little of their hair. They wear their beards long. Their habits are made plain; a leathern belt is girded about them ; and three yards of beads hang around their necks, which they make use of in counting the Saints, when saying their prayers. That is, for every Saint they address a prayer to, they move a bead, and for every time they call on the same Saint, they also move a bead. Then the sum of their prayers is told by the number of beads they have pushed along on the string.

They wear no stockings, but half sandals. Those Priests were brought into my sick room, and *death-candles* lighted up, as they call them. These candles are very large, and one is placed at each of the four corners of the table.

When I saw this, I soon lost my senses. At this time some of my American female friends came in, and objected to my being christened. This caused a great confusion ; but they left me as they found me, only they frightened me out of my senses.

But the Lord had mercy on me, and I was restored to my health again.

I soon forgot that I had been brought so near to death, and entered again on the scene of amusements and wickedness with him. My conscience often told me that I was very wicked, and that I was committing a great sin in living with him as I did. I have often told him that when we died, we should both go to hell. He then would tell me, if I would be christened, and become of their persuasion, I then should be a Christian; I then could go to the Virgin Mary with all my burden; that she would relieve me; that all Protestants would be lost; that none would or could be saved, except those that belong to the Holy Catholic Church. But as ignorant as I was, I knew their religion could not save me. During this time he was very kind to me, and provided every thing for my comfort, but would not consent to my seeing any of my country people. His wish was, that my society should be amongst his country people. I was obliged to submit to his wishes; for if you put yourself under their protection, you cannot gratify your own wishes, but must always gratify theirs. And by this time I was brought under his control entirely. I durst not think or do any thing without consulting with him first.

I have often asked him if he did sincerely believe that he could forgive the sins of those that came to him to make Confession, and say Mass for them. On conversing seriously with him, he would tell me that he should try to save his own soul first, and then would do all that he could to save others; that no one would be lost that belonged to the Holy Catholic Church, even though they should sin daily, if they would but go to the Virgin Mary, and beg for mercy.*

* The famous Popish Cardinal Cajetan says, "Cessante scandalo," &c., "that the Virgin Mary can be worshiped with supreme adoration, only on account of her having touched, (the Savior,) provided it can be done without scandal. But the more modern Divines maintain, that she can be worshiped with supreme adoration, not only on account of her having touched the Savior, but also, on account of her maternity, inasmuch, as the same blood flowed through her veins as flowed through the Savior's." Vasq. L. I. Disp. 8, C. 1, N. 195, 196.

Their great St. Thomas Aquin, otherwise styled the Angelic Doctor, tells us also, that the "Cross of Christ is to be worshiped with the

The Priests do lead the people so much in darkness, that if any commit murder, and only goes to one of the Priests, and takes with him a sum of money, and Confesses what he has done, they make him believe by their Masses and burning candles, that God will forgive the murder; but let any criminal go to one without money, and the Priest will not hear him Confess; without the requisite sum, he will go to hell. This drives criminals to new thefts and murders; for I have known instances of the kind, and have seen and heard Confessions by them, when on the gallows to be hung—that such and such a Priest was the cause of their death. They were not permitted to tell the Priest by name. They still die in the fear of the Priests; for if they have any friends to give the Priests money, to buy candles, they are led to believe that the Priests by burning candles can light them through Purgatory. This I have heard himself say, that they could not save them without money. In Cuba they think nothing of going to public executions. I have often attended. Sometimes a number would be hung every week. I have myself heard them, on the gallows, charge their crime on the Priests, always concealing their names, to purchase whose Masses and prayers they committed the robbing and murder. And I have heard others, attending when I did not, tell of the convicts Confessing the same thing.

It is natural for the Priests to be possessed of a jealous disposition. Manuel began to be unkind to me, but still provided every thing for my comfort. He would often have supper parties at my house, of other Priests, his friends, who would likewise bring their ladies with them, who were living with them in the same capacity. Among them were Father Antonia, Father Gabrilla, Father Zoda, with their ladies; and Father Hosa. Father R——, and Father Truman, were in the habit of visiting Father Canto familiarly at my house without their ladies. These last had their ladies, and I knew them, and met

same adoration with Christ, that is, with the adoration of latriæ, supreme worship." Thom. Aquin III. Ques. 25, Art. 4.—ED.

them at home, and at the gambling-houses, and at the
masquerades. Father Senor, Father Varela, and others,
visited often at my house. The Priests never call one
another Father, but always, Canto, Antonia, &c. I will
not be sure that I spell their names right, but I can pro-
nounce them right, and tell the Convent to which each
one belonged. Canto belonged, as I have said, to St.
Francisco Convent, so did R—— and Hosa. Senor belonged to the Cathedral, St. Catalina. Antonia belonged
to St. Domingo Convent, Gabrilla belonged to St. Clare,
Zoda belonged to St. *Wanadou*.

The Priests are very partial to foreigners, as they say
it is not so much sin, as to take their own countrywomen,
because Americans are of a fairer complexion, and of
more virtuous habits, and more pardonably tempting
than the natives of the island. They admit it, that the
Virgin Mary will have more mercy on them, for the
temptation by foreigners is greater ; and I have been told
by respectable persons, that they can put all the curses of
the sin on the woman's head that lives with them, by saying Masses, and burning candles on her head.

Any one can go to the Convents, and buy those candles
of the Priests, to try *malediction*, as the Priestcraft
term it.

If a young lady is desirous of gaining the affections of
any gentleman, she will go to the Priest, with a sum of
money. He will sell her those candles, and bless them
too, that in burning them she may gain a victory. And
they have other candles to sell you, if you want to torment any one, or to set any one crazy with love. The
malediction candles are not burned in the Saint's presence, or before their images ; that would be sin ; but
they burn them in small rooms by themselves. The
red candles usually have nine new pins stuck in each, in
the form of the Cross. The Priests instruct them how to
place the pins, which are the common pins, only they
must be new.

Their rule is, to burn them nine days and nights, and
nine Masses are to be said, on that individual. This I

do know to be the fact, that they deal with Priestcraft;
and, in that way, make their people so much afraid of
them. Seeing so much of their wickedness and Priestcraft, was one thing that led me to see my lost situation.

7*

CHAPTER IV.

" Cautious and swift the Indian went,
" His head was raised, his bow was bent,
" And as he, like a wild deer, sped,
" So light, so silent, was his tread,
" That scarce a leaf was seen to move,
" Of flower below, or branch above."

          Miss L. M. Davidson.

Rosamond attacked in her house by robbers.— Wounded and supposed to be dead.— One robber killed.—Another taken.— His punishment.—Loses her senses under the shock from Manuel's entering her room.—She recovers, and removes to another house.—Learns who sent the robbers to her house.—Altars of private devotion to the Saints.

I HAD been living in Havanna about three months, when on the third of October, 1828, at seven o'clock in the evening of a rainy day, I was assailed by the robbers in my house. I was alone sitting in my *boutak*, or Havanna armed chair, at the window, looking into the street. My servant girl, Sarah, had put the front door a jar, on her way to the grocer's, and then turned back for a few moments, to the yard. As she re-entered the back door, three ruffians entered the front door, throwing it wide open upon its hinges. The first that entered was a white man, who flew and seized me by the throat, and presented a knife to my breast; while a black seized the colored girl, and presented a knife to her breast, and a mulatto guarded the front door, walking to and fro. I screamed aloud; for, at the first sight, I knew they were robbers. The Commissaries, with the city guards, are not usually stationed before half past seven or eight o'clock; and at seven is the hour of evening prayers, or oration in the Convents, when the Convent bells ring, and the Priests must all be in their Convents; and when the devout or even formal Roman Catholics, in their houses, or in the streets, riding or walking, stop; or, sitting and eating, rise up, and Cross themselves, and offer a prayer. And this hour of common devotion, is the precise time for the robbers to be on the alert.

I could not understand Spanish, and the robbers did not understand English. My servant begged of them for me, and begged of me, to cease screaming, or they would certainly kill us both, and to give them what money I had, and they would leave the house. My servant could speak three languages, and she pleaded with them for our lives, while I cried murder ! help ! robbers ! But all my crying was of no avail; for when the robbers make an attack, all the neighbors close their shutters and doors, and no one dares to come to your assistance. There is but little chance of any one's coming to your assistance, because they fear to be taken for the robbers themselves. They do not open the shutters again until the robbers have fled, or have been secured. And the custom of the place is, not to cry an alarm, or make any noise, when attacked by robbers, but silently to give them what money you have, in the confident expectation that if you do this, they will spare your life; but that if you make an outcry they will kill you. I had not yet learned the customs of the place.

Seeing the shutters of the neighbors all closed, and myself all a gore of blood, I asked my servant what we should do—if they were going to kill us. She said, no, if I would not halloo any more, and would give them what money I had. For the robber had removed my left earring; and in his effort to take out the right hand one, he was embarrassed by the spring; and when I raised my hand, to take it out for him, and I saw my hand and arm were covered with blood, I shrieked, O, do come ! he has killed me ! so loud, that it is said I was heard to the *Place de Amos*, which was distant several squares. He rent out the ear-ring, tearing it through the flesh; and I found myself stabbed in my mouth, in my side, and in my hand.* I did not know when I received these

---

* The scars of these four wounds which she received upon this occasion, are now distinctly seen upon her body. Her right ear is slit by the wrenching out of the ring, the length of about one third of an inch. The other scars are about an inch long. One is on the right side of her cheek, near her mouth; one on the right hand; and another on her side.—ED.

wounds, but the flowing blood made me think I was
surely killed. Then, for the first time, I thought of calling on my God for help; and I cried: Lord! have mercy
on me! for 1 felt that I was going in a moment to eternity. Instantly I was calm,—I stopped crying,—and it did
appear to me, as if God was with me. I went readily
into the next room, the robber still holding me fast by the
throat, and I gave him what money I had in the house.
I became perfectly resigned, and expected every moment
to be launched into eternity.

By this time the Commissaries came. A noise was
heard in the front room. The robber let go his grasp on
my throat, and ran. In passing out, he wounded the
Commissary who stood guard at the door, while the soldiers had pursued the two other robbers. The white robber came unexpectedly upon the Commissary, who supposed there were but two robbers in the assault; and the
wound he gave the Commissary, enabled that robber to
escape. But the mulatto was stabbed and killed by one
of the soldiers in pursuit, and the black was taken. I
have seen the end of the soldier's sword, which was
broken off in the body of the slain mulatto.

After they had left the house, I heard my servant girl
crying in the street, " they have killed my Mistress!"—
She escaped unhurt into the street, as soon as the robbers
had gone. I ran towards the sound of her voice, and fell
senseless to the ground in the middle of the street.

Here no one dared to lift me up, until the head Commissary and a Physician were called. The crowd
gathered round, supposing, from the quantity of blood,
that I was dead. But after the Commissary and the Surgeon came, I was removed into my house, and my
wounds were dressed.

These robbers neither put out the lights of my house,
nor shut the door, nor shutters; and people were passing
in the street all the time. But in Havanna, the people
will neither stop, nor gather in a crowd, nor look round,
if there is a robber in the way. One American lady saved
herself, when her house was assailed by robbers, by going

upon the roof, and crying *fire! fire!* This brought the people out, and the robbers fled; when, if she had cried " *Robbers!*" every door and window shutter would have been closed, and the robbers would have plundered the house, and perhaps murdered the mistress.

The black robber who was taken in the attack on my house, was put in prison, and kept until his trial. Then he was condemned, and sentenced to be exposed half naked on a mule, and whipped at the corners of the principal streets, and afterwards to be sent five years to the Spanish mines.

The mode of whipping is this.—The criminal is taken by the Commissary, and placed on a mule, on a wooden saddle. The Commissaries and their soldiers walk on either side. The multitude follows behind, to see the whipping. At every corner of the street, where the Commissary passes, he stops the mule, rings a bell, and proclaims the crime of the convict, and then he strikes him on the naked back, one blow, with an instrument resembling, in shape, a common hand-card for carding cotton or wool. It is full of sharp iron points, which at every stroke make the blood flow. After the one blow, he drives on to the next corner, and there repeats the same ceremony.

After I was relieved, and my wounds were dressed, my Priest came. He was in his Convent at the time the robbery happened. As soon as he entered my room, I lost my reason. I remained in this situation three months. In this time, I was removed to a friend's house, Mrs. A——— T———'s, a Spanish lady, where Manuel provided for me every thing to make me comfortable. It was said that he was kind to me, and mourned much about me. This became all public, up to the governor, and down to the lowest class, who I was, and who I was living with. It excited more attention, on account of my being a foreigner, and of my living with a well known and respected Priest.

At the time that I was brought to my reason, which was three months after, then I was brought to see what a sinner I was, and what wicked people I was living with. I then told him, that I could never go to live with him again; that it was more wicked for me to live with him, than if I was with any one else. I felt so; for I knew that he was very wicked, and have often told him, that when we died, we should both go to hell; that their religion could not save them.

He replied, that it was not so dangerous to the soul, to live with him, as with a common citizen; for if I would become a Catholic, he would save my soul; but unless I became a true Catholic, neither he could do any thing for me, nor could any of his friends.

I then thought to myself, if I was only a Christian!— Oh, the sound of the voice of a Christian! And would often think and say, if I could only go and find some Christian, to go to tell them how I felt! For I knew it was the mercies of God, that saved my life, and rescued me from the wicked hands of those robbers: and I felt and knew that if I persevered in my way of living, that I should be lost, not only in this world, but through eternity for ever and ever. Oh! I can well remember those feelings; and they still make me shudder, when I see how near my feet were in the gulf of wo; *and to see how much mercy the Lord has had for me, and what he has done for me*, O, that I may always lay at the feet of Jesus, and have it always in view, how much the Lord has done for me!

It was not my wish to live with him again; but as I have said, when you put yourself under their protection, it is not so easy to leave the Priests, as one might think; and I was brought into so much fear of him, that I felt like a criminal in his presence. After I recovered, I did not return to live in the same house, but Manuel provided another one, No. 16 Cuille, O' Havanna, for which I paid 3¼ ounces, or about $59.

My girl was so terrified by the robbers, that she would never return again to live with me.

Shortly after this, I was informed how and why I was attacked by the robbers, and I had every reason to believe it to be true. The person who informed me, was a Spanish officer's wife, who was then living next door to me. She appeared to feel much for my lost situation, and often urged me to leave him, telling me how wicked it was to live with one of the Priests; that he could pray for all the curses of the sin upon my head, and that God would have no mercy on me.

When I told Manuel of this, I was obliged, through fear, to tell him my author; for, although I knew it to be true, I also knew, that if I lost his friendship, I would be undone and lost myself, since I had no kind friend where to find a shelter.

> " O! that I had a faithful friend,
>   " To tell my secrets to,
> " On whose advice I might depend,
>   " In every thing I do!

> " How do I wander up and down,
>   " And no one pities me!
> " I seem a stranger quite unknown,
>   " A child of misery."

The Spanish officer's wife informed me, that I was attacked by the robbers by the direction of a Spanish lady, who was the wife of a certain marquis belonging to the nobility, with whom Manuel had been intimate for a number of years before I had become acquainted with him. This lady had an independent fortune, and kept a private altar of the Saints in one of her rooms for her own devotions. It is customary for all the nobility, to have their altars and Saints, for worship in their houses; and also for the Priest to go to their houses, to hear their Confessions. This Priest of mine was her favorite Priest, and she had supported him, and supplied all his wants of money, which he bestowed on me and on others; and in those countries it costs not a little to live. This lady had learned that he was living with me, he paying his visits to her daily, as her Priest, in the eyes of her husband and family. Her jealousy and her wicked heart, had hired these robbers to attack me; but through the mercies of the Lord, I was delivered out of their hands. It was sometime after I heard this, before I had strength or resolution through fear to tell him.

CHAPTER V.

"Hé stood on Sinai, wrapped in storm clouds, wild
"His loose locks streamed around him, and his eye
"Flashed indignation on a world defiled
"With sense and slavery, who lost the high
"Prerogative of power and spirit, by
"Their longings for their flesh-pots. O, 'tis lust,
"Which robs us of our freedom, makes us lie
"Wallowing in willing wretchedness."

PERCIVAL.

Masquerades.— The habit of attending.— The wealth of the people of Havanna.— Their silent stab.— Their stilling hiss.— Their calling hiss.— The mockery of the Priests in Masks.— Manuel's remark on his habit.— His urging Rosamond to pray to the Virgin for good luck.— Their universal superstition.

EVERY Sunday evening in Havanna, and often on other days of the week, there is a public masquerade ball, to which all go, who will pay their admission dollar, and behave civilly in their way. Sometimes a thousand people attend in the several saloons; people of the genteel class, from the Governor and Priests, down to the poor gentleman. I was not regular in my attendance at the Mass-house on the Sabbath-day, but was punctual, on that day, at the masquerades; and so was Manuel.* The

---

* Plays are allowed by the Church of Rome on the Sabbath, "Because," (as Ligori teaches,) "they are for the recreation of the mind, and by way of rest from servile labor." Ligor. Theol. de. 3. Prac. Dec. C. 1.
They do not stop here, but advance so far in iniquity as to teach, that "the commandment to sanctify the Sabbath, *does not oblige us to worship God in Spirit.*" This, Saint Ligori attempts to prove, by quotations from a multitude of their best divines; and, among the rest, he quotes the Angelical St. Thomas, who says, that "*we are not bound to worship God interiorly by this commandment.*" Thom. I. 2. Q. 122. C. 4. "The same doctrine," (he says,) "is taught in the Roman Catechism." Ligor. de 3. Prac. Dec. C. 1. N. 264. "Hunting, hawking, fishing, are allowed on the Sabbath." Id. N. 283;—also, "merchandizing, and selling goods at auction, is allowed." "IT IS ALSO PERMITTED ON THE LORD'S DAY," (says this same great Saint Ligori,) "TO SELL LIQUOR AND EATABLES, EVEN TO THE MAKING OF THOSE WHO BUY DRUNK; also, to sell shoes, candles, and such like things, likewise houses, horses, and merchandize, these are all allowed,"—(and behold his reasons!!)
8

chief expense of attendance, was in the hiring of the dresses for the different evenings, and in the cost of refreshments, suppers, and gambling at these balls. The cost of a common mask-dress, for an evening, is four dollars, and from a dollar to a dollar and a half, for the mask. For any stylish dress, the cost is half, or three quarters, or a whole doubloon, or *ounce*, as they call it. An ounce of gold in Havanna, is no more than an ounce of silver here in the expenses of the people. They think little more of a doubloon, than we do of a dollar.

Foreigners, strangers, and sometimes ladies, appear without masks. Manuel and other Priests used to frequent the balls and gambling-rooms, (which latter are in saloons, opening from the ball-rooms,) in a citizen's dress without a mask.* He used to give me money for gambling, as he was unfortunate in the gambling-houses himself. In the Convents he was more successful; but he never was vexed if I lost, even though it were twenty dollars of an evening; for I paid up my losses when I won, and kept the money, if any thing was over.

" both *because* by use, the timid and scrupulous are brought to bear it; and also, because the Church only prohibits selling in public shops on account of the scandal." Ligor. Theol. de 3. Præc. Dec. Dub. 1. N. 286.

P. S.—The above seems almost incredible;—but I am willing to prove the correctness of these quotations before the whole United States. The authority of this Saint, not a Popish Priest dare dispute. —Ed.

* Capt. J. E. Alexander, in his " TRANSATLANTIC SKETCHES," testifies, that the Priests in the West India Islands pass much of their time in gambling, cock-fighting, and bull-baiting. Vol. I. p. 339. " Many of the country *Padres*," (Holy Fathers,) says he, " are excessively idle, and openly vicious, and a perfect disgrace to the Church." Id. ib. " I heard," (continues he,) " a liberal Ecclesiastic lament over the sins of his brethren, and regret that marriage was not permitted in the Church. Many of the *Padres* have a handsome *Niece* to keep their houses in order; but it is better this, than exciting the jealousy of husbands."

" What respect," (exclaims the same writer,) " can a Clergy be held in, when they are too often bold and eager gamblers! From Mass, they go to the cock-pit; and from the cock-pit to Mass; and sometimes delay the Mass to see the end of a fight. They might be seen at Guanabacoa, in full Canonicals, watching with intense interest, a combat between a favorite cock and that of a negro slave, who had staked his money against that of the unworthy Priest."—Transatlantic Sketches, Vol. I. p. 340.—Ed.

When any man attending the ball, in his passion at a loss, or at an attempt to cheat, draws his knife, and stabs another, he does it without a word of alarm, or any noise. The dealers of the cards do not stop, nor does a female scream. The only notice taken of the act, by the company present, is, that every one places his fore-finger across his lips, shuts his teeth, and blows a long stilling hiss; as much as to say,—" *never mention it* "—and the soldiers, who are always in attendance, take the hostile parties out, and all things are as if nothing violent had occurred.*

This gentle hiss is a common one in Havanna, for many purposes. If one would stop a friend passing in the street, he never speaks or calls his name, walking or riding, but breathes short hisses, to obtain his attention. But the hiss of silence is long and gentle, with the finger placed on the lips in token of silence.

The life of the masquerade, depends on the novelty of the characters assumed by different persons, and the spirit with which each one sustains his character. Manuel used to be very fond of appearing in the character of a lady. It is no matter that he is known for a man, if only he plays well the woman's part. Oftentimes, people would appear in the habits of the Priests, and make great diversion of the long visages of the Father Confessors. It always disturbed the Priests very much, to see themselves played off in Crossing, Confessing, and absolving the various penitents that were readily found in the ball-room. The Priests, when the imitation would be fine, were always very much distressed at it. They thought it wicked in the extreme, but they never thought it wicked to be

* This same bloody disposition is conspicuous wherever Popery domineers. Petrarch, the celebrated Popish writer, speaking of the manner of the people of Naples, in Italy, says, that "they kill one another at the public games, for mere diversion. To these barbarous spectacles, the people run in crowds, and shout, and rejoice at the sight of human blood. Kings, princes, and even ladies, are amused by it." (Life of Petrarch, in a Letter to Cardinal Colonna.)

Capt. J. E. Alexander tells us, that "all the inhabitants of Cuba go armed; such is the lawless state of society in that place, *aujourd'hui.*" —Transatlantic Sketches, Vol. I. p. 371.—ED.

themselves present. I have known them so much excited by the fairness of the mask in their own character, that they would gather together, and chafe away the pleasure of the whole evening in view of the perfect imitation of themselves, and in planning how to discover who wore the mask. They would say one to another, glancing an eye to the mask, " *I'll mark ye !*" and would follow him home, and sometimes get a sight of him after his mask was off. What revenge they took, I never knew ; but no Spanish Priest would fail to have it, in some form or other, of any one against whom he entertained a grudge.

Their *Alcowaters* will do any thing for them that they are bid to do. Be the sin what it may, they believe that the Priests can and will absolve them from it.

The masquerades are kept up all night. Those go home who choose, at an early hour ; but the saloons are not closed until daylight. In the midst of preparation for these scenes, I have sometimes asked Manuel, if he did not think it was wicked for a Priest to engage in them. He would take his habit by a fold between his thumb and finger, and extending it from him, reply, " Why, Rosetta," (for so he always called me,) " this habit cannot change our feelings, we have the same feelings with other men."

In the course of the day previous to going to the masquerades, while talking together of the expected pleasures of the evening, he would tell me, I must pray for good fortune at the gambling-table ; that I must make a fortune this night; and I must pray to the Virgin Mary through the day, and bear her on my heart, with constant prayers for good fortune at night. Whenever he told me this, it was not done laughing, but in seriousness ; and if I had bad luck upon it, he would tell me, it was because I was a poor Protestant at heart. I did not know what a *Protestant* meant, and he would get angry with me, because he said I knew, and would not tell him, all that Protestants believe, and how they worship, and what our ministers do in the churches. But this one thing I always noticed, that when he told me, that he had what he called a forerunner of my good luck at gambling, I was almost sure to lose ; so that I learned to stop him, when prophesying good fortune, and to charge him not to spoil my prospects.

People here may not believe we could be so superstitious, but it is true every word of it; and, in Havanna, all are superstitious. Those who do not use Priestcraft, will use sorcery ; and those that refuse to sprinkle Holy Water, for keeping off bad luck, will yet sprinkle salt and pepper, to keep it off, especially if a Priest had been in the house : for the Roman Catholics all use Holy Water,* and the Protestants, living in sin, often use salt and pepper, to resist evil spirits ; so accustomed are all classes to superstitious ceremonies of one kind or another in Havanna.

And it is not only so in Havanna. The superstitious observances of the Roman Catholics are much the same in all the world, I fear. In the "SIX MONTHS IN A CONVENT," published at Boston, Mass., it is written, that in order to keep off the assaults of the Devil : "I must watch and pray all the time, and banish entirely worldly thoughts from my mind, and throw Holy Water at the evil spirits, and challenge them to come if they dare. Perceiving the unpleasant effect this had on my feelings, he (the bishop of Boston,) portrayed, in lively colors, the happiness which would flow from my resisting the evil spirits, and what a crown of glory would be placed on my head by the Angels."

The music and dancing at the masquerade ball is kept constantly going from eight o'clock, when the saloons open, to the end. A full band is kept playing, and the company are all assembled by ten o'clock. There are rooms joining the masquerade room, furnished with every variety of meats, fruits, drinks, and confectionary, for the

---

* " Ah ! nimium faciles, qui tristia crimina cædis,
"Flumina tolli posse putetis aqua." Ovid. Fast. 2. 45.

"Ah! easy fools, to think that a whole flood
"Of water e'er can purge the stain of blood."—ED.

persons who attend the balls. Manuel used to decline the dance altogether. Other Priests danced, but he never did. And he often drew me from the dancing-rooms, to the promenade, where they walk, and sport, and joke; and he preferred most of all, to be with me in the gambling-rooms.

CHAPTER VI.

" The supplicating hand of innocence ;—
" That made the tiger mild, and in his wrath
" The lion pause ; the groans of suffering most
" Severe, were nought to Popish Bigotry ; she laughed at groans ;
" No music pleased her more, and no repast
" So sweet to her, as blood of men."   POLLOK.

' PRELIMINARY.

WE here introduce a chapter on the Island of Cuba, taken from the "ENCYCLOPEDIA AMERICANA," that the reader may have some general idea of the country, in which the events related in this Narrative occurred ; and for the sake of the correlative testimony which it bears to that of the authoress.

Geographical description of Cuba.—Animals.—Soil.— Vegetable Productions.—Minerals.— The Spaniards exterminate the Aborigines of the Island.— The Chieftain put to death for refusing to be baptized.—Corrupt morals of the people.—Ignorance of the Clergy.—Cock-fights.— Bull-baits.—Gambling.—Murders frequent.— Description of Havanna. —Religion a mere show.— The shrine of Columbus.

CUBA is the largest and most westerly of the Antilles. Its configuration, extent, geographical position, great number of ports, fertility, and climate, contribute to render it an interesting country. Its length, from Cape St. Antonio to Point Maisi, in a direction from W. S. W. to E. N. E. and then from W. N. W. to E. S. E., is 257 leagues, and its greatest width, in the direc tion north to south, is 38 leagues. The learned geographer, Don Felipe Bausa, calculated in June, 1825, that the surface of Cuba contained 3615 square marine leagues. Cuba is situated between longitude 73° 56' and 85° W., and between latitude 19° 48' 30" and 23° 12' 45" N. It lies 14 leagues west from Cape Nicolas, in the Island of St. Domingo, 34 south from Point Morant, in Jamaica, and 37 south from Cape Florida.

The gulf of Mexico, which is very nearly of a circular form, of more than 250 leagues in circumference, is closed by the Island of Cuba, with the exception of two narrow passages, the one . to the south, between Cape Catoche and Cape St. Antonio, and the other to the north, between Bahia Honda and the Florida shoals. Along the coast of Cuba, are many keys and small islands, which are included in the same government with the large island. The navigation of the coast is very unsafe, on account of the rocks and shoals which encompass it almost without interruption, and often extend from two to three miles into the sea. The broken outline of this vast extent of coast, however, affords more than fifty ports and anchoring places, which are equally safe and easy of access. The most remarkable, in a commercial point of view, are those of Havanna, Matanzas, Nuevitas, Jibara, and Baracoa, on the north; St. Jago, Manzanillo, Trinidad, Jagua, and Batabano, on the south side of the island. There is another port between Manzanillo and Trinidad, called *Santa Cruz*, which, in February, 1829, was declared a free port, and which, undoubtedly, will be much frequented, furnishing great facilities for trading with Puerto Principe, (the second city of Cuba, in point of population,) being the only good harbor in the vicinity of the south side of the island, and distant from it but twenty leagues.

A ridge of mountains traverses the whole of the island, from the east to the west, dividing it into two parts. At the foot of these, the country opens into extensive savannas. A considerable number of small streams from these heights, water the island on both sides. These streams abound in fish of different kinds, and are said to bring down considerable quantities of gold. There are likewise many salt ponds, which furnish abundance of fish and game; also, several springs of mineral water, which have proved very useful for the cure of many diseases.

The island is very rich in minerals, particularly in copper, iron, and loadstone. In 1813, some persons endeavored to work a mine which they found near the city of Trinidad, and from which they obtained good gold and silver. They were, however, obliged, from want of funds, to desist, though it was highly probable that, with a sufficient capital, it would have been made profitable. For the same reason, together with the want of protection from government, a very rich mine of coal, which was opened in 1816, near Bacuranao, was abandoned. In 1827, a silver mine was discovered, yielding 7-5ths of pure silver to a quintal of ore. Loadstone is found in the mountains of Paragua, and on the northern coast. Marbles of various kinds, serpentine, chalcedony, of excellent quality, quartz, mineral bitumen, &c., are likewise found in the island. Our knowledge of the geological and mineralogical structure of Cuba, however, is comparatively small, on account of the thickness of the forests, and the asperity of the mountains, particularly on the eastern part.

The soil of Cuba is so productive, that it yields two, and even three crops of corn in a year. The fields, during the whole year, are covered with aromatic plants and trees in blossom. The climate is dry and warm. It never freezes, not even on the highest mountains.

The coasts of the island are well known to be unhealthy; but this is not the case with the mountains. Among the animals indigenous to the island or the surrounding sea, are the cayman, or alligator, the manati or sea-cow, the iguana, (a species of lizard,) the turtle, &c. Many of the domestic animals of Europe, have also been introduced. A great number of swine, and also of bees, are raised. Birds are numerous. The rivers, though they have but a short course, and are deficient in water, abound, at certain seasons, with excellent fish. Reptiles are extremely numerous.

The vegetable kingdom of Cuba is extremely rich. Here are to be found, the mahogany tree, the cedar, lignum-vitæ, various kinds of ebony, besides numerous woods suitable for building houses, ships, &c.; and also palm-trees, among which the *palma real*, is remarkable for the utility of every part to man and various animals; sarsaparilla, and many other plants useful in medicine; also, the chestnut, the pine-apple, the annana or custard-apple, the medlar, plantain, orange, and various kinds of melons. Among the agricultural plants, maize is the most important; rice, beans, peas, *garbanzos*, are also cultivated.

The culture of wheat is abandoned. The true riches of the country consist in its great articles of export, sugar, coffee, tobacco, wax, cacao, molasses, rum, maize, &c.

The trade of Cuba is carried on chiefly through Havanna, its capital. The island is subject to the king of Spain. It is divided into two Ecclesiastical jurisdictions, the one governed by an Archbishop, who resides at St. Jago, the other one by a Bishop, who resides at Havanna.

Education is in a very *low* state. The *morals* of the people are *loose*; the *police* is *weak or inactive; murders are frequent*. The laws are very numerous and contradictory, and *much bribery* and corruption prevail *in the administration of justice*. In 1821, the importation of slaves was prohibited by law; and, though it is yet carried on, and tolerated by the authorities of Cuba, in spite of the laws against it, there is no doubt that it has diminished a great deal, in consequence of the efforts and vigilance of the English cruisers. The *emancipation* of Columbia, Mexico, and the Spanish part of St. Domingo, has *brought to Cuba almost all the Spaniards* who were settled in those countries, together with many of the creoles. The population of Cuba, according to the census of 1827, was 311,051 whites, and 393,436 blacks.

Cuba was discovered in 1492, by Christopher Columbus. In 1511, Don Diego Velasquez sailed from St. Domingo, with four vessels, and about 300 men, for the conquest of the island. He landed on the 25th of July, near the bay of St. Jago, to which he gave its name. The natives, commanded by the Cacique Hatuey, who had fled from St. Domingo, his native country, on account of the cruelty of the Spaniards, in vain endeavored to oppose the progress of the invaders. The noise of fire-arms was sufficient to disperse the poor Indians. Hatuey was taken prisoner and condemned to be burned alive, which sentence was executed after he had *refused to be baptized*. This diabolical act filled all the other Caciques with terror, and they hastened to pay homage to Velasquez, who met with no more opposition. The conquest of Cuba did

not cost the Spaniards a single man. The *conquerors*
not finding the mines sufficiently rich to induce them
to work them, gradually *exterminated the natives*, whom
they could not employ.

Havanna, the capital of Cuba, contains 112 thousand
inhabitants.   It is the residence of a captain-general, and
the See of a Bishop.   It is the most important commercial port in Spanish America, and is considered as the key
of the West Indies.   The harbor is not only the best in
the island, but is esteemed by many as the best in the
world, on account of its strength, and because it is ca-
pable of containing commodiously 1000 ships, without
either cable or anchor, there being generally six fathoms
of water in the bay.   The entrance into the harbor is by
a narrow channel, about 1000 feet wide at its entrance,
so difficult of access, that only one vessel can enter at a
time.   It is strongly fortified.   The city stands on a plain
on the west side of the harbor.   The streets are, in general,
narrow, crooked, unpaved, and dirty.   The want of common sewers, and of cleanliness, and the vicinity of marsh-
es, contribute to the insalubrity of the city, which is much
exposed to the ravages of the yellow fever.   Havanna
contains eleven churches, which are magnificently ornamented, especially the cathedral, with gold and silver
lamps, images, &c.   There are seven Monasteries, and
four Nunneries, a theatre, a place for bull-fights, and two
agreeable promenades.   The houses are almost all of one
story, and of a Gothic structure.   The principal ones are
built of stone, and covered with terraces, having large
apartments, yet little ornamented.   The great square is
one of the principal ornaments of the city.   The *morals*
of the place are *loose.*   *Gaming, cock-fighting*, &c., are
carried on to a great extent.   The customs are Spanish.
Foreigners who go there, seldom intermarry with the natives, as they rarely intend to make Havanna their per-
manent residence.

The lower *Clergy are ignorant*, and the ceremonies of
religion are surrounded with a *puerile show*.   The Havanna has the honor of containing the bones of Colum-

bus, the illustrious discoverer of America. In consequence of an order contained in the Will of Columbus, his body was removed from the Carthusian Convent of Seville, and deposited, along with the chains with which he had been loaded at Cuba, on the right of the high altar of the cathedral of St. Domingo. His body, in a brass coffin, was removed to Havanna on the 19th of January, 1796. His bones are now preserved in a silver urn on the left of the altar of the cathedral.

This description of Havanna, and the manners and customs of the people, will throw some light on the Narrative of the authoress, whose important and interesting disclosures we now lay before the public.

CHAPTER VII.

"Most guilty, villanous, dishonest man!
Wolf in the clothing of the gentle lamb!
Dark traitor in Messiah's holy camp!
Leper in saintly garb!—assassin masked
In virtue's robe! Vile hypocrite accursed!
I strain in vain to set his evil forth,
The words that should sufficiently accurse
And execrate such reprobate, had need
Come glowing from the lips of eldest hell."
                                POLLOK.

Manuel is sent to Puerto Principe.—Is accompanied by Rosamond, and his Alcowater, a pimp.—Alcowaters kept in all the Convents.— The poor burn pitch-pine to the Virgin Mary, instead of Candles.—Manuel becomes jealous of the Alcowater.—Manuel's tricks with Rosamond.—Manuel seduces the daughter of his host.— The Priests' oath or Hoorie.— Mode of doing penance.—The paying of money for the forgiving of sins.—Manuel sends Rosamond back to Havanna, who being chased by Pirates, has to put in at Matanzas.

MANUEL had orders from the Bishop, to go to Puerto Principe, on the south eastern part of the Island of Cuba, and the seat of justice for the Island.   As he would not consent to leave me behind, fearing, I believe, that in his absence, I should escape from the Island, this arrangement was made:—he hired an old man, who was an *Alcowater*, as they call them, (in this country, they are called pimps.)   He lived in St. Francisco Convent; as the Priests have them in all their Convents, to aid them in all their iniquity and seductions.*   He was to go with us to disguise me as a friend, under his protection, and prevent it from

---

* The Pope of Rome patronises public brothels as a necessary evil, as they term it.   His annual revenue from this source in the city of Rome, is considerable.   Having been educated a Protestant, previous to my perversion to Popery, this part of the discipline of the Romish church, I could never cordially reconcile to my mind.   Whenever I expressed my disapprobation, however, in regard to this part of their discipline, the Romish Clergy invariably defended it.   The law of the Romish Church, however, in this, as in all other things, is made paramount to the law of God, which expressly says, "*There shall be no whore of the daughters of Israel.— Thou shalt not bring the hire of a whore, or the price of a dog, into the house of the Lord thy God for any vow, for even both these are abomination unto the Lord thy God.*" Deut. xxiii. 17, 18.—ED.

9

being known, that I was with Manuel. I had then been living with him about four years. We took our passage in a Spanish brig, commanded by Captain Joan, a Catalan Spaniard, bound for Puerto Principe, Manuel, the *Alco-water*, and myself, where we arrived in eight days. We all put up at the private house of a wealthy Spaniard, of the name of Zobrisco, whose servants sell dry goods in the streets. I think there are no Americans living there. It is a heathen, wicked country. You will find in all their houses, from the highest down to the lowest, wooden, and sometimes marble images, representing our Saviour, the Virgin Mary, and different Saints, in their rooms, painted to resemble life, and candles burning before them. Those that are poor, and not able to buy candles, will burn a piece of wood, similar to our pitch-pine, cut in the form of a candle. These lights are specially kept before the images of the Virgin Mary, and the Saints. When they feel that they have done wrong, or committed sin, they kneel down to the image of the Virgin Mary, and pray to her ; as all the Roman Catholics believe that she has more readiness to forgive them, than God, or any of the Saints.* We were there about three weeks. During

---

* The Popish church, in her Breviary, salutes the Virgin Mary with the epithet, "SALVE REGINA!—AVE REGINA CŒLORUM!—DOMINA ANGELORUM!"—"Hail! Queen of heaven!—Hail! Lordess of the Angels." (In Officio B. Virginis.)

In their " PRECES ANTE ET POST MISSAM, AD USUM SACERDOTUM," which is a small formulary of prayers, recommended to be said by every Priest, and which is in common use among them, we find the following expressions, "O! Our Lordess!—Our Mediatrix, and our Advocate! render us worthy by *thy mediation*, to participate in the glory and happiness of thy Son, Jesus Christ." Preces. p. 46.

To which we add the following blasphemy from the same work, "ACCIPE," &c. *Receive* what we offer!—Bestow what we pray for! —Pardon our fears!—because thou art the ONLY HOPE of sinners." Preces. p. 150.

The Popish church styles the *Virgin Mary, the Queen of Heaven;* and in every Popish country on the globe, incense is burnt unto her. This burning of incense to the Queen of heaven, we maintain, is forbidden by the Word of God, and we prove it. See Jeremiah, Chap. XLIV. 17. 22, where the Lord forbids the people of Judah, from "*burning incense to the Queen of heaven.*"

Ridiculous and wicked as may seem the devotion of the poor deluded

that time, I was still growing more unhappy and wretched, at my lost situation. To look forward, I dare not, and to look back, every thing would appear frightful and hateful to my mind.

Papist towards the Virgin Mary, their devotion, however, is altogether consistent with their principles, and is sanctioned by the practice of all their own Saints. For the truth of what I here assert, I will merely adduce two testimonies, which no Papist can reject. The one is of their great Saint Epiphanius, and the other of the celebrated St. Bernard.

The following is the prayer of St. Epiphanius to the Virgin:

"Πρόβατον," &c., "O! sheep," (says the Saint, addressing the Virgin,) "O! sheep, that produced a Lamb! O! cow, that bore a calf! you produced, not a temporary, but an eternal God, who, incarnated in you, was before you, and before all things! O! light, illuminating the sun with your splendid lamp, and irradiating the ends of the earth! O! Holy Virgin, who, as a spiritual bush without combustion, held the fire of Deity! O! spiritual oven, that brought the Bread of Life into the world! O! maiden candlestick, that shines in darkness, and brought fire and oil for burning! O! unpolluted womb, which comprehended the incomprehensible God! O! ——— bigger than the heavens, which pressed but lightly on the Deity within!" Epiph. de Laud. 2. 291.

St. Bernard's prayer to the Virgin:

"Omnibus firmamentis firmius firmamentum." "O! firmament, firmer than all firmaments! Him, whom the heaven of heavens could not contain, thou, O! our Lordess! didst contain, conceive, beget, feed, suckle, and educate. Thou, in the midst of waters, dividest the waters from the waters. The light of thine eyes dispels darkness, expels legions of devils, purifies the vices of the mind, and warms the coldness of the heart. Happy, O! Lordess! are they, who behold your eyes. Turn, therefore, O! Lordess! those eyes to us, and show us Jesus, the blessed fruit of thy womb." (Here I have to supply the indecent strain into which the Saint has run with a dash ———.) He continues, "O! elevation of minds, intoxication of hearts, and SALVATION OF SINNERS! O! Lordess, gentle in consoling, mild in soothing, and sweet in kissing!" Bernard, Serm. IV. P. 1739—1747.

Among other expressions of this Saint to the Queen of heaven, we find the following:

"O! Lordess, Holy Mary, thou art Heaven, earth, pasture, Paradise, bread, drink, manna, oil, wine, cinnamon, balm, myrrh, frankincense, olive, spikenard, saffron, gum, a temple, a house, a bed-room, a bride, a lamp, a kingdom, a Priesthood, a trumpet, a mountain, a wilderness, a field, a vine, a floor, a barn, a stable, a manger, a warehouse, a hall, a tower, a camp, an army, a bird, a palm, a rose, a river, a pigeon, a garment, a pearl, a candlestick, a table, a crown, a sceptre, a tree, a cedar, a cypress, a pipe, a reed, a daughter, a sister, a mother, a sun, a moon, a star, the city of God, the rod of Aaron, the fleece of Gideon, the gate of Ezekiel, the morning-star, the fountain of gardens, the lily of the valley, and the Land of Promise, flowing with milk and honey."—Idem.—Ed.

"From fear to hope, from hope to fear,
 "My shipwrecked soul is tost,
 "Till I am tempted, in despair,
 "To give up all for lost."

While we were there, his wicked heart became jealous at seeing me talk with the old man, the *Alcowatcr*, as I was obliged to do, to seem to be under his protection, in order to blind the people. Often, when in the presence of the family circle, Manuel would pinch me in such a manner, that I was black and blue. Often, I have had to halloo out, when, on being asked by some of the family, "what was the matter?" I would turn it off, and say, I had the cramp in my hand or foot. I have had to do this not only there, but also in other places. Here I was brought to be an eyewitness of some of his wickedness, in seducing the eldest of the daughters of the private family where we were staying; her name was Mariettee, a young girl only fourteen years old. I think there were five children, two girls and three boys. She retired with him into a room, for him to hear Confession.* She Con-

---

* The Roman religion requires every sin committed, or thought of being committed, by a Roman catholic, to be Confessed privately to the Roman Priest; and empowers the Priest to impose upon the penitent, some penalty to be often inflicted on his flesh, and generally some fine, if he has money, to be taken out of his pocket; and, furthermore, empowers the Priest, to give him absolution from the pains due to the Divine law, for the sins Confessed; the absolution to take full effect, from, and after the discharge of the penance imposed by the Priest. The rehearsal of his sins by a Roman catholic to his Priest, is called *Auricular Confession;* the penalty imposed by the Priest, is called *Penance;* and the forgiveness of the penitent's sins by the Priest, is called *Absolution.*

It is a little remarkable, that with so ready a way of discharging the penalty of every transgression in the flesh, so few Roman catholics yet reach heaven, without laboring some time in Purgatory, and without giving often much money for Masses, to help the souls of their deceased relatives through Purgatory. It would be unaccountable, if the Priests had not an income of no small value from the aid they profess to give the suffering souls of the dead by Massos, to relieve them from the flames, and to *lift them out of the pit, into heaven!* But there is a great gulf between Dives and Lazarus, according to the Scriptures, which no soul can pass.

The use which Roman Priests *can* make of this doctrine of the Roman church, is mournfully exhibited in the painful story of Ma-

fessed to him, among other things, that she had stolen two shillings from her mother. He told her that he would not have her be forgiven, unless she would consent to all his wishes: that he would be a witness against her, that would send her soul to hell. All this Manuel himself told me. Her parents saw her dejected spirits, after her violation, but thought she had been committing some sins, and was preparing to undergo penance for them, which they all do, under the direction of their Priests.* Some have their heads shaved,

---

riettee. The Priest must see his penitent alone. The sinner must tell him all his guilt, or there is no remission, but a fearful curse; must tell all the guilt he has done, or thought to do, else there is no remission. To aid the young in particular, long lists of questions from the Priests are printed and put into the hands of the penitents, on which they are to prepare their hearts, to answer the Priest, as before the Searcher of hearts. Some of these questions are indelicate and corrupting; and the whole exercise is one of the master keys of Roman power, over the conscience of Roman catholics; and is a systematic drill of the young mind under the command of disciplinarians, accomplished and skilled in all the arts of "the Mother of harlots and abominations of the earth."

* We are accused by Papists of calumny when we state, that the Romish church holds that "*ignorance is the mother of devotion;*" their great St. Ligori, however, confirms it.

"How many simple girls," (says he,) "*because* they have learnt to read, have lost their souls!" Ligor. Theol. Prax. Conf. de Person. Devot. C. VII. N. 101. By losing their souls, in Popery, means losing their Popish faith. What the *Saint* therefore says, is, in this sense, true enough, since, after having learnt to read, they may steal an opportunity of looking into the Word of God, and therein be instructed in the true way of salvation.

How many of these poor, deluded, and Priest-ridden souls, (may we, on the contrary, truly say,) have lost their souls! and how many are still losing them, for the want, indeed, of learning to read, and for being led by Popish Priests, instead of by the Word of God!

Such is the extreme ignorance to which Popery reduces her subjects, and in which she keeps them, that many of them absolutely do not know the prayer-book from a Bible. Some time since, in a conversation which I had with a young woman from Ireland, who belonged to the Romish church, among other questions, I asked her if she ever read the Bible, " Yes," (she replied,) " I read the Bible every day." I asked her if she would show me her Bible. " I will," (said she,) and, running up stairs, exulting at the thought of proving her versatility in the Sacred Scriptures, she returns with a prayer-book in her hand:— " There," (said she,) " it is." Why, my dear woman, (said I to her,) this is not the Bible, it is nothing but a prayer-book.—" O, no," (she exclaimed,) " it is the Bible." Have you no other Bible but this?—" No, I

9*

and wear a coarse tow gown, with a leather belt round their waists; some go barefooted; and others do penance in various different ways.*

It was the evening before his barbarity, that Manuel told me all his plan and purposes with Mariettee; what he had made her believe, and what he wished me to do. And he threatened me in various ways, and specially with transportation to the mines, if I withstood him, or made an alarm, or warned the family.† And he hooried

have no other, and I want no other:—your Bibles are all forgeries:—my Priest told me so."—I asked her, then who wrote the Bible? Here the poor creature was completely at a stand.—After some pause, however, she replied, "Why, it was written by the Pope."

Having spent some time in endeavoring to convince her of her errors, I found all my arguments of no avail. She still persisted that her prayer-book was the Bible; that I was a heretic; and heretics were not to be believed. I left her as I found her, as ignorant of the truth as a mere heathen.—ED.

* This *barefoot penance*, (as has been related in the "RENUNCIATION OF POPERY," a pamphlet published by myself shortly after my renouncing the Popish church,) was, by Rule, enjoined upon the Nuns of the Convents of Loretto, in Kentucky. Their Rule forbade them from wearing shoes or stockings, from April till the first of November. Many of these deluded devotees died in consequence of the severe penance imposed upon them. The Rule, however, in consequence of the repeated and urgent solicitations of the parents and relations of the Nuns, was eventually mitigated.

The *leather-belt penance.* This penance, or one somewhat similar to it, I was once, when in the fervors of Popery, zealot enough to practise on myself. The belt I wore was a bed-cord, which was knotted in such a manner, that, by wearing it drawn tight around my body, the knots sunk into my very flesh, and inflamed it to such a degree, that I was under the necessity of mitigating the severity of the penance in order to save my life.

The *hair-shirt* is the ordinary penance which is enjoined in Popish countries to subdue the rebellion of the flesh. This rough *Monkish saviour* has not yet been introduced into the United States.

Previous to my departure from New-Orleans to France, a certain zealous Papist, who was sorely beset with temptations which he wished to shun, begged me to procure and send him one of these hairy *soul-saving machines.* I promised to do it; but as Bonaparte had been purging France of most of the Monastic nuisances, I was unable to procure one. However, in order that he might have a substitute, I wrote to him, and advised him to wear a *coarse coffee-bag* in place of it. —ED.

† How Manuel came to terrify her with these fears, she relates thus. Having threatened the child of Zobrisco, Mariettee, for her wickedness, with the terrors of hell, in her Confessions, privately; he then

to it, that is, he took the Priests' oath, to do as he said he would, and made me *hoorie*, or take the Priests' oath, to

brought her two days before they left Puerto Principe, into the room of Mrs. C—— (who appeared to the family, only under the protection of the Alcowater,) and there brutally violated the child, threatening positively, that if the poor and distressed Rosamond interfered, or cried aloud, or said a word to alarm the family, he would send her to the mines. So he effected his infernal purpose, carrying the terror of hell to the heart of the child, and the terror of the Spanish mines to the heart of his miserable and dependant companion.

Of all the forms of vice, not one is so fatally corrupting, as that which assumes the sanctity of a preacher of righteousness, and robes itself in the mantle of the Lord Jesus Christ. The security of the public virtue and the honor of our Redeemer, constrain us to expose the wolves in sheep's clothing, who prey upon the lambs of the flock, and lead down to hell poor souls committed to their care, to be trained up for heaven.

It is not the purpose of this Narrative, to excite the angry passions, or to wound the feelings of a living soul; but rather by *pointing* to wounds, (for who can lay them bare?) which the Authoress has herself personally received, deep in the heart, to warn the young from trusting to the hypocritical wretches, who, in the profession of Priests of the Lord JEHOVAH, give themselves to the most wanton indulgence of the worst passions of our fallen nature.

It would seem as if angels must weep over the scenes of Puerto Principe; and the blood rushes to the heart and to the head, while the wicked fruits of the celibacy of Roman Catholic Priests, are developed in forms too monstrous to be described, and in colors too black and diabolical to be conceived. How truly has the Apostle declared of them, '*who, being past feeling, have given themselves over unto lasciviousness, to work all uncleanness with greediness.*'

The unparalleled crime of Father Manuel Canto, taught the wretched dependant upon his will, that nothing was too bad for him to do; and his own security evidently required him to deprive the eyewitness of his cruelty, of the power on earth to testify against him. Hence, it was, that she so certainly expected at this time, to be landed at the Spanish mines; and her spirit was tossed, and shaken with alarms, like the ocean heaving in the calm, that suddenly succeeds the hurricane.

Of the horrors she has passed through, that of the robbers, and this of Puerto Principe, leave the most painful impression on her mind. The former is described, the latter cannot be even imagined. I find vent for my own feelings in the words of an impassioned poet, which may also relieve the pressure upon the heart of the reader.

"Weep all of every name! Begin the wo,
Ye woods, and tell it to the doleful winds;
And doleful winds, wail to the howling hills;
And howling hills, mourn to the dismal vales;
And dismal vales, sigh to the sorrowing brooks;

observe what he told me.   My obligation, however, did not restrain me ; my fear of him, and of the Spanish mines, and of instant death, restrained me ; for, although I did not much regard the oath he put on me, I never knew him fail to observe that *hoorie* which he took.

He told me that he could tell any Christian to take me off, saying, " *Take away that wicked woman !*" and it would be done at the word.*   I never saw his countenance so malicious towards me before ; though it often appeared as much so afterwards ; and I was obliged to promise him, in order to be rid of his malice and his threats.

Such was my dread of Manuel, that I dared not whisper a word about what had happened to the family.   Had it been an American family, I would have died to tell them; but to tell this family, would not save them from the devouring wolf in sheep's clothing ; and it would have brought the revenge, both of the family and Priest, on me.   The Alcowater, under whose protection I appeared, had gone.   I never knew what became of him ; but suppose from what I have seen of them, that he came to no

> And sorrowing brooks, weep to the weeping stream;
> And weeping stream, awake the groaning deep!
> Ye Heavens, great archway of the universe,
> Put sackcloth on ! And ocean, clothe thyself
> In garb of widowhood, and gather all
> Thy waves into a groan, and utter it,
> Long, loud, deep, piercing, dolorous, immense!
> The occasion asks it !"
>
> POLLOK, BOOK VI.

"Could a civilized man be guilty of such a deed ?" exclaims the reader, his countenance flashing with shame and indignation!

"I wish you knew all about it," Rosamond replies.   "Manuel told me beforehand what he was going to do, before he brought Mariettee to my room ; and told me, how he had wrought upon her fears, and how I must do, or he would send me to the mines."

* St. Theresa, and with her, the great St. Ligori, says, that "God desires nothing of the soul who proposes to love him, except obedience to the Ecclesiastical Rules, to the Superiors, and to the Spiritual Fathers, the Priests." Ligor. Theol. Prax. Conf. C. ix. N. 167.

"Irrational obedience," (say the Popish divines,) "is the most complete and perfect obedience; for instance, when a person obeys in the same manner, that an ass obeys his master." Cusan. Epis. 2. ad Bohemos. Excit. L. 2, and 6.—ED.

good end, or to a natural death.   I was alone, among
strangers ; and I had not strength to lift so much as my
voice aloud against the Reverend Priest : Reverend to
outward appearance, and consecrated, and holy in the
eyes of the family and of all the people.   Mariettee was
in and out of my room, continually ; but I would not say
any thing to her, for fear of Manuel.   If her own parents
could not afford her protection, to which she might confidently fly, it was in vain for me to attempt to caution the
child.   After dinner he came at five o'clock, to the meeting appointed ; for she had consented to meet him in my
room, knowing what he wanted, and being taught that
it was necessary for the remission of the sins she had committed, to give way to the will of the Holy Priest.   It was
dusk, when he drew a Spanish knife, and threatened both
me and the child, with a spirit such as took away my
senses.   I could not support the horrible scene, but
fainted.

Whether it was my fancy, or whether it was actually
so, I cannot tell, but to my eye and mind, Manuel's countenance after this was changed.   There was a wild, and
horrible expression in his countenance afterwards, that he
never got over ; something that spoke murder in the
heart.*

* To what dreadful crimes, does the Roman Catholic religion lead
its deluded followers !   Led to believe and trust in his superior power
with the Lord and the Saints, the Roman Priest, continually pampered
with adulation, at length gives vent to the wicked passions of the
human heart in every form of indulgence first, and then in forms of
the most beastly excess.   Manuel goes into temptation by the duties of
his office, without regard to danger ; and whatever fall he may seem to
make, it is yet the fall of a Saint, easy to be restored to Divine favor !
He is made to forswear the world, and then is put in the way to gain
the world, so as few could withstand, who condemn him for gaining the
world.   He is made to forswear wedlock ; and then is exposed to
temptations, to which no man should be exposed, and which any man
might not find it easy to resist.   He is set apart to the service of God ;
and still is taught that the Mass and the image, to which he is made
from lisping infancy to bow, receive and transmit this service to the
Father of Spirits.   He is bred up in the belief of lies, and why should
he not serve the father of lies ?   The whole system of Romanism is most
accursed ; and, chiefly for this, that it leads both Priest and people
under the curse of those who neither know God, nor obey the Gospel of

During the three weeks we were at Puerto Principe, Manuel had upwards of two hundred people under pen-

the Lord Jesus Christ, while they blindly profess to proclaim the Gospel, and to possess the sole inheritance of the kingdom of heaven.

One circumstance I mention to the praise of Rosamond. In the way she had first prepared this part of her Narrative, only enough was told, to warn the reader of a most villanous outrage, committed before her, in the name of the Roman Religion, by a Romish Priest in the exercise of his official duties. Most of the circumstances were concealed, from the obvious difficulty of enumerating particulars. They were introduced from time to time, into the Narrative, from her own lips, in the order in which they now stand precisely; and that last expression in the narration, " *I could not support the horrible scene, but fainted,*" was never used by her, nor hinted at, until it came out, as it is written, in the order, and in the place it is written. I mention this, because every one in her situation, who wished to *appear* refined, and who sought to hide her shame, and pain, and deep mortification; who sought to excuse her degradation, in being compelled to witness this most barbarous offence against natural affection and common humanity, would not have postponed that expression to the very last word of the last interview relating to it; but she would have thrown out that particular to view, in the very outset, at the first mention of the subject; and would have carefully kept it in view, at every successive explanation of the inhuman crime. And I notice this striking fact, not for its singularity in her case; but for its harmony with her whole conduct, and spirit, in the preparation of this work for the press, and for the American public.

Under the Pontificate of Paul II., a bull was emitted from Rome respecting the conduct of the Clergy, particularly those of Spain, in reference to the Sacrament of Confession :—" Whereas certain Ecclesiastics in the kingdom of Spain, and in the cities and dioceses thereof, having the cure of souls, or exercising such cure for others, or otherwise deputed to hear the Confessions of penitents, have broken out into such heinous acts of *iniquity,* as to abuse the Sacrament of Penance in the very act of hearing the Confessions, not fearing to entice and provoke females to lewd actions, at the very time when they were making their Confessions." The introduction of this document into Spain, brought to light in a most appalling manner, the wretched condition into which domestic society had been reduced by the influence of the Papal institutions. When this Bull was first introduced into Spain, the inquisitors published a solemn edict in all the churches belonging to Seville; that any person knowing or having heard of any Friar or Clergyman's having committed the crime of abusing the Sacrament of Confession, or in any manner having improperly conducted himself during the Confession of a female penitent, should make a discovery of what they knew, within thirty days, to the Holy Tribunal; and very heavy Censures were attached to those who should neglect or despise this injunction. When this edict was first published, such a considerable number of females went to the palace of the inquisitor, only in the city of Seville, to reveal the conduct of their infamous Confessors, that twenty notaries, and as many inquisitors, were appointed to minute down their

ance in different ways, and I was informed by a Mrs.
S——, that a certain lady, whose name, I think, was

several informations against them; but these being found insufficient
to receive the depositions of so many witnesses: and the inquisitors
being thus overwhelmed, as it were, with the pressure of such affairs,
thirty days more were allowed for taking the accusations; and this
lapse of time also proving inadequate to the intended purpose, a similar period was granted, not only for a third but a fourth time.

The ladies of rank, character, and noble families, had a difficult part
to act on this occasion, as their discoveries could not be made at any
particular time and place. On one side, a religious fear of incurring
the threatened Censures, goaded their consciences so much as to compel them to make the required accusations; on the other side, a regard
to their *husbands*, to whom they justly feared to give offence, by affording them any motives for suspecting their private conduct, induced
them to keep at home. To obviate these difficulties, they had recourse
to the measure of covering their faces with a veil, according to the
fashion of Spain, and thus went to the *inquisitors* in the most secret
manner they could adopt. Very few, however, escaped the vigilance
of their husbands, who, on being informed of the discoveries and accusations made by their wives, were filled with suspicions; and yet, notwithstanding this accumulation of proofs against the Confessors, produced to the inquisitors, this tribunal, contrary to the expectations of
every one, put an end to the business, by ordering that all crimes of
this nature, should be consigned to perpetual silence and oblivion!

What a picture of domestic life, in Papal Havanna, does this Narrative present! The Priests hold one portion of the people in the bondage of fear, and another portion in the bondage of sinful appetite, and
all in the Egyptian bondage, and the Egyptian darkness of the "proud
woman, which is that great city, which reigneth over the kings of the
earth;"—that city which, for above twelve hundred years, subdued the
world by the Roman armies, and for about twelve hundred years more
has subdued the world by the Roman religion. Be reverent before high
Heaven, and be astonished all inhabitants of the earth, that one city in
the thousands of this world, has contrived, by force of arms, and by
professions of religion, to tyrannize over the nations, to reign over the
kings of the earth, to deck herself with the riches of all people, and to
break to pieces, and to stamp with the feet, both the tables of the laws,
and the charters of the civil and religious liberties of mankind, and the
rights of conscience, for a term little short of 2500 years! And Rome
has done it, not by her own strength, but by the subserviency of her
allies, and her vassals, and her dependent nations; by the soldiers and
the Priests of Italy, Austria, Gaul, and Spain. Under the command of
Roman IMPERATORS and Roman Bishops, the liberties of the world have
been and are still trodden under the foot of haughty Rome.

And what place is so trampled on as Cuba; where the whole
people are subject to Roman Priestcraft, from their cradle to their grave,
from the lighting of their birth candles to the lighting of their death
candles, from infant baptism to extreme unction! Where the cry of
robbery and murder is answered by a closing of shutters and a barring

i

Madame Castillo, or some such name, had whipped and starved her servant maid (who was a mulatto girl) to death.   This Mrs. C—— was a lady of fortune, about fifty years of age.

Her penance for that, was, to wear an iron collar round her neck, and go barefooted.   Her collar was put on in such a way, that whenever she turned her head, it would be like so many pins going through her.   She was led to believe by this Priest, that by suffering six months, and having so many Masses said, and burning candles before the images of those Saints, God would forgive her.   The clothes of the girl she whipped to death, were stuffed in the form of a person, and placed in the room where the images of the Saints were, with the candles burning before them.   At the end of six months, she was to be relieved, and to be forgiven, by paying a large sum of money to the Priest.   It would be useless for me to say, how many different ways I have seen them undergo penance.   I did not see Madame Castillo, but Manuel did, and confirmed all that Mrs. S—— told me ; although it was a

of doors against the voice of the cry !   Where the rich have their family altars, and Roman Priests, in the eyes of the husband, the father, and the brother, go into the secret chambers with the wife, and the daughter, and the sister, seemingly to assist in their heavenly aspirations, and to guide their devotions, and to aid them in the true worship of the living God !   Where the same Roman Priests, in honor of chastity, affect to despise the marriage covenant, and do actually cast it utterly away from their own order, while they openly live in shameless concubinage !   Where the people of good common sense, and wide information, are generally persuaded that the same Roman Priests have power to make a scape-goat of their concubines; and, when wearied of them, to Confess all their sins upon the head of the woman, and to send her away crazy to hell.   And where the same Priests seize on young virgins under their parents' roof, and, with threats of eternal judgment in the name of their Apostolic power, joined to personal violence, wantonly and wickedly perpetrate the most beastly crimes, not shrinking from the presence of an earthly witness, nor before high Heaven !—"*How long, O Lord, holy and true, dost thou not judge and avenge our blood on them that dwell on the earth !*"

'Oh, horrible delusion of Romanism, surpassing, in the lives of Roman Catholic Priests in Cuba, all that we read or hear of the mental blindness of the ignorant heathen ; and all that we can conceive of the depravity of man !—But it is written here, "*to let the world know, believing it will be also written in heaven.*" ·

resident Priest, and not Manuel, who imposed her penance. Her penance was not finished when I left the place.

By this time he had got ready to leave Puerto Principe, to return to Havanna; but, previously, he had sent away, in his jealousy, the old man, the *Alcowater.* He put me alone on board a Spanish brig, under the care of the captain, with whom he was acquainted; as he thought it would not be prudent, himself, to leave in the same vessel with me. I was alone, with no other passenger; and the captain, whose name was Gosha, a creole, a native of Havanna, treated me like a sister. The mate was an Italian.

You can in some measure judge of my feelings,—I considered myself lost in despair beyond all mercy. Manuel had brought my feelings to such a state, by his conduct and his threats, that I thought he was going to send me to the Spanish mines, there to be exiled. I thought it was for this he had sent away the old man, and I expected to be confined for life.* I was then brought to see what a

---

* The abhorrence of Manuel, and desire to abandon him, were most natural to a bosom that had a spark of feminine feeling left. A perfect loathing of the unholy wretch was most natural to the abused sex. His threats show that he was thoroughly prepared for this state of Rosamond's feelings; and his Priestly associate in crime was at hand in Matanzas, to present her his commands to come to him at Havanna, under pain of that death which Manuel, the Priest, knew how to inflict, and which Padro, his fellow Priest, had the hardihood in his name to threaten. "Though hand join in hand, the wicked shall not be unpunished." They triumphed over the poor wanderer that time, and led her back to the sorrows of a sinful life with Manuel. But the very enormity of his crimes, while it bowed the spirit of the vexed Rosamond, still inspired her with a hope, that she would one day escape from his hands, through the mercies of an overruling Providence. Such transgressions she felt in her heart could not escape the judgment of God, although they do escape the observation of men; and that the righteous One would help her against the oppressor, was a secret hope that found, sometimes, a place in her thoughts, and began after awhile to be cherished there with frequent misgivings.

But what an exhibition of the Roman Priesthood is here! Wolves they are in this Narrative, not singly and alone, but, also, by the pack; howling to make a prey of the innocent, and joining together in aid of the wicked schemes which one could not accomplish alone! The state of society in Spain and Cuba, is altogether, from the testimony of travelers, more corrupt than can be conceived of here.

10

wicked sinner I was, and what wicked people I was w
To look forward, I dare not ; and I thought my mi;
was near at an end, as I expected I was going t
landed on an island beyond the reach of all mercy.

CHAPTER VIII.

"But laymen most renowned for devilish deeds,
Labored at distance, still behind the Priest;
He sheared his sheep, and, having packed the wool,
Sent them unguarded to the hill of wolves;
And to the bowl deliberately sat down,
And with his mistress, mocked at sacred things."
                                        POLLOK.

On her voyage from Puerto Principe, is chased by Pirates.— Takes refuge in Matanzas.— Receives a letter from Manuel, desiring her to come to Havanna.— Her mental sufferings.— Is threatened with death, if she refuse to go to Havanna.— Leaves Matanzas and arrives in Havanna.— Is taken sick, anointed, and baptized for death.— Description of the ceremony of her baptism.— Becomes deranged.— The Priests are in dread of her.— The people pity and deplore her lost condition.

WHEN we had been at sea three days, we were chased by a pirate, by which we were driven to Matanzas. Here I found myself landed in a strange and wicked country. When I left New Orleans, this was the first place I landed at; but I then stopped but a few days before I went to Havanna. Here, I now found an American female living, who belonged to New York. I found great comfort and consolation in informing her of my lost and forlorn situation. I was there but a few days, before I received a letter from my Priest, desiring me to come to Havanna immediately. He had me in his power in such a way, that I felt as if I must obey him, as if he were something more than a natural being; not through love, but through fear. I had forgotten my friends and myself; I had forgotten I was in existence, aiming and planning to please him. I can truly say, that he has made me, at times, feel like a criminal, brought to the gallows, when in his presence.

He wrote a letter to a Priest, Frederick Padro by name, a friend of his, who lived at Matanzas, desiring him to call on me, and threaten me with what would be the result, and he did threaten me with death, if I did not go immediately to Havanna. Father Padro called on me, and delivered the message, which was: " *That if I was not in Havanna, in three days from that day, that I should not be alive ; that he was acquainted with people in Matanzas, who dare not disobey his orders ; and if I divulged this to any one, my life would be in danger.*" Father Padro, who called on me, and made me this communication, took me to his house, where he had a young girl, nineteen years old, with whom he was living. He had been the cause of her ruin. She was a person of a fine mind and beautiful. He had persuaded her parents to give her to him. They, being poor, and she being young and beautiful, he made them believe, that it would not be any sin to live with him, as he had so much power with the Virgin Mary, that he could save her soul; this she told me herself. She had one child by him, but it was taken away from her soon after it was born. He told her that he was going to put it into a Convent, under the care of the Abbess. This is all she knew about the child. I could see that she was unhappy, and lived in much fear of him; but she could relieve her mind, at times, by going to the Priest, and making her Confession, as she believed in the Catholic church, and all that the Priests told her.

I left my American female friend, with whom I found so much consolation, for Havanna. Here I found myself with Manuel more unhappy and wretched than ever. I had given up all hopes of ever leaving the island, or getting away from him. I felt myself lost, and gave up to despair. Then I would say to myself, " Oh! if I could only become a Christian, or could find some Christians to tell them of my trouble !" For I had no one around me, but what appeared so wicked to me, that I dare not tell them what my feelings were.

Shortly after, I was taken very sick, and was brought very low. How to prepare myself to die I knew not, as I was as ignorant as any heathen of the way of salvation, and hell presented itself before me. Oh! judge my feelings from what your own would be.—Manuel then persuaded me, and insisted on my being christened, and

ROSAMOND CHRISTENED.

p. 113.

said I should then become a Christian, and would die
happy. I consented to be anointed and christened, not
believing that it could save my soul; but as I was living
in the manner I was with him, I thought it could do me
no harm in the sight of heaven. He said if I died as I
was, he could not bury me.*

The preparations were accordingly made, and I was
removed from my bed to a death-table, as they call it,
which is about four feet high, and seven feet long. Four
death-candles were placed, one at each corner of this table, and the images of different Saints, with the Virgin
Mary, were brought from the Convent into the room, and
I was placed in the centre, laid out on the table. The
image of the Virgin Mary was placed at the foot of the
table, in full dress, with candles lighted up around her.
Then there stood around two of those Capuchin Priests,
and my physician, (who lived in the Convent, and dresses like a Priest in habits,) with a gentleman and lady, to
stand my Godfather and Godmother, and my Priest and
other individuals, who came in as friends.—I was very
sick, near unto death, but in the terror and excitement it
caused, I did not feel my weakness, or disease.

On looking around me, as I laid on that table, I thought
that those Priests were so many devils; and that I was
truly in Purgatory: I was afraid to look at them, as they
went through their ceremony. But I know their customs: First, they burnt incense in the room, in an ark,
which they take to be very holy. This is to burn the
evil spirits out of the person, and out of the room.

---

* "*He could not bury me.*" This feature of Romanism, that refuses
the charity of a burial to a Protestant deceased, is traced by the poet
Young, smarting with grief for the loss of a loved daughter, in these
lines:

> "Denied the charity of dust to spread
> O'er dust! (a charity their dogs enjoy ;)
> What could I do? What succour? what resource?
> With pious sacrilege a grave I stole!
> More like her murderer, than friend, I crept,
> With soft, suspended step; and muffled deep
> In midnight darkness, whispered my last sigh."

10*

Next, they rang a little bell, which they carry with them on such occasions. Then they knelt down, and *laid my body*, as they term it, by offering a prayer, a few words in Latin. Next, they sprinkled me with Holy Water; anointed me with Holy Ointment, Crossing my forehead, my breast, my hands, and my feet, with this ointment, all the time ringing the small bell, and repeating over something to themselves in Latin.* After they got through with this ceremony, as I have said, the excitement and terror it gave me, made me almost forget that I was sick ; and they then said I was a holy Christian, and that all the sins I had ever committed were gone from me ; and they rejoiced over me, and said I had been weighed down and oppressed with evil spirits, which now were cast out of me, and I was made whole. They then put a Cross† round my neck, and told me, whenever I committed any sin, that I must take this Cross, and go to the image of the Virgin Mary for mercy ; that she would always have mercy upon me ; but charged me, whenever I felt as if I had done wrong, to go to some Priest, and to Confess it to him. I did recover immediately from my sickness, and I do believe it was owing to the effect this had on my system ; but the Priests all said it was because they had made me a Christian ; I was restored to my health again, in some measure, so that I was able to be about. I did truly feel as if I was another person, for my mind and feelings had now become stupified.

I had now become foolish, like a child; so much so, that I could not remain in my house, wanting to be wandering, in the streets, alone. When out, I knew not where I was going ; and when I saw any of the Priests, I would go up to them publicly, and cry to them, weeping, and tell them, they had set me crazy, that they had put Priestcraft on

---

* "At the time of my baptism, I was anointed with oil ; a piece of salt was put in my mouth, the Priest breathing three times upon me, and touching my eyes, ears, and nose with spittle, speaking Latin all the while. They profess to take these ceremonies from the Scriptures." *Miss Reed's six months in a Convent, p.* 66.

† This individual Cross is now in the Asylum at Yorkville.

ROSAMOND FRANTIC.

P. 115

me. I got so lost at last, that I would not consent for my
Priest to come to my house ; and if I saw him in the
street, I felt as if I wanted to tear him to pieces ; and
when I was laboring in this state of mind, I once tore
his habit off him in the street.   He at last got afraid of
me, and all the other Priests would try to shun me, when
they met me in the street.

It became public to all, from the oldest down to the
youngest, who I was ; and the cry was with them publicly when I went into the street : " *Look at that poor
American girl, who lives with Father Canto ! He has
made her crazy by malediction and Priestcraft !*" This
had become so public, that all the people were ringing it
in each other's ears.   And they pitied me, and blamed the
Priest.   The old Bishop, and some of the Priests, consulted
together what could be done.*   There was a respectable
family, that would send for me, and talk and plead with
me, to leave the Priest.   I remember the kindness of that
family.   Their name is Soutan, and they live in Cui St.
Phillipe.   Mr. Soutan transacts business in the Alcada's,
or chief judge's office.   He is an intimate acquaintance of
my Godfather.   They made me an offer, to take me and
give me a home with them, telling me it was so wicked
to live with him ; that God would never forgive me.   I
then asked them, if it was not wicked for *him* to do so.
They would say, yes, yes ; but that he could save his own

* For all this was a very public matter, so much so, that I was myself annoyed in the streets, when I had my reason, by people pointing
at me when I passed, and hissing to each other, as their custom is when
they would arrest attention, and saying one to another :—" That is the
poor American girl the Priest's have made crazy with their Priestcraft." [They all knew that she was living with Father Manuel Canto,
and knew that it was a sin ; and they believed that the sin was visited
wholly on her head, through the prevailing power of the Holy Priest
with the Virgin and the Saints, to save his own soul. While this served
to confirm their opinion of the Holy Priest's power, and filled them
with fear of the men, who have such power with the Gods of Rome,
the Virgin and the Saints, many still felt sympathy for the interesting
young stranger, who wandered among them a monument of Divine
wrath, smitten and broken, by the influence of the prayers of
that man, for whose pleasure she lived, and to whose pleasure she
ministered.]

soul; that he could pray all the curses of the sin, on the woman who had any thing to do with him; and the curses would fall on her. This was all the comfort I could get from them.

CHAPTER IX.

"How poor, how weak, how impotent, is man !—
Cradled in imbecility, the prey
Of those who love him fondest, who will fan
His passions by indulgence, and will sway
To sense, and self, and pride, and fear, and play
Their apish tricks upon him, till his soul
Has lost its native innocence."

PERCIVAL.

Rosamond disguised as a Priest, by Father R——.—Pays a visit to Father Canto, in St. Francisco Convent.—Her surprise at the thought of being confined there.—Manuel receives her gladly, and desires to know all her history, and her religion, and her mind.—She opens her mind freely.—His confessions.—His contrition.—His advice to her to become a Nun in St. Claro Convent.—Manuel about to prepare to go on penance.—After three days, Rosamond returns from the Convent, in charge of the same Father R——.—Tells her Godmother where she had been.—Her horror at this unpardonable sin.—Rosamond attempts to escape from Cuba.—Prays to the Virgin Mary.

AFTER a little, I became more reconciled in my mind. God was so merciful to me, I enjoyed my natural reason in some measure; but I was still wretched and unhappy. Soon after, my Priest was taken sick in the Convent, and confined to his room. It was his wish for me to go to the Convent, to see him; and he sent a Priest, Father R——, who lived in the same Convent with him, to call on me with a letter, stating, that I must go to him in disguise, as a Priest, in their garb of a habit and a wig. They have wigs in the same form, as they shave their own heads, for the purpose of getting married, and enticing young ladies into their Convents, as I have heard the Priests themselves frequently say; for, in this disguise, they can pass them in, without notice from any one.

The same Priest, Father R——, who came for me, I saw only the day previous, next door to me, hearing the Confession of a dying lady.

I knew and felt that it was wrong for me to put this disguise on, and to go to the house of God, as I thought it; but as I was so much in their power, I did not dare

to refuse to go. Oh, how plain I can look back on my
wicked pilgrimage! and how plain I can see that God's
Holy Spirit was with me! for how often, when I have
been doing wrong and wickedly, there would be a moni-
tor within, that would tell me it was wicked in the sight
of God, and I would feel bad and unhappy! But, oh!
how soon these feelings would leave me, and I would go
on- and do those things, which I knew, but a few moments before, were wrong and wicked in the sight of
God, and, about which, I had been unhappy.

> " The more I strove against its power,
> I sinn'd and stumbled but the more ;
> My grief and burden long has been,
> Because I could not cease from sin."

After I had dressed myself in this habit, and put the
wig on my head, the Priest, Father R——, took some
black chalk, that he had brought with him, and blacked
my eye-brows, and around my chin.—I then wanted to
go and look in the glass, but this he refused me ; and said
it would be so wicked for me to look in the glass, and to
make fun of my Priest's habit. I could not persuade him
to let me go to the glass ; but he said he could pass me
any where in the day-light ; no one would take me to be
a woman.

When we entered the Convent, it was about eight
o'clock in the evening. The doorkeeper, who keeps the
keys, met us at the door. Not one word was said by
either of us. We followed him up five stair-cases, and
he unlocked five iron doors. I judged they were iron
by the sound ; and I have often heard the Priests say
they were iron. The only light we had with us, was
from the cigar the doorkeeper was smoking. Oh! I
could not describe the feelings which I had when the
first door was locked upon us. I never thought, nor
reflected on what I was doing, until then ; it came to my
mind, that he had sent for me, to put me in some vault,
there to die. All appeared silent as the grave, only I
could hear the beating of my own heart ; and when he

unlocked those doors, they would give such a doleful
sound, as would make the whole Convent ring, which
still made it appear more horrible.

When we entered Manuel's room, I felt somewhat relieved.* I found him in his bed, sick. He appeared to
be glad to see me. I never saw him look so unhappy in
his mind, as he was at that time. He desired me to speak
my mind freely to him, and tell him all my history ; who
I was, and what first led me to come on the island ; what
my feelings were towards him, and whether I had felt
different in mind, since I was christened ; and if I had any
desire to leave him, and come to America. I did feel able
at that time, to open my heart wholly to him ; for I felt as
if my time was come, and that I was brought there to die.
I told him I was not prepared to die ; but if I died as I
was I should go to hell ; that their religion could not save
my soul ; and I did wish to come to America to die with
my friends. He then wanted me to tell him all about
our religion ; but I could not tell him any thing, for I
knew nothing. I was as ignorant as a heathen of the
right view of eternity, or the way to seek the salvation of
my soul ; and I told him so. I pleaded with him to do,
and to live differently ; that he could not be a Christian ;
and it was so wicked to lead the people in so much darkness. He then told me, that he never wished to be a
Priest from the first, but was compelled to become one by

* The natural repugnance of Rosamond to put on the habits of a man
for disguise ; the blacking of her eye-brows and chin by Father R——;
her curiosity to see herself in this new attire ; the Priest's double assu-
rance, once, that it would be wicked for her to make fun of her new
habits, (and he knew her disposition too well to trust her at the mirror)
and again, that nobody would take her black habits, and black brows,
and chin, to belong to a woman, even by daylight ; form a group of in-
cidents not easily counterfeited by any ingenuity ; but when to this is
added, the thoughtless step with which she entered the Convent, the
sudden reflection produced by the clang of the iron door, as it bolted
her from the world, that she would go no more out of it forever ; the
only light, the light of the keeper's cigar, and, the only sound, the sound
of her beating heart, to whose aching pulsations the presence, even of
Father Manuel Canto, afforded some relief ; these details altogether,
are so grouped by the simple hand of plain truth, as no artist could design, no genius could invent.

the wish of his father, who was then living in Spain, and one of the head Monks there. I asked him if his father was ever married; he said no. He told me he did not know who his mother was; and I have frequently heard him curse her, whoever she might be. He never before, nor since, appeared to feel, or see, that he was living and doing so wrong. He did not tell me so; but I could see his countenance bespoke it.* He wept like a child, while he thought and spoke of his wicked course, and that he had been led to commit crimes against his conscience, through the office of a Priest, which was forced upon him, and which he never had a wish to take. And he openly expressed a wish to escape himself from Cuba, which it is no easy thing for a Priest to do, and to come to the United States, if only he had any means of obtaining a support there.

He then told me I must prepare myself to die;

---

* This interview with Manuel in St. Francisco Convent, is one of rare interest. The reader may suppose, that in the retirement of his sick chamber, the reflections of Father Canto were not free from the stings of a guilty conscience; and the recent extravagance and craziness of Rosamond, came to arouse his doubts of the sufficiency of his doctrine and ceremonies to save a soul. The conviction that this Convent door would never be re-opened to her, inspired Rosamond with courage and resolution to lay open to him her whole heart. The compunctious visitings of his conscience aided her, and the Priest learned righteousness from her lips. He rather excused himself for his guilt in the Priesthood by charging the assumption of that office on the will of his father; and the guilt of his life, he was so hardened as to cast on the strange mother that gave him birth.

Possibly, the freedom with which Rosamond addressed him, was instrumental of changing his purpose to confine her within the prison walls of the Convent vaults. It certainly brought him to exhibit some of the signs of penitence; and his desire to know all about Rosamond and her religion, was evidence of a momentary distrust of the faith he professed. His confidence returned, however, while he parried her remonstrance against his wicked life with exhortations to become a Nun, and to put herself under the tuition of his aunt, in St. Claro Convent.

Having written this, and spoken of the contrition Manuel manifested here, Rosamond added, that she had not told all; for she feared bringing the vengeance of the Priests upon Manuel, and subjecting him to persecution for the frankness of his speech; but when the further relation seems honorable to Manuel, I venture to give it, hoping that the spark of independence and of honest feeling it manifests, may yet be blown into a flame.

PURGATORY ROOM. P. 121

that if I died as I was, my soul would be lost for
ever, and asked me if I did not want to be an
Angel in Heaven. I told him yes, that I wanted to
become a good Christian before I died. He then told me
he had an aunt, who lived in St. Claro Convent, where
there are a great many Nuns, all Christians and holy ;
that they lived next door to heaven ; and if I would consent to go there, he would put me under the kind care of
his aunt, and he could come and hear my Confessions.
He told me also, that he was going to prepare to go on
penance.* I replied, that I would make up my mind,
and go there. I would go and die there. I did not feel
so, but thought I should never be allowed to leave the
Convent, and was obliged to answer him as I did.

I remained in the Convent three days. A number of
Priests, his friends, would come into his room, and would
partake in eating, and in drinking wine. I could hear
and see it was his friends, the Priests, who wished to
have me put in confinement in St. Claro Convent, more
than himself. While in the Convent, I would partake of
nothing, that Manuel did not taste with me. I put confidence in him, while I feared poison and death in every
form. He knew it too, and used to laugh at me ; but he
always indulged me, by tasting with me.

On the third day I came out, by promising I would prepare and go to St. Claro. The same Priest who took me
there, Father R——, came out with me. It was twilight
when we passed through the rooms, I was dressed in the
habit of a Monk, and Father R—— led me through by the
arm. I could just perceive one of them was full of figures

---

* This "*going to prepare to go on penance,*" exemplifies both the confidence of the Priests in the efficacy of their own better remedy for sin,
and the reluctance with which these spiritual physicians swallow the
prescriptions they are every ready to administer to other souls. The
Priests do go on penance under direction of the Father Confessor of
their Convents. Manuel's late course might well call for some atonement, such as the guilty conscience, led by deluded Priests, requires to
be self inflicted on the penitent. But the Father Confessor of St. Fran-
ciso Convent, seems to have been himself too deep in the mire of pollution to lay any very heavy burden on his penitent Priests. He kept
himself his lady in the Convent, Manuel often said.

11

in different forms, one of which was the image of the Old Adversary, with a blue flame issuing from his mouth, with all his troop. Another was the figure of a man, dressed like a Monk, with a horrible and frightful countenance, who stood near the jar of sulphur, brandishing a torch in his hand, which burnt with a blue flame. They were all naked. When we entered, we were almost suffocated by the burning of sulphur, which was placed in a jar in the middle of the floor, around which were burning several small lamps. They call that room " *Purgatory.*" The next room we entered, was in total darkness. By this time, I had become perfectly resigned. I never expected to see day-light again, so sure was I that they meant to destroy me, for that, I believe, was their plan. I was so wretched, and troublesome to them, and Manuel was likewise so unhappy, that they wanted to get rid of me ; and but for him, they would have done it. I do believe they would have confined me in St. Claro Convent, while I lived.

I cannot express the feeling I had, when I found myself out of this Convent, and once more in my house again. When reflecting, this all appeared to me like a dream ; I could not bring to my mind the reality of the late scenes which I had witnessed and gone through. This Priest, Father R——, told me, that my house was full of evil spirits, and I must have it cleansed and purified ; must burn incense, and have some Holy Candles lighted immediately, and cleave to the Virgin Mary for mercy ; and through my weakness and blindness, I did as he told me. He left me at my house, on my promising that I never would mention to any one where I had been.

I had brought my mind to such a state, that I was become afraid of myself, and of every one around me. If any one would call and see me, to talk with me, and comfort me, I imagined they were trying to lay some plot, to put me to death, or into confinement.

Being asked by my Godmother, where I had been, I told her that I had been in St. Francisco Convent. She then said, that I had committed an unpardonable sin; that the "Mother of Mercies" never would forgive me, unless I went immediately and heard Masses, and made Confession to some Priest; that I had run great risk, not only of being put in confinement for ever, but had committed the unpardonable sin.

My mind had become so distracted and weak, that I was led to go to a Priest to Confess. I went to several Convents before I had courage to enter one. In those Convents they have the Sanctuary for worship, and rooms where you go to give in Confession. The Priest that I went to, was between fifty and sixty years old. As soon as he learnt who I was, he told me he could not hear my Confession at that time. I must come to him on Good Friday, which was in the following week. That day they take to be very holy. It is the day the Catholics all burn incense in their houses and churches.

On my return home, I found my Priest there waiting for me. It appeared to me, that I was fenced in by many evil spirits all around me. I was like a person in a house all on fire, and myself, placed in the middle of it; for when I would look around, it appeared as if they all wanted to put me away in some confinement, there to die. I would go to this one, and that one, but none could relieve my mind, nor my conscience.

"When iron slumbers bind your flesh,
    With strange surprise you'll find,
Immortal vigor springs afresh,
    And tortures wake the mind.

"Conscience, the never dying worm,
    With torture gnaws the heart,
And wo and wrath in every form,
    Is then the sinner's part.

"Sad world indeed, ah! who can bear
    For ever there to dwell,
For ever sinking in despair,
    In all the pains of hell."

It then came to my mind, what my female friend had

told me in Matanzas, that there was a place here in New York, a home for a penitent female to reclaim her character ; and the way pointed out to her, in which to seek the salvation of her soul.   My burden of conscience was somewhat relieved, upon the hope that I should be able to escape from the Island of Cuba.   I made several attempts to leave, but was detected by my Priest ; and at every attempt I made, I felt more encouragement to believe that one day I should succeed.

Although every thing appeared so dark and gloomy before me, behind me, and all around me, in all my troubles, wretchedness, and difficulties, I never thought of, or went to my God, to beg for mercy and assistance.   No, I went to men, wicked people.   I have, at times, when melted down in sorrow and misery, not knowing what to do, gone to my room, knelt down to the image of the Virgin Mary,* and poured out my feelings to her for mercy ! Oh,

---

* The folly of image worship is so rank, that, to an American, it seems impossible to dwell in an enlightened mind.   But here is an instance of an American of no mean spirit, bowed down with sorrows, and destitute of a right knowledge of the Holy God, blindly adopting the customs of the people that surrounded her, and pouring out her heart at the feet of an image, representing the blessed Virgin.   This idolatry gained faster hold of her affections the longer she indulged it; for the relief which she experienced in unburthening her heart to the image, was a sensible pleasure, and, no doubt, if the fixed purpose of her soul to escape from the island, had not been favored of heaven, she would have become a perfect devotee of Romanism.   It was long after her escape, months passed, before she rose superior to a profane veneration of the image of the Virgin and the Crucifix.   " *Thou shalt not make unto thee, any graven image, or any likeness—thou shalt not bow down thyself to them, nor serve them.*" Exod. xx. 4.

The reader may think of the generous Greeks and the haughty Romans; of the wise men, and brave, and intellectual, of every age, who have bowed to images, and worshiped the work of men's hands.   They knew that the wood was yet wood, and the stone, stone ; but they acknowledged the god which the wood and the stone represented; they bowed and confessed and prayed before it; they praised and adored the ethereal spirits, which they supposed to hover around the images called by their name ; and so they gave, as the Roman catholics of all countries now give, the glory which is due to Jehovah alone, profanely to the images and pictures representing deceased men, and departed spirits.

We are in the habit of pitying the distant heathen ; of striving in the meekness of the Gospel, to turn them from the worship of idols, to serve

what a life of darkness and blindness mine has ever
been ! I knew that there was a God who made us, and
that was all I knew or thought about it. I may well say
that I was a heathen. Oh ! blessed be his holy name,
that he did bring me to New York, that he did have
mercy upon me, and has opened my blind eyes, and enlightened my dark understanding, and brought me to see
the right way to seek the salvation of my soul. Oh, that
I may always sit low at the feet of Jesus !

the living God; but we do not sufficiently regard the heathen in our
midst; we do not pity, as we ought, the poor Roman catholic, who is
led as certainly in the ways of the heathen, to the end of the heathen,
as any Hindoo. Many offend them rather by their zeal, than win
them by their charity to forsake images, and to serve the anointed of
God.

11*

CHAPTER X.

" And tell, hopeless bigot, why ?
For what, for whom did Jesus die ?
If pyramids of Saints must rise
To form a passage to the skies ?
And, think ye man can wipe away
With fast and penance, day by day,
One single sin, too dark to fade
Before a bleeding Saviour's shade ?
O, ye of little faith, beware !
For neither fast, nor Saint, nor prayer,
Would aught avail you without Him,
Beside whom Saints themselves grow dim."

Miss L. M. DAVIDSON.

Attempts to escape from Cuba.—Was detected by Manuel, who threatens to have her confined.—Burning Holy Candles to the Virgin, and the Saints. —The pay of the Priests for laying evil spirits, and sprinkling Holy Water.—The ceremony of laying out and burying the dead.—Burning their bones.—Procession against the cholera.—Fly to the Convents as a refuge from the cholera.—The Priests entice two hundred females into the Convents.—No escape from the Convents.—The conduct of the Priests too indelicate to be told.—The amours of the Right Rev. Bishop, who was near 100 years of age.—The lamentations of the females at the death of the Bishop.

IN one of the attempts I made to leave the island, I had my passage bespoke, and my passport in my pocket, and my trunks put on board ship. On leaving my house, to go on board myself, I felt like one who had committed some dreadful wicked crime, and was afraid of being detected. When I got to the wharf, I was met by the captain of the port, who said that I could not leave in that vessel, nor the island at present ; and my trunks were brought on shore. I made no inquiries of him, where they were ; for I well knew I was detected by my Priest. I was then obliged to return to my solitary home, where my trunks had arrived before me. I had succeeded in getting off without my servant girl knowing any thing about it, until I returned. The Priest accused her of knowing it. Shortly after, she left me suddenly, and I never knew what became of her. I felt myself so much in danger, that I dare not make inquiries about her.

My Priest then told me, it would be useless for me to

try to leave the island; for I could not. He said he could bring me in a lunatic, and have me confined; and many times he threatened me he would do it. His reasons for wishing me not to leave him, I could not see clearly at that time; but since I have become enlightened, I can see it was because he was afraid of being exposed, as he well knew what state of feelings I was laboring under, and often, yes, often, he has heard me say; Oh, if I could only become a Christian! But I still felt encouraged, that I should one day be able to get away.

He wanted me to go into the country, to a friend of his, who was an elderly lady, a widow. He brought her to my house, to see me. I still kept on promising I would go whenever he wished. During this time, and the past year, I was seldom without some Holy Candles, as they call them, burning in my bed-room, with the image of the Virgin Mary, and other Saints, and a bottle of Holy Water, to sprinkle my house with. The Catholics all have them in their houses, and I had got such a habit, that I felt lost without them.

Seeing so much of their Priestcraft and malediction, would stupify the most refined feelings of mind; that is, if a person was a heathen, as I was. If you are placed among them, you are led to believe by the Priest, that the candles they buy out of the Convents are so blessed by the Priest, that burning them in your house will keep out all evil spirits. Every Good-Friday you must go to the Priest, *to lay* the evil spirits; and then you start afresh for another year. But you must take the Priests a sum of money to compose the evil spirits. They cannot lay them, and bless you, without money. I have known my Priest to take from one hundred, to a hundred and fifty dollars, on a Good-Friday, by Masses,* Confessions, and laying the evil spirits in different families.

When any of the Catholics have a new house built, be-

---

* "The price of Masses," (says Ricci, who was himself an Italian Bishop,) "varies. The Priest turns every thing to account,—a *privileged altar*,—the devotion of the people towards a particular Saint,—a relic,—an image reported to be miraculous, &c." Tom. i. p. 284.—ED.

fore they move into it, they must have it laid, and Mass said, and pay a sum of money to the Priest for the service; or, if you move from one house to another, it must be done for the house you move to, before you go into it. Each family, and person, generally, have their favorite Priest. When a rich person dies on the island, after the corpse is laid out, there is preparation made in the room for all the Priests to go and say prayers over the dead body, (a few words in Latin,) and sprinkle some Holy Water in the room. Afterwards each Priest would receive two dollars before he would leave. The friends of the deceased are led to believe, that those prayers by the Priests will help them through Purgatory.*

The way they lay out the dead there, is in a full suit of new clothes, shoes, and stockings; the same as when living. When a lady dies, she is laid out in a suit of black; the same as when going to church with her Holy

---

* By endless exactions of this sort, the Roman Clergy, in those countries where they are not much restrained by the eyes of Protestants, load and harass their people without mercy. What is to hinder them ? They have all power over the consciences, and even over souls, of the living and of the dead, not to forgive the sins of the one, or to pray out the suffering spirit of the other from Purgatory, unless they see cause, according to the faith they teach, and as the Roman catholics believe. Why, then, should they not tease the people to the very extreme of suffering ? Man is by nature a tyrant; and never did any succession of men, in any age, hold the reins of power by what they call divine right, without grievously oppressing the people. Manuel Canto well said, extending his habit between his thumb and finger; " These habits do not change our feelings; we have the same feelings with other men." —And any set of men, even Americans, would become corrupt, as the Roman Priests in Popish countries assuredly are, if they were exposed to the same temptations.

The fault of their excesses belongs not to this age of Priests; not to the Spanish, or Irish people; but it belongs to the Roman catholic system; which inevitably would lead any people into their vices, as it has led them, provided they were exposed to the same instruction and example from their youth.

Let us see our parents and holy Priest always adoring the image of the Virgin, and should not we, too, adore ? Let American youth be separated to celibacy in the Convent and the Nunnery, in early life; and then put to Confess to one another in secret; and would not they become vile ?—The fault is in the Romish system. The Roman catholics are neither more nor less than other men, except what that system makes them.

Beads and Cross. Strict Catholics in Havanna, always wear black at Church, and at no other time. When a young maid, or a young child dies, she is laid out in white; her face is painted; and her head is dressed with white artificial flowers. They carry the dead in coffins to the grave-yard; then they are taken out of the coffin, and laid in the ground. They are covered with lime, before the earth is put over them. The lime is put on, to eat the flesh; for, once a year, in these countries, they take up the dead bodies and burn them. The bones are gathered together, and then buried. Three days previous to burning the dead, the Priests and the friends of the deceased make a great holy-day. The Priests get a great deal of money on those days for Masses and candles. The grave-yard is illuminated with candles, which they get from the Priests. Each one of the friends of the de-ceased, will take a candle and a bunch of flowers, and place them on the grave where their friends lie. When they carry their dead to the grave, any one, who will fol-low, is presented with a candle by the Priest. No one is allowed to follow in the procession without a candle, which must be bought of the Priests.

The Catholics do not think it any harm to go to the theatre, or masquerade-balls, nine days after they have buried a near relative. They are led to believe that after nine days their bodies are at ease, and their souls are happy with their holy mother, the Virgin Mary, in hea-ven. Some of them, however, have Masses said for many years, for fear they may still be in Purgatory. The same custom of illuminating the grave-yard annually, and of burning the dead, prevails in the French grave-yard at New-Orleans: and the day is a holy-day for the slaves as well as their masters, there.*

Shortly after the last attempt I made to leave Manuel, and Cuba, which was in the Spring of 1833, the cholera broke out on the island; this woke up all the Priests and

---

* To this statement respecting the annual burning of the bones of the dead at New-Orleans, I can add my incidental testimony. Such was the custom some few years ago when I visited the place.—ED.

people. They had been expecting it, as it was visiting every other place : and, for a month before it broke out, the Priests all became very holy in going through their ceremonies of worship in their Convents; and, for a month, they every day came out into the streets, in large processions, with images of the Virgin Mary, our Saviour, and the Saints, burning incense and candles, and praying that the cholera might not visit the island.—The images are as large as grown people, decorated in the richest apparel. The Virgin Mary's image would be placed on a couch, carried by four Priests. This couch would be decorated with gilded leaves, and artificial flowers. The image would be placed in the centre of the couch, standing and weeping with the tears on her cheek, and a white handkerchief in her hand.—By her looks you would think it a natural being. How they contrived the tears, 1 do not know. The image of our Saviour would be placed on a similar couch, carried by four Priests.—He would be standing up with his bleeding wounds. It would appear as if the blood was actually gushing out from the body.—They bring the image of the Virgin Mary from one Convent, and that of our Saviour, from another ; and when the two processions meet in the street, the Priests drop on one knee, Cross themselves, and pray in Latin ; and then the Virgin's image leads the way, and both processions go together to some Convent, where they place the images together. When the processions have left the images of the Saints, they disperse.*

* The Roman catholics deny that they worship images. They deny that they bow down before them.—The simple truth is known to them, and also to the Judge of all.

Their catechisms of instruction do not always contain the *second* commandment. They give the first and second as one ; and, for brevity's sake, they repeat the first, and omit the second. To maintain the number good, they divide the *tenth* : 9. " *Thou shalt not covet thy neighbor's wife.* 10. *Thou shalt not covet thy neighbor's goods.*" They have ten commandments in this way; although they sink the second into the first, or sink it out of sight.

When introduced, it reads thus : " thou shalt not make to thyself a *graven thing,* nor the likeness of any thing;" &c. " Thou shalt not adore nor worship them."—And the Roman catholics all maintain that they do not adore, nor worship the graven thing, the image, not they.

The week before the cholera came, the Catholics were all crying out, that the cholera would not come there, and were led to believe it was the influence of the Priests, and the Holy Prayers they offered to the Virgin Mary, and other Saints, that kept it from them; and when the ignorant class met the Priests in the streets, they would kneel down to them, Cross themselves, kiss their habits, and take them to be their Gods.* But at length the cholera came; and the Priests were more alarmed than the people, for fear they should die with it. I know how it was with Manuel, and he told me how it was with the rest. The people still clung to them for mercy, and offered them large sums of money for Masses, burning candles, and praying to the Virgin Mary, that they might be spared. The rich people fled to the Convents and churches, to remain there during the cholera, until the churches were all filled. They believed that by living in the Convent, and the influence the Priests had with the Virgin Mary,

—They worship the *spirit* represented by the graven thing; certainly.—

. Suppose they do.—All idolators worship the *spirit* represented by the idol, while they prostrate themselves before the *graven thing.*

But suppose Roman Catholics do not break the second commandment, or any commandment, by kneeling to, and invocating the images of departed spirits, still they break the first commandment, which ordains: " *Thou shalt have* NO OTHER *or strange Gods before me.*"—When they invoke the blessed Virgin, or St. Peter, they break this commandment.

" By no means," (exclaims the Jesuit;) " we do not invoke them as Gods; but only as Saints."—

So they pray *before* images, but not *to* them; and they have many *Saints,* but no *Gods,* before the Lord of Lords. They bow down unto the images, and call them by the names of spirits, and ask their aid and pardon, their counsel and favor; and they have more faith in their mercy, than in the mercy of God. They rob the most High of his attributes; and ascribe them to their favorite Saints. " *Ye hypocrites! well did Esaias prophesy of you, saying, This people draweth nigh unto me with their mouth, and honoreth me with their lips, but their heart is far from me. But in vain do they worship me, teaching for doctrines the commandments of men.*" Mat. xv. 7.

* Well did Petrarch, in a letter which he wrote to Cardinal de Cabassole, say, alluding to the Popish Clergy, " You are not like *most of* your brethren, whose heads are turned by a *bit of red cloth,* and who forget that they are men and mortal."—Dob. Petrarch, L. V. P. 479.—En.

that they should be more safe there during the time of the cholera. The Priests persuaded about two hundred young females, belonging to the first families, to enter the Convent, and take the veil for life.* Their parents dare not refuse any request the Priests would make in the time of the cholera.

The young ladies are obliged to enter the Convent, whether it is their wish or not. I saw eight enter on one day. It was one of the most solemn scenes I ever witnessed. They went through the streets in a large procession. About one or two hundred Priests walked before the convicts, as I term them, for I have heard what they must suffer, after they enter there. They looked and appeared as solemn as if they were stepping into eternity. Their parents, brothers, and sisters, followed them with a band of music, playing a very solemn or death march. It is not uncommon to see them faint away, when entering the Convent, before they are put out of sight by the Priests.

> In vain for mercy now they cry,
> In lakes of liquid fire they lie;
> Their minds, in bitter anguish tost,
> For ever, oh! for ever lost.

This taking of the veil always creates a great bustle

---

* Such is the infatuation of the Popish Clergy in recommending their deluded female followers to immure themselves in Convents, that their great Saint Ambrose went so far as to eulogize the crime of suicide in support of chastity. Amb. 4. 478. Euseb. VIII. 23. The following history is from Godeau: "During Maximin's persecution in the 4th century, Pelagia of Antioch, with her mother and sisters, rather than suffer violence to their persons, put themselves to a voluntary death. Pelagia, adorned, not like a person going to death, but to a wedding, leaped, as she *was inspired of God*, from a lofty window on to the pavement; and, by her fall, mounted to heaven. Her mother and sisters, says the same historian, jumped into a deep river, where they found a baptism which purified them from every stain. The water, concealing their bodies, respected the bodies and martyrs of its Creator. Marcellina asked the opinion of St. Ambrose on this melancholy, but unwarranted action. The Bishop spoke commendably of the dreadful deed as a duty owed to religion, a remedy inoffensive to God, and an achievement which entitled these virgins to the crown of martyrdom." Godeau. 2. 65. —ED.

among the gentlemen: and, especially, among the military officers there at the time. They will curse the Priests, and expose them and their wickedness, for they know that no one will be ever allowed to see or hear again from those who have entered the Convent: no one, except their Priests and their Abbess. The Priests have often been at my house with Manuel, drinking wine; and it would be their whole conversation about any young lady who was going to take the veil. They would be contemplating with each other, whether she was young and handsome; and if she was not young and handsome, their expression would be: " *Ka sta mallo esta no recevo !*"—that is, that she was not pretty: that she will be ȵo prey for them; or is not worth having.*

* **More of the Interior of Convents.**—The following documents in relation to the Convent in Baltimore, are taken from the Baltimore Literary and Religious Magazine. The witnesses are credible and respectable persons, and no explanation has yet been given of the mysterious circumstance to which they relate. The whole system of Convents, the subjecting of American women to the despotic control of a Superior and a few Priests, and the cruelties which they are taught to endure as meritorious in the sight of Heaven, are inconsistent with the spirit of the times, they belong to the darkest ages of the world, and are paving the way to the introduction of a mental and spiritual tyranny, that has, for centuries, stained the pages of history with the records of its licentiousness and crimes. We believe there is but one paper in Baltimore that has published the statement, and without intending to impeach the press of that city, we fear that very few would dare publish it, such are the influence and terror, which the Roman catholic religion already carries in the public mind.

STATEMENT.

We, whose names are subscribed hereto, declare and certify, that on or about the — day of ——, 183—, about nine o'clock at night, as we were returning home from a meeting in the Methodist Protestant Church, at the corner of Pitt and Aisquith street, and when opposite the Carmelite Convent and school in Aisquith street, our attention was suddenly arrested by a loud scream issuing from the upper story of the Convent. The sound was that of a female voice indicating great distress—we stopped and heard a second scream—and then a third, in quick succession, accompanied with the cry of HELP! HELP! OH, LORD! HELP! with the appearance of great effort. After this there was nothing more heard by us during the space of ten or fifteen minutes—we remained about that time on the pavement opposite the building from which the cries came.

12

If a Nun has any fortune, she takes it with her into the Convent; and also, her instruments of music, whatever

When the cries were first heard, no light was visible in the fourth story, from which the cries seemed to issue. After the cries, lights appeared in the second and third stories—seeming to pass rapidly from place to place, indicating haste and confusion. Finally, all the lights disappeared from the second and third stories, and the house became quiet.

No one passed along the street where we stood, while we stood there. But one of our party was a man, and he advanced in life—all the remainder of us were women. The watch was not yet set, as some of us heard 9 o'clock cried before we got home.

Many of us have freely spoken of these things since their occurrence, and now at the request of Messrs. B. and C. and M. we give this statement, which we solemnly declare to be true—and sign it with our names.

> JOHN BRUSHCUP,
> LAVINIA BROWN,
> SOPHRONIA BRUSHCUP,
> HANNAH LEACH,
> SARAH E. BAKER,
> ELIZABETH POLK.

Baltimore, March 13th, 1835.

CERTIFICATE OF THE MINISTER.

This is to certify that John Brushcup, Hannah Leach, Sophronia Brushcup, Lavinia Brown, and Sarah E. Baker, are acceptable members of the Methodist Protestant Church, of Pitt street station.

(Signed,)   WILLIAM COLLIER, *Superintendent.*

We take leave then to say in conclusion:—1. This whole subject must be perfectly familiar to the Superior of the Convent, and to the Priest who resides there as Confessor to the establishment, and we demand of them an explicit and satisfactory account of this affair; in default of receiving which, we shall put upon their silence the only construction it can bear.

2. The Archbishop of this diocese ought to know that such transactions are perpetrated in this establishment. And if all his American feelings are not swallowed up in his vows and duties to the head of the Holy Roman state, we expect and call upon him to ferret out this transaction and relieve the public mind, by a full statement of the affair.

3. To aid him, in his humane labors, (for which we trust he has leisure, as the Terrapine feasts of Lent must now be over,) we have to say, that we are well assured that two females have died within six months in the Carmelite Convent; and if he will furnish us with the date of their deaths, then we will furnish him with the date of the terrible affair, to which we now call his paternal notice.

P. S.—We have never yet heard of any explanation of this mysterious affair.—ED.—December, 1835.

they may be. When they enter those Convents, they come out no more; being so well guarded by the wicked Abbesses and Priests. I have been told by my Priest, that the Nuns have their own servants in the Convent, (Mulatto maid-servants,) and that their employment is making artificial flowers, and needle-work. These are sent out of the Convent, and sold by the Abbess. Their work is very handsome, I have seen it, and bought it. You can go on the Sabbaths and holy-days, to the Convents of the Priests, and hear the Priests sing, when there is public worship; but you cannot see them. But no females are allowed to sing in any of the Convents of Havanna; none but the Priests are allowed to sing in public worship there : and they have so many kinds of musical instruments, that you can scarcely perceive the human voice. The great delicacy of the Priests is assigned as the reason for this separation. Delicacy forbids having a female in the choir with them.

I could relate more of their wickedness ; but a delicacy, different from that of the Priests, must prevent me. One thing, however, I will observe ; that whenever I saw those Priests praying, or going to hear the Confession of the dying, or saw them in their processions, I would think to myself ; oh, how wicked they are !—How they are deceiving the people !—During the time I lived with this' Priest, until the last year, he used to inform me of a great deal of their proceedings, and of their intrigues of wickedness ; and, as his friends among the Priests were in the habit of coming to my house, to partake of suppers and wine, I could, and did see, and hear from them, the way they managed their seductions. The old Bishop himself, who died during the time I lived on the island, and who was nearly a hundred years old, was in the habit, until a few months before his death, of having young females come to his house for evil purposes ; and he was very partial to foreigners. If he found a female that pleased him, he would keep her at his house a number of days at a time ; and would bestow handsome presents upon her. I have heard the American females, who reside on the island, lament how they missed the old Bishop; for they often used to be invited to his house. He lived about two miles out of the city, at the *Place de Toros.* They used to go there for a treat, as they called it; for he always gave them wines and cakes of every description; and it never cost them any thing for the ride; for he often sent his *kitterrine* for them, and always made them that pleased him, handsome presents. I have seen diamond pins, and diamond rings, that he has given to different American females. When I informed my Priest of this, he would appear to rejoice; for he knew more than I could tell him, not only about the Bishop, but all the Priests; how they are always aiming and plotting intrigues to seduce the young females, and married ladies.

CHAPTER XI.

"It was a strain of witchery,
So sweet, yet mournful to my ear,
It lit the smile, it waked the sigh,
Then startled pity's pearly tear;
There was a ruffle in my breast,
It was not joy, it was not pain,
'Twas wild as yonder billow's crest,
That tosses o'er the heaving main."

                             PERCIVAL.

Description of the dress and amusements of the inhabitants of Cuba.— Their mode of sanctifying the Sabbath.—Frequency of Assassinations. Slothful habits of the natives of Cuba.

I WILL endeavor to give you, as near as I can, some of the customs, and the mode of living, of the citizens of Cuba; although my mind does not bend to the subject; for the view of this world, I have laid aside. In the first place, there is very little moral and virtuous principle possessed by the natives of Cuba; neither by males, nor females.* Their principal study is dress, and public amusements, such as masquerade balls, the theatres, gambling-houses, and bull-fights. These are all visited by male and female, old and young. And I must include the Priests among the visiters of all those places, except the bull-fights. The bull-fights they attend not; because they are exhibited in the day-time.†

* Lest this might seem to be the fruit of the observation of one who was not likely to be acquainted much in the circles of the virtuous, it is proper to add, that from the testimony of others who have personal acquaintance at Havanna, the remark is fully and fearfully corroborated. And how can it well be otherwise, when the shepherds who feed the flock, are not only robbing them, but are leading them into all manner of snares and devices, to the corrupting of their morals, and their habits.

The remark is generally a sound one: Like pastor, like people. This being true of Cuba, and as those say who have visited the island long enough to be thoroughly acquainted with it, the society of that island must be in a deplorable state, in regard to all the domestic relations, and the private virtues.

† Moore, in his tour through Italy, tells us, that "all of the Clergy, the Monks not excepted, attend the theatre, and seem to join most cor-

12*

The first object of females there, is dress, which is very tasty, and very rich. They wear a great deal of jewelry.

dially in other diversions and amusements. The common people are no ways offended at this; nor do they imagine that they ought to live in a more recluse manner." MOORE's VIEW, Vol. 2. Lett. 59.

We have seen, from the note extracted from the Theology of St. Ligori, on the subject of sanctification of the Sabbath, that the Romish church allows theatrical representations on the Lord's Day as well as on any other day. Consequently, if it is not wrong to perform plays on the Sabbath, it is not wrong for the Clergy to attend them. So far are the Popish Priests from thinking it sinful to frequent the theatre on the Sabbath, that I have frequently heard them condemn the Protestants for their ignorance, and Pharisaical strictness, in maintaining it is wrong.

The following Bull, however, which was issued by the late Pope Pius VII., on the 1st of January, 1815, ends all further controversy on the subject. The 24th article of this Bull runs as follows : "Every Ecclesiastic, Deacon, Subdeacon, &c., is forbidden to appear at any playhouse in his religious habits. The play-houses are to remain SHUT EVERY FRIDAY throughout the year. No Ecclesiastic is to go into a play-house, in any habit or dress soever, on Wednesdays and Saturdays, but HE MAY ON SUNDAYS ! ! !"

The reason why the Romish church does not allow her Clergy to appear at any play-house on Wednesdays, Fridays, and Saturdays, is, because on these days the laws of that church enjoin universal abstinence from flesh meat; and Saturday is the day appropriated to the honor of the Virgin Mary, their " Queen of heaven."

Thus it is, that they officially exalt a creature "above the Creator, who is God, blessed forevermore." On the Lord's Day, the Lord who is King of heaven and earth, Priests can innocently frequent the playhouse; but on the Virgin's Day, the Virgin, their Queen of heaven, it would be sinful ! ! !—It seems almost incredible !—Surely, indeed, the prediction of the Apostle is verified, when he says, " God shall send them strong delusion, that they should believe a lie." 2 Thes. 11 : 11.—ED.

Capt. J. E. Alexander, and other tourists, who have visited the West India islands, testify, that the Priests do frequent the bull-fights. See Alexander's " TRANSATLANTIC SKETCHES," Vol. 1. p. 339.

The apparent discrepance between the authoress of this Narrative, and Captain Alexander, can very easily be reconciled, without the slightest disparagement to the veracity of the latter, and much to the favor of the testimony of the former. The authoress, ever tenacious of the truth, describes nothing more than what she knows, or what she has been witness of. She says the Priests did not attend the bull-fights; —evidently meaning thereby, that she did not know of their attending. She never was in their company at those fights; for the simple reason, as she states, because they were " exhibited in the day-time." The time the Priests take to gallant their Mistresses about, is under the shades of night. When they attend the bull-fights, they leave them at home.

On reading what the authoress has stated on this subject, who is there that cannot see that she writes under the dictates of truth, candor,

They wear no hats, but ornament their head with gilded artificial flowers. They never wear any but satin shoes and silk stockings, with their clothes very short. Instead of hats, they wear lace veils over their heads, either white or black. Their dresses are made with short sleeves, and their necks are bare. They wear no gloves, in order to display their bracelets and rings, which are mostly of diamonds. The females are small in size, with small feet and hands. The natives have generally dark complexions, but they make use of whiting and red. When they are dressed, they are very beautiful to look at. The elderly ladies wear no hats, or caps. Their dresses are also made with short sleeves, and their arms ornamented with bracelets and rings. Fathers, mothers, and daughters, all mix together in the public amusements.

The gentlemen likewise are very neat in their dress. They are, in general, possessed of a lively disposition, very easy, open, and polite, in their manner, both male and female, as much so, if not more, than the French. They are, very fond of music, singing, and dancing. You will hear instruments of music in all the houses of rich and poor, from the heads of the houses down to the poor slaves. Their principal and favorite instruments, are the piano-forte, and the guitar. These two instruments you will hear in their houses, from morning till late at night; likewise, singing and dancing. In this way, they pass their time.

The servants are also permitted to indulge in their instruments of music, which are of their own manufacturing; consisting of a *Banjou*, and some other instruments. Of an evening, their houses will echo with the different music, from the masters and mistresses, to the servants. They are very holy on the Sabbath mornings, until 11 o'clock;

and impartiality? If she had wished to paint the frightful picture of the moral depravity of the Romish Priesthood, in colors darker than could be drawn by the pencil of truth, why did she withhold her pen from giving it such a touch as that of their frequenting the bull-fights?—Evidently, because she was unwilling to sacrifice the truth for the embellishing of a tale.—Ed.

going to their churches, and to the altar; dipping their
fingers in Holy Water; and kneeling and Crossing themselves; and going to the image of our Saviour, and kissing its feet.   After they return to their homes, they take
off their "*Sacred black-dresses*," which they all wear at
church, and decorate themselves in their usual tasty
dresses.   The remainder of the Sabbath will be spent in
talking, laughing, singing, and playing, until the evening.
Then they prepare to go to the theatre, or masquerade
balls, or to the gambling-houses.   All these places of public amusement are open on Sunday evening; and not
only the citizens will go, but the Priests.   I have been
often, yes, often, with my Priest; and have seen other
Priests there, and talked with them, on the Sabbath.

The Sabbath day is considered a holy-day for amusements.   The soldiers are out, going through the streets
with music.   On Sunday evening, at five o'clock, they
will prepare to ride out in their *kitterrines*, to the *Place
de Toros*, about two miles out of the city.   It is a beautiful place, where they resort to ride, called the king's *Pas-
sour*, or Garden.   This garden is about four or five miles
of level ground, along the sea-shore, laid out with oranges,
and lemons, and flowers of every description.   Here there
will be, on Sabbath afternoon, a number of bands of music
playing.   At six o'clock, they will return to the city, to
prepare for the theatres, where they stay till eleven or
twelve o'clock.*   After returning home from the theatres,

---

* In all Popish countries, the Sabbath-day is a holy-day. It comes
to be the same among the Papists of this country. In New-Orleans the
places of public amusement are open on the Sabbath-day. In the city
of New-York, the cake shops, and orange women, present the usual
temptations of the week in a vast many cases, where Roman catholics
are the proprietors. The review day of the soldiery is the Sabbath-day,
in all the dominions of the Roman religion. The reader shall know the
ground on which Rome ventures to abate the fourth commandment,
and to turn the Lord's day into a day of carnal amusement.
Rome affirms that the church has all power through its ministers, to
alter or amend the Divine commandment, according to the exigencies
of the case; to appoint a day, and make it holy, or to make the day
common and secular. The immemorial custom of the Romish church
is taken for the common law of that church; and the custom of Romans, having been, time out of mind, to be devout on Sabbath morning

they will partake of supper and wine, and smoke cigars. It is customary for females, as well as males, to smoke cigars. They are made of fine tobacco wrapt up in white paper. When a gentleman makes his calls on the ladies, after entering the house, and passing the compliments of the day, he will present his cigars to them. It is customary for the Priests to do the same, when calling on their friends, only their method is to Cross themselves, when presenting the cigar to a lady. And the people would think it a sin, if they did not present wine and refreshments to the Priests, when they called on them.

They generally rise at half-past five, in the morning, or six, and prepare to go to Mass or Confession ; and return to their homes in about an hour.* At eight, they

while attending one Mass, and to spend the remainder of the day in amusement, this settles the question of the sanctity of the Sabbath, and removes the obligation of the fourth commandment. Moreover, the Saints' days, appointed to be observed by the Romish church, are, many of them, of the same sanctity with the Sabbath-day : and, as it is very inconvenient to give several days in seven to Divine worship exclusively, they are accustomed to clip holy-time, on every holy-day ; and, finally, to convert that season which they intended to sanctify, into a season of amusement. And they treat the Sabbath, precisely as they treat the days of the greatest Saints. They make it also a *holy-day*.

* The Mass is this:—The Romish Council of Trent, the last and greatest of the Romish Councils, say, that although Christ was offered once on the Cross, to procure eternal salvation, he left in the Last-Supper a sacrifice, which the nature of sinful man requires to be applied to the atonement of the *daily* sins, which Christians commit : and that the same Christ who was sacrificed on the Cross with his blood shed, is daily sacrificed without blood in the Mass, to make reconciliation for the true penitents, on account of their daily sins. And that this offering is not only effectual to remove the stains of guilt from the living, but also to make atonement for the sins of the deceased believer, who has not yet paid the full price of his offences in the fires of Purgatory.

In performing the ceremony of the Mass, which should be done every morning, in all Roman catholic churches, for the sins of the people, there is some part of the service to be pronounced aloud, and some only to be spoken in a whisper, and all to be said in the Latin tongue, with a display of burning candles, incense, and changes of the Priest's garments, to excite the attention of the worshipers.

The Mass is a mingling of wine and water and particles of bread in the chalice, which the Priest consecrates, as the flesh and blood of our Lord, and, having offered it up to be adored by the worshipers, he reverently drinks it off, and thrice rinses the cup, and drinks, that no particle of the sacred elements may remain in the cup ; and then, he

take their strong coffee. They never use tea, except as medicine. They take a little brandy in the coffee, instead

carefully wipes it out with a consecrated napkin, and restores the chalice to its place in the altar.

This is the Mass, "*the unbloody* sacrifice," as the Romans call it, which is daily offered for the sins of the living, and of the dead, if there is any money to be had for the service.

And so tenacious is Rome of this monstrous rite, and of the circumstances here connected with it, that she pronounces an awful curse on the man who denies that the Mass is a true and proper sacrifice of Christ to God; and also on him, who says that the service is only useful to the Priest who performs it, and that it ought not to be offered in atonement for the sins of the living and of the dead; and, on him also, who says, it is an imposture, to offer the Mass in honor of the Saints, to obtain *their* intercession with God; and even on the man, who says the ceremonies, and changes of raiment, and external signs used by the Roman catholic church in celebrating the Mass are more vain than pious.

Therefore, in Cuba, and in all Roman catholic countries, the devout are particular every morning to attend Mass, and to pay the Priests well for Masses to be read, said, and offered for the sins of their deceased friends, to help them through Purgatory; and to leave a bequest to the Priests to the same end.

How much profit this may be to the dead, no one has returned to tell, but it is evidently profitable to the Priests.

But, in all the Holy Gospel, not a word is said of the Mass, or of a daily sacrifice of Christ, except it is, that the apostate by their sins crucify the Lord afresh: "*Seeing they crucify to themselves the Son of God afresh, and put him to an open shame.*" Heb. 6:6. "*Who needeth not daily, as those high Priests, to offer up sacrifice;—for this he did once, when he offered up himself.*" Heb. 7:27.

"Under the idea that the Priest, who performs *the bloodless sacrifice*, as they call it, can appropriate the full benefit of it to the individual whom he mentions in his secret prayer, before and after consecration, the Roman catholics are eager, all over the world, to purchase the benefit of Masses for themselves; to obtain the favor of Saints, by having Masses done in their praise; and, finally, to save the souls of their friends out of Purgatory, by the same means."

This miraculous change of the wafer, by which the Lord in heaven becomes every day offered up in sacrifice, according to Rome, at the hands of her Priests, on the account of that person, or thing, that the Priest is pleased to name in the prayers of the Mass, constitutes the brazen forehead of "*the Man of Sin*," the most imposing feature of the Antichrist. All Roman Priests are clothed with this power, as they think, by virtue of their office; and the supposed possession of this power, makes them the terror of the poor flock, over which they are placed as pastors. To gain the exercise of this divine gift for the saving of the soul, is the anxious desire of every good Roman catholic; and the worst of them fear the spell on their prospects, both for time and eternity, which the Priest is believed to have it in his power to lay for his enemies, by virtue of the Mass.

of milk; and, afterwards, smoke a cigar. This is customary, both with old and young. They breakfast at nine
or half-past, and take wine, instead of coffee. They take
luncheon at twelve, which will be of confectionary, jel-
lies, wines, and cordial. They dine at three. Their
cookery is very rich; mostly fricassees. After drinking
their wine, smoking, and cleaning their teeth with snuff,
they retire to their couches, to refresh themselves. I have
heard my Priest, and others, say, that *tobacco* was a *holy
herb.* The first that ever was known to grow, was on
our Saviour's tomb. At five o'clock they decorate themselves for some public amusement; and return and take
supper at ten.

They are fond of fish, eggs, or something hearty for
supper. The native females seldom do any kind of work;
neither the rich nor poor families teach their children to
make so much as their own clothes. There are a great
many foreigners living there, Italians and French, who
do their principal sewing. They employ their leisure
time in singing, dancing, playing on musical instruments,
and smoking cigars. You will see little girls and boys,
as soon as they can walk, with cigars in their mouths.
The parents do not mind holding conversation on any
subject, good or bad, in the presence of their children.
They say it will make them wise, to know all things,
both good and bad. A poor man will have money to support his family in idleness, if he has to rob or murder to
get it; this I have been told often. Frequently persons
hung for murder, (which you will see more or less every
week,) will confess that they had taken the lives of ten to
fifteen persons, before they would be detected; as the
men are too lazy to work, especially the natives. The
native Spaniards will not work; but the emigrants from
old Spain, especially the Catalan Spaniards, are indus-

For the power to appropriate it to whom he will, is accompanied with
the power likewise to appropriate it for whatever he will. Masses are
known to be offered in the Popish countries for the benefit of brutes,
even of dumb beasts, as well as man; and also, to curse, as well as to
bless, the souls of the deluded Roman Catholics.

trious.   These Catalan Spaniards are numerous i
vanna.   They are dark complexioned, have a lan
of their own, and come from Catalonia in old ;
They constitute the great body of the wealthy,
trious, and enterprising inhabitants of Havanna.

CHAPTER XII.

"See superstition crouched in some rude rock,
Books, beads, and maple-dish, his meagre stock;
In shirt of hair, and weeds of canvass dressed,
Girt with a bell-rope that the Pope has blessed;
Adust with stripes told out for ev'ry crime,
And sore tormented long before his time:
His pray'r preferr'd to Saints that cannot aid;
His praise postponed, and never to be paid;
See the sage hermit, by Popery admir'd,
With all that bigotry adopts inspir'd,
Wearing out life in his religious whim,
Till his religious whimsey wears out him;
His works, his abstinence, his zeal allow'd,
You think him humble,—God accounts him proud."

COWPER.

Manuel's confidential communications to Rosamond.—Penance in the Vault; in an iron coffin.—Fasting on bread and water.—Penance in the Purgatory-room.—The penances end with presents to the Priests.— How the Priests put young females on penance too shameful to be told.— Some of the licentious Priests sent to the Mississippi to propagate their faith.

For the first two years that I lived with Manuel, he used to open his mind very freely to me, as to how and what the Priests had done, and were doing : but when he saw that my feelings were changing to a gloomy and unhappy state, he was more cautious. He used to tell me when such and such a Priest would go on penance ; and in what way he himself used to go on penance, at different times, while I lived with him, when he knew that he had treated me cruelly. They are obliged to Confess every morning to the head *Comparthra*, or Superior Confessor of the Convent. The Superior puts them on penance, according to what they have done. Manuel has told me some of the forms in which they go under penance, according to what they have done.* Some will be confined in a vault under the Convent, and will remain there nine days, fasting on bread and water. Some will

* "A man who is not yet reconciled to God, (says Bellarmine,) can, by works of penance, pray for, and obtain as a right, (' de congruo,') the grace of justification." Bellarm. de Just. L. V.—ED.

13

go to the Purgatory-room, and be laid in an iron coffin ;"
some for three, and some for nine days, fasting on bread
and water. I have heard Manuel say, that, before the
Constitution, hundreds of Priests have suffered death in
that vault. When he talked about it, as he did much in
the year the eight or nine Spanish prisoners, confined on
charges of treason, escaped from Moro Castle by night, in
a boat, during a thunder-storm, he would devoutly Cross
himself, and repeat : *" Ka sta mallo !"* "How very
bad !"

My Priest has told me that the most respectable, and
elderly men, when they wish to go on deep penance,
(that is, if they have hired a person to murder an individual ; for if they have a lawsuit with any one, and are
afraid it will go against them, they will get their opponent
murdered,) then they will apply to their Priest Confessor,
how to go on deep penance ; and their Priest will take
them into the Convents, and put them on penance in this
room, which is called Purgatory-room ; but I have heard

---

* This penance of the Priests is an evidence of the iron consistency
of Romanism, and of the confidence of the Priests themselves in the
nostrums for expiating guilt, which they prescribe in much heavier
doses for the guilty people, than for their own plague-spots in the soul.
It is easy to laugh at their stupid folly ; but possibly it is not right ; for
to them who are called to it, the lying in an iron coffin for successive
days, in the midst of the fumes of sulphur, with no better food than
bread and water for a dainty stomach, is truly a serious affair : and
since the poor souls have always been taught this mode of repentance,
and know no better ; and for their labor have only their pains, and a
false license to sin afresh ; they rather deserve our tender pity, and our
most earnest and kind efforts, to save them from their own torments in
this world, and from the endless torments of the wicked in the world to
come. It is natural and common to despise the errors of other men, and
the men who maintain the errors ; yet, we admit, that it is cruel to
mock at one born blind, because he cannot distinguish colors. And
how much is a poor soul, born and educated in the delusions of Rome,
better than one mentally blind to the holy perfections of God, and to the
tender compassions of Jesus, and to the sanctifying power of the Holy
Spirit ? He is made blind to the salvation which is offered in the Gospel, by folds of mystery, and abominable delusion, drawn over his sight
from the time he can distinguish between a living man, and a senseless
image. Therefore we ought to have compassion on the souls that wear
the hard yoke of Rome, and in the kindest spirit to ease them of their
cruel burthen of senseless ceremonies, and deceitful penances, and false
hopes.

Manuel say, it depended a good deal on who the persons were that they would take into the Convents, to go on penance. It must be a respectable man, and one whom the Priest knows to be a strict Catholic, and wealthy. When these offenders have gone through their penance, they are obliged to make handsome presents to all their Saints in the Convents, and which are numerous. The images of Abraham, David, Solomon. Peter, Paul, and John, a great company dressed in habits ; these are not decorated ; only the Virgin Mary's image is dressed rich. I have seen a crown placed on the head of the Virgin Mary's image,* set with diamonds, in the most costly manner, which he told me was presented to her, by a very wicked man, a pirate-captain and a murderer, who had been in the Convent on penance, and who presented it when leaving.† I saw this man when afterwards he was

* " *Seest thou not what they do in the cities of Judah, and the streets of Jerusalem ? The children gather wood, and the fathers kindle the fire, and the women* KNEAD THEIR DOUGH *to make cakes to the* QUEEN OF HEAVEN, *and to pour out drink-offerings unto other gods, that' they may provoke me to anger.*" Jerem. VII. 17. 18.

The Papists universally in their Offices, and everywhere, style the Virgin Mary, the "QUEEN OF HEAVEN."—"AVE ! REGINA CÆLORUM !"— "*Hail ! Queen of heaven !*" says their Breviary in the Office of the Virgin. Offic. Parv. B. Mariæ. Antip. ad Magnif.

The cake of which the Scripture speaks in the above text, is made in the Popish church, and offered to the Virgin Mary, their "*Queen of heaven,*" every Saturday in the Mass. This day the Romish church appropriates, in a special manner, to the honoring of the "*Queen of heaven,*" and the Mass that is then enjoined to be said unto her, is called a *Votive Mass*, "MISSA *Votiva*." Vide Offic. B. Virgin. in Sabbato. in Breviar.

The cakes are made in the form of a large wafer, and the "*dough is kneaded,*" precisely as the text declares, by "*women.*"

The drink-offering is the wine in the Mass, which, in the Popish church, "*is poured out*" or offered every morning to their different Saints, which they call *honoring the Saints.* Vide Breviar. Rom. Passim.—ED.

† The greater the sinner, and the greater his offence, the greater is the price of his pardon, and the greater is the Priest's fee. It was fit for the captain of a piratical crew, to adorn the head of the image of the Virgin with a costly crown : for no small acknowledgment was due to the supposed remissions of his multiplied offences.

The natural fruit and inevitable consequence of this state of things is, to make the Priests rejoice in the greatness of the iniquity

hung for murder; and seeing him, led my Priest to tell
me he was the person, who, at one time, had been in the
Convent on penance, and had presented this crown to the
Virgin Mary.

My Priest was always reserved in informing me in
what mode these men would afflict themselves, when on
penance in the Convents; but, always when they had one
there, he would often speak of him, and appear to pity
him, but he would say he wished it was the rule for females to go into the Convents on penance, and he was
their Father-Confessor for ordering the penances upon
them.

I could here relate in what ways the Priests put young
females on penance, which I have been informed by Manuel; but delicacy must prevent me. I wish the world
knew of their deception and intrigues, seductions and
wickedness, as I do. I even pity the Priests; and how
much more do I pity and feel for the people they are deceiving, and ruining, and leading into darkness; and not
only the natives, but even American females who are
there. For the Priests of the island, the very same I
knew to love licentiousness at heart, were ordered away
by the Bishop to some other settlement; some of them to
the villages on the Mississippi river, to remain there, to
preach the Roman religion.*

penitents, so long as their copious treasures enable the criminals to pay
for their pardon a sum proportionate to their transgressions. And for
this joy a man who is educated to the Roman Priesthood is not so much
to blame, as the system which exposes him to the temptation of taking
pleasure in that which mightily increases his means of procuring pleasure. The Priests are but men: their garments do not change their
hearts. They rejoice and must rejoice in those things, which lawfully
fill their pockets with the means of increasing their worldly comforts.
* This I confirm in regard to licentious Priests in the United States.
—Ed.

CHAPTER XIII.

"——The unfaithful Priest what tongue
Enough shall execrate ? His doctrine may
Be passed, though mixed with most unhallowed leaven,
That proved to those who foolishly partook,
Eternal bitterness :—but this was still
His sin—beneath what cloak soever veiled ;
His ever growing and perpetual sin,
First, last, and middle thought, whence every wish,
Whence every action rose, and ended both—
*To mount to place ; and power of worldly sort ;
To aid the gaudy pomp and equipage
Of earthly state, and on his mitred brow
To place a royal crown : for this, he sold
The sacred truth to him, who most would give
Of titles, benefices, honors, names :
For this, betrayed his master ; and for this,
Made merchandise of the immortal souls
Committed to his care—this was his sin.*"

POLLOK.

Father Hosa's execrable conversation with Manuel respecting the Nuns.—Lived some years in concubinage with a Quadroon girl.—His barbarity towards her.—He interrogates Rosamond respecting the beauty, &c., of the females of the Mississippi valley.—His and Manuel's desire to have all the Protestant ministers in Moro-castle.—An American imprisoned in Moro-castle 40 years.—Description of Moro-castle.—Priestcraft.—The Priests refuse to intercede with the Virgin without money.—Superstition in regard to dreams.—In default of money for Masses, jewelry is taken.—The laying of souls.—Priestly exactions and impositions.—The Cassa or house of the Virgin Mary.—The room in which were the devil and other horrible images.—The people's superstitious fear of the Priests.—Mode of performing penance.—Jealousy among the Priests.—Seduction of a young girl.—All compelled to kneel while the Host or consecrated Wafer passes.—The common people kiss the Priest's feet.

I KNEW a Priest well, at the time he left the island to go to the Mississippi, about the year 1830 ; whose name was Father *Hosa*. He was a man about thirty-five years of age, tall, slender, and of a delicate appearance, dark complexion, with full black eyes, and very heavy eyebrows. His left hand was deformed by the loss of the 4th finger, which was taken off close to the palm of the hand. Father Hosa was an intimate friend of Manuel. They were both natives of Spain, and educated for Priests in Spain, as I have heard them say. Father Hosa used to visit my house often ; and I have heard him say things,

13*

in conversation with Manuel, which he ought to be hung for, relating to what he had done, and what he wished to do, with the Nuns, who were in the Convents on the island. He had been living then about seven years with a Quadroon girl, as his Mistress, and had two children by her, who were living. She was young, when he first became acquainted with her, and he was the cause of her ruin, as I have been informed by my Priest, and other individuals. While living with her, he made her a perfect slave, by his cruel and harsh treatment. The food he provided for her and the children, would be the remnants that were left of his luxurious suppers, which he would have at her house.* I was informed she grieved much at his leaving the island without making any arrangements for the support of her, or his children. He told her, when he was settled on the Mississippi river, he would send for them.†

A few days before Father Hosa left the island, for America, he was at a supper-party at my house; and knowing that I had formerly lived in the Mississippi country, he wanted to get some information about the customs, and manner of living there; and if the females were handsome, and open and easy in their manners; and asked me, if I could not put him into the way to get into their favour. I told him that the females were generally virtuous and chaste in that country. My Priest made reply, that he was very glad it had fallen to Father

---

* Six months in a Convent, apple-parings.

† Rosamond spoke of the pitiable situation of this poor girl, more than once, in a way to show how much she felt it; but never intimated the hardest feature in her case, until an apothecary of this city, who has spent a season in Havanna, was descanting upon the vices of the Priests; their notorious habits of concubinage, gambling, and crime, and added, among other things, that they were known to keep girls to hire out for vicious indulgences. Then she explained that this same Quadroon was so abused by Father Hosa. He would be jealous of her in the extreme; for fear lest she received company without his knowledge, and yet he would send her foolish souls on sinful hire, which he received for her. This is an enormity that only could be committed by a man under the blind delusion of "*The Mother of harlots and abominations of the earth.*" Vile as this is, it sorts but too well with the other traits of Father Hosa's conduct recorded here.

Hosa's lot to go, instead of him.   He said that he had
been informed the same by others.   Manuel advised him
to be very prudent here in America ; as there were so
many *poor Protestants* living there, whom their Protestant ministers were leading in darkness : and they would
all be lost.   They said they wished they had all the Pro
testant ministers on the island, in the Moro castle, where
the old man was.   This man that they spoke of, was an
American, who was found in the Moro castle, not long
before Father Hosa left the island.   He had been there
about forty years.   I cannot inform you who first learnt
he was there, or for what purpose ; but when he was
found, they said that he was elderly, but in health.   I re-
collected a few months previous, that there was great talk
about some one finding him in this prison.

Moro castle is the principal fort, and station for soldiers, and the prison for desperate criminals.   It is on a
small island, close to the harbor of the city.   They keep
the prisoners in it : those who have committed murder,
and those who are waiting to be transported to Spain,
and to the Spanish mines.   I know, at the time the old
man was found in the castle, the Priests were very uneasy about it.   I asked my Priest, if they could not set
him free, and let him come to America.   He said it would
be just as the Bishop decided ; and charged me not to
mention it to any of my country people.   What I learned
from my Priest, at the time, led me to believe this poor
man had been put into the prison, for some of the wicked
purposes of the Priests.   I can not tell his name, nor the
part of the United States he came from : but he was from
the United States, and was very old, and Manuel pitied
him much.

Since I have been writing and reflecting about these
Roman Priests, so much of their wickedness comes to my
mind, which I was eyewitness of, during five years I was
on the island of Cuba, that my mind is overwhelmed ;
and I feel as if it was my duty, and as if it was serving
the Lord, in writing, to let the world know about them ;
not, that I believe it will be so much for the benefit of the

souls of the Priests, (although God is able,) for they all know, that their lives are full of evil purposes ; but it is for the love I bear for the souls of the many people they are leading in darkness.

Their religion is perfect witchcraft. They have a most peculiar way of enlisting you into it. You may think it strange that there is so much murder and robbery in those countries, but it is because the Priests make the people believe there is no harm, which they cannot heal, in committing murder, robbery, or telling a lie; if, when you are committing any of these wicked deeds, you have your mind, your thoughts, and your heart, fixed on the Virgin Mary ; and it is no sin, if you go immediately to some Priest, and Confess it to him.* This was common doctrine among both Priests and people, so far as I knew them. But they cannot intercede with the Virgin Mary, unless you take them a sum of money, to have your pardon. Money with them is necessary to buy salvation for the soul.

They are also very superstitious. If you dream about any near relative, who may have been dead for years, you are led to believe by the Priests, that their souls are unhappy : and that they can put them to rest, by saying Masses and burning Holy Candles. If a person has not got money to pay for them, they will take jewelry. I have had given me by Manuel, while living with him, at different times, jewelry, which he has got in such a way. When I asked him if he thought it was not wicked to do so, he would reply : "If I did not take it, some other Priest would."

In this city the souls of the dead are also sought " *to be laid.*" If any rich lady, or gentleman, be in bad health,

---

* All the evils of the world, are, by the Apostle, reduced to three heads: "The lust of the flesh, the lust of the eyes, and the pride of life." 1 John 11. 16. The Popish Doctors, however, say, that these are only "evangelical COUNSELS." Thom. Aquin. L. II. Quest. 9. Art. 3.

"To disobey an evangelical counsel," (they say,) "is no sin." Vega de Justif. L. XIV. C. 12. Navar. C. XXIII. N. 49. and C. XXI. N. 43. —ED.

RICH LADY DOING PENANCE.

and think they are going to die soon, they will sometimes put their money into the Priest's possession, believing that he will pray more sincerely for their souls, on account of the money.

I knew a rich widow lady who had given her wealth to a Priest, Father Antonia, belonging to the Convent of St. Domingo, to keep. This is not the Father Antonia that used to visit at my house. They both belonged to the same Convent; but Manuel's friend was a· young, small, light framed man, with a Roman nose ; while this Antonia was a large, fat man, with a red face, forty or fifty years of age. This Priest would make her believe that she must live in such a secluded way, that she would not allow herself the necessaries of life ; but every cent she could get, she would give to this Priest. He made it a rule to call at her house every day at eleven o'clock, to hear her Confession. Her retired room for worship had images of the Virgin Mary, our Saviour, and other Saints, as large as grown persons. The Virgin Mary was placed in a small house, they call it, *de Cassa*, the house, (similar to a cage, or show-box, to contain the image,) decorated with artificial flowers ; and dressed in the richest manner with pearls and diamonds. The room was always illuminated with Holy Candles. Precisely at the hour her Priest would come, a table was placed in the centre of the room, with a bottle of wine, cakes, sweetmeats, and fruits of every description. A large candle, placed in the centre of it, would be lighted up. They would remain in this room, alone, about an hour.

Afterwards, Father Antonia would go to another room which she had appropriated to the servants. In this room would be the Virgin Mary and our Saviour, and one candle. In a corner of this room, was placed an image representing the devil, a most horrid figure. Here he would every day hear the Confessions of the servants, to keep them in subjection through fear. These scenes I have witnessed, as I used to go to her house often ; and she has often taken me into her room of worship, and kneeling down with me to the image of the Virgin Mary, she would pray, among other things, for me, that I might leave the Priest, and become a Christian. And in talking with me, she would say, that he could save his own soul, and had that power and influence with the Saints above, that he prayed for all the curses of his sins to be laid on my head. This rich lady's name was Madame Pelori, the widow of a dry-good merchant of Havanna. She was an old lady, and lived in " *cui le Vorispa*," as they call the street where her house stands. This impression of the Priest's power to curse the head of the woman, is universal among the people of Cuba, with whom I was acquainted : and what gives ground for it is, that it is so common to see those females who are long in their vile and wicked company, exposed to their sorceries, and their Priestcraft, and their lewd conversation, go crazy. I have myself known many females who lost their reason, as I myself did, while living with Roman Priests. The people are so afraid of displeasing one of the Priests, even if they know the Priests do what is wrong and wicked, that they dare not tell them of it, for fear they should pray a spell, or curse upon them.

I have known this rich widow lady to go on penance often, and have seen the forms of her suffering. Sometimes she would wear a coarse tow-gown, made in the form of a habit, with a leather belt round her waist, and would go barefooted, with her head shaved like a Priest, during from three to six months ; and her diet would be chiefly plantains and bannanas. At other times, I have seen her on penance with a steel collar round her neck, placed in such a way that she could not turn her head. This she wore, night and day, for nine months. These penances were ordered by her Priest. This lady died, leaving no children, and giving all she had to the Priest. While I lived on the island, the Priest, Father Antonia, came to her house, and removed her corpse to the Convent. It remained there four hours, and then was taken to the grave, in the same form as one of their poor, and buried without honor. Her Priest took possession of her

XIII.]   MUTUAL JEALOUSY OF THE PRIESTS.   155

servants, and all her property, which was thought to be great.*

When an occurrence of this kind took place, as it often did, I have heard Manuel say it would create a jealous feeling among the other Priests, towards the Priest who would be the gainer of these treasures, which they are always aiming at.

* In reading this to the authoress for correction, it was observed that this part is so unnatural in itself, and so contrary to all our habits and laws, that it deserves some explanation. She replied, it is not unnatural in Cuba, and needs no explanation to the residents of that island. Whether the sick in the Convents make any Will in this case, she never heard; but thinks she should have heard, if this were the case. Her impression is, that the dying give it by a word to the Priests, to pay them for praying their souls out of Purgatory; and that the customs of the Roman catholic church, and people, confirm this mode of conveyance, with the same certainty, as if it were devised by a sealed instrument, a deed acknowledged, or a last Will and Testament. But it is not in Cuba alone that this iniquity is practised. Mr. Stevens, a Methodist Minister of Boston, holds this language respecting the case of *Patrick Ward of Baltimore.*

"Look at the following, with scores in one of your cities, in one of the middle states, known to be true, as the fact came out in the open court.

"About four years since, a member of the Methodist church, who was a native of Ireland, accumulated by his industry a handsome property. He was taken sick, and remained so a long time. The officiating Roman Priest visited him, and was, apparently very kind to him, and his family, and won their confidence. The sick man at length became insane. The Priest advised a removal to the dispensary, of which the Papists have the control. The family consented, and he was placed under the care of the 'Sisters of Charity.' His Will was made previously to his removal. He died, but behold! another Will appears, in which a large sum was left for the Priest in question, a large sum for St. Patrick's Church, and the rest for his lawful wife in Ireland! The distressed family knew not what to do; there was his last Will with his signature. No money to support an action, their friends doubted the propriety of bringing one; and it rested awhile. At length the case was tried, and it was shown that the deceased never was a Papist—that he had no wife in Ireland—that the plaintiff was his lawful wife, then a widow, and that the Priest got the instrument drawn up, and obtained the deceased man's signature when in a state of insanity!! The counsel for the Priest was so affected, that he refused to plead against the poor, distressed, cruelly-treated widow.

"The deceased brother was a member of the church where I preached in turn with other ministers. *Must Popery be let alone?*"

This is not a tale of the 15th century; but of the Roman catholics of our own times and country, affording evidence of the depravity inherent, through all time, and under every form of government, in the Roman catholic system of faith and worship.

When they meet with a rich man, who they think will not live long, they will persuade him to go to the Convent, and prepare to die ; but he must leave them all his wealth.*

I knew another trait of the wickedness of a Priest who belonged to St. Domingo Convent. I do not recollect his name. He persuaded a rich man, whose name was Don Vesta, a native of old Spain, who lay low with a consumption, to go to the Convent, and prepare to die. This man had a wife and three children. When he went to the Convent, he took all his money, and left nothing for the support of his family, except the house and furniture. He lived but a short time after he was taken to the Convent ; and, at his death, the Priest went and took possession of the house, and turned out the poor widow with her three children, to seek a living for themselves. This family lived in the same square or street that I then lived in, which was the Pontra-street, leading out of the Pontra gate. The cruelty of this Priest was talked about very loudly.

Shortly after this, he placed his Mistress in the same house, a young girl about sixteen, who had been led away by him ; and I was informed, by my Priest, that Antonia was formerly her Father Confessor in her father's house. They both have been at my house, when my Priest would have supper-parties. If I were to tell all I know about them, I should never have done ; I don't know one Convent on the island, where the Priests reside, but I have heard, or seen the intrigues, snares, and traps of wickedness carried on there. Still the church laws are very strict in regard to the obedience of the Priests.

Whenever they go to hear the Confessions of a dying person, the Confessor will be placed in a Kitterine, that

---

* So determined are the Priests to get possession of the money of their credulous followers, that many Popish divines teach, that the Bishops of the church of Rome have the power and the right of altering a man's last Will and Testament, whether the heir agrees to it or not. " *Posse id facere Episcopum illo, (herede,) contradicente.*" Ligori, Theol. de Privilegiis, C. III. N. 68.—Ed.

is, a carriage, or Havanna chaise, with a candle burning in one hand, and a prayer-book in the other. He will be praying, while two young Priests are walking by his side; one, with a death-lantern with a candle burning in it, and the anointing-oil, and the consecrated host, or Communion bread; and the other, with a small bell, which he keeps ringing. This bell is to summon the people to the doors and windows, while the Priest passes, where they must kneel and Cross themselves. It is considered a great sin by the Catholics, not to perform this duty. If you are in the street, and meet the procession, you must stop; and if walking or riding, the men must take off their hats, and Cross themselves.* When the elderly or strict Catholics meet the Priests in the streets, they kiss their habits in speaking to them; and the poor and ignorant class of people, and especially the slaves, will kneel down in the street, and kiss their feet. This I have often seen done.

When a young person, or a child, has been very sick, on recovering, it must go on penance from three to nine months. If a boy, he must put on a habit made in the form of the Priest's, with white cotton-cord round his waist, and a gospel-piece suspended round his neck by a white cord, and his head shaved like a Priest's.† His

* The Journal of Commerce of this city, July, 1835, gives an account of two Americans in Mexico, who were violently seized and cast into prison, where they remained in confinement under the charge of the offended Priest, for refusing this homage. The following is a notice of the same event, which is found in the Pittsburgh, Pa. *Times,* 22d July, 1835.

"*Insults to citizens of the United States !*—Great excitement is said to prevail in Metamoras among the foreigners, in consequence of the imprisonment of Messrs. Boyd and Lee, American merchants, and the subsequent harsh treatment they received. The Mercurio of Metamoras, says, that a few days before, the Parish Priest, while conveying the Sacrament in the usual cortege to the house of a sick person, was met by the above named gentlemen, who did not pay the procession those marks of reverence which are customary. The Priest, irritated, appealed to the spectators, ordered them to seize Messrs. Boyd and Lee, and throw them into a dungeon, which was done without the least hesitation on the part of the people, or interference on the part of the magistrates.

† " The Papists pretend they borrow their ceremonies from the Jews. If true, bad enough.—Not true, however :—they are borrowed from Pagans.—All the Egyptian Priests, as Herodotus informs us, ha

habit must be the same color as his Priests'. The Priests'
habits are of different colors and different cut, according
to the Convent they belong to; so that, when you see
them, you may always know the Convent they belong to.
A little girl, when recovering from sickness, must put on
a habit, with a white cord round her waist; and many
other different forms of penance, they are put under.

heads shaved and bald. (Herod. Lib. II. 36.) Thus, the Emperor Com-
modus, that he might be admitted into that order, got himself shaved,
and carried the god Anubis in procession." Lamprid, in Com. 9.
    The Jewish Priests were commanded, *not to shave their heads.* Le-
vit. XXI. 5. Ezek. XLIV. 20.—ED.

CHAPTER XIV.

> "Stop! ye are on the brink
> Of endless wo and ruin—sleep no more—
> The charm will soon be broken—ye will wake,
> And find the alluring hours that wooed you, o'er,
> And, rising like a fury, Vice will shake
> Her smoky torch, and in your heart's blood slake
> Its hell-lit fires; and you will seek in vain
> The young days that have vanished."
>
> PERCIVAL.

Father Manuel Antonia and his Mistress.—His love-letters.—Prize in the lottery consecrated by the Priest to the Virgin Mary.—Lottery prizes are the gifts of the Saints in Heaven.— The Virgin Mary will not hear the prayer of Protestants.—Rosamond in deep despondency.—Intrigue of Father Panterilla to obtain the property of his Mistress.—Suspicions against Panterilla relative to the sudden death of a certain wealthy foreigner, who died on Panterilla's plantation.—In consequence of which Panterilla is banished to New-York, where he continued to exercise his Priestly functions.—Is eventually recalled to Havanna, and resumes his functions.— While in New-York, prevails upon two young ladies to accompany him back to Havanna.—Mode of living in the Convents.— The Priests disguise themselves in citizens' dresses.— The Priests use no perfumery in their Sacerdotal habits, but use it profusely in their dress of citizen.— The Priests' koorie, or oath.—Manuel's amorous playfulness.— The Priests' shaven heads a shield against robbery.—Priestly pastime. —From carousing they go to Confession, and to the celebration of Mass, or to visit the sick, or bury the dead.

I KNEW of another Priest belonging to St. Wanadou Convent, whose name is Manuel Antonia. He was about thirty years of age; a Creole of very light complexion; large black full eye; round featured; black hair; and a rare instance of a Priest who looked well in his Priest's habit. He was born and educated on the island, to be a Priest. He had been living with an unmarried female about nine years, as his Mistress. This female belonged to New York, and has a mother and sister now living here. I have seen them, and have been at their house in New York. They are of the Jewish persuasion; and this female was brought up in it. When she left New York, she was going to New Orleans with the child of a lady in her charge, to take it to its mother, who liv[...] New Orleans. When on her way, the vessel [...]

commanded by Captain Andrews, was taken by some pirates, and carried into Matanzas, on the island of Cuba, where she first became acquainted with Father Antonia. After being detained a few weeks, the vessel left the port, and she went in it to New Orleans. Antonia was continually writing to her, wishing her to come to him, which she did, and placed herself under his protection, and was living with him when I left Cuba. She had become a complete idiot. Her mind was perfectly stupified, and sometimes crazed, by the influence of the Priest, and of his cruel and superstitious conduct to her. She has no desire to leave him ; as she believes, if she remains with him, until she dies, he can save her soul. He makes her believe she will remain in Purgatory a short time, but he can pray her out of it into Heaven. I know this to be true, for I was well acquainted with them, while living there. I know at one time, she drew a prize in the lottery of five hundred dollars. The Priest persuaded her to lay the money aside, as he believed it to be a gift from the Virgin Mary, to help to prepare her soul for heaven. When she died, it would purchase Holy Candles and pay for Masses, to be read, to help her soul out of Purgatory. This poor female believed him, and gave it to him, to keep for that purpose, when she dies. He has brought her to believe, that when he treats her unkindly and cruelly, it is for the good of her soul ;* and her soul must always be persecuted, while in this world. When I told my Priest all this, he would tell me it was all right, and that she was wise ; that the money was given to her by the Saints above for that use ; and that I must pray to the Virgin Mary for the same gift.†

* I remember to have heard the editor of the DOWNFALL OF BABYLON, Samuel B. Smith, who is a converted Priest, say, when explaining the cause of a weakness on his lungs, that he took cold while preaching in an unfinished chapel in Michigan, where the roof along the eaves, was open directly over his head, and the cold air came in a current upon him, from Sabbath to Sabbath, while preaching. He knew that he was suffering dreadfully for it, " but," (said he,) " I did not mind it ; for I thought it was good for my sins."

† See " SIX MONTHS IN A CONVENT," *bushel of gold,* to be sent from heaven.—Ed.

He would frequently give me money to buy lottery tickets; and while these tickets would not be successful, he has often persecuted me, and told me that the Virgin Mary would not hear my prayers, because I was still a poor dead Protestant at heart; (and he has compared me to the dumb beasts;) that he believed this female was a true Catholic Christian; that I was to be lost, and she would be saved. My feelings have been brought to such a state by what he would tell me of heaven and hell, that I became bewildered, and would sink down in despair, and remain so for weeks. In this state I would kneel down before the image, and cry out to the Virgin Mary for mercy. Oh! then I could well repeat these lines:

> " Beneath the poisonous dart
> Of Satan's rage I fell;
> How narrowly my feet escaped
> The snares of death and hell!

> " Darkness, and shame, and grief,
> Oppressed my gloomy mind;
> I looked around me for relief,
> But no relief could find."

While writing this to the world, to let them know of my misery and suffering, and how blind and ignorant I have been all my life, until now, as to the right view of eternity, my heart is melted down. Oh! I can truly say, I feel myself to be nothing; that I can and do repent, with this frail body of mine, in dust and ashes, before the Lord; and praise him, for the loving mercies he has showed for my poor immortal soul, in sparing my life, and bringing me out from among those Roman abominations, and placing me in this Christian country; he has, I hope and trust, placed me on the rock of safety; and now I can say,

> " Deep on my heart let memory trace
> His acts of mercy and of grace;
> Who with a father's tender care,
> Saved me, when sinking in despair."

14*

I have written to this female several times, since I have been brought here; but I have received no answer from her; I am informed that she died last summer. I have often, in this country, reflected on the fact, that the Priests do not cast off their crazed companions, as other men, under the same circumstances, would certainly do; and I do believe it is partly owing to their superstitious fear of the Virgin Mary, lest she should avenge their cruelty to the poor victims of their vile lusts; and partly owing to the cherished belief that the female in this case is evidently bearing on her head the punishment of their sin of living together. While they behold their iniquity thus borne by another, they are content to put up with some inconveniences, rather than risk a change, that might expose their own heads to a possible curse.

I knew another Priest, Father Panterilla, who belonged to St. Francisco Convent, and was chaplain to the soldiers stationed there, outside of the Pontra gate. He had, by his snares and traps, for her money, gained the affections of an American lady, who had accumulated a good deal of property; but whose principles were as depraved as his own. Not long after she had put herself under his protection, he persuaded her to purchase a plantation, about six miles from the city, on which they both went to reside, as he said his health was bad, and he thought the country air would be of benefit to him. He purchased a number of slaves, to work on the plantation, with the money of the lady; but as she had been living on the island about thirteen years, she had some knowledge of their intrigues and wickedness, and some art herself, and she took the deed, and held her money fast, only giving it to him, as he wanted to make purchases. They had lived together on the island about two years; and, during the time, he seldom came into the city, to perform his duty as chaplain to the soldiers; so that his friends thought he remained in the country to recover his health.

During this time, a friend of his from Spain, arrived on the island, who was said to be very rich, and had then a large amount of money with him. He was in bad health, and far advanced in a consumption. Father Panterilla took this friend to his plantation, to remain there a few months, it being thought more healthy than the city. He had been there but a few months, before he was suddenly missed. He had an uncle living in the city, who made many inquiries, and searched about for him ; but he could not be heard of or found. This created a great stir and confusion among the Priests. Shortly after, his body was found, *buried on the plantation.* I never heard who found it, whether his uncle, or some other individual ; but I was informed by my Priest, that the Bishop, and the Priests, had made arrangements with his uncle, to keep silent, for fear of a persecution against the Holy catholic church ; and that, if the Priest had taken the man's life, he must have been tempted by the devil ; and some other remarks he made upon it, such as these,—that if Father Panterilla had murdered and robbed the man, if he had not his heart on the deed, it was no sin ; and while the Old Adversary led Father Panterilla to be the instrument of his will in committing this murder, if Father Panterilla kept his heart fixed on the Virgin Mary, it was no sin.

This Priest was obliged to leave the island ; and he came to New York. This was in the first year I was in Cuba, A. D. 1828. He stayed and boarded in this city, in Walker-street, near Centre-street ; and remained about a year ; and learned to paint landscapes beautifully, while here. During the time he was here, he sent for the American female, who came to him. I saw her the morning she sailed, and also saw and read letters she wrote to her friends on the island, while she was there, stating that her Priest was preaching in the Catholic churches of New York ; and if arrangements could not be made for him to return, he would settle in New York, as he had offers made by the Bishop to preach in the city. But I was informed by Manuel, that the Priests had made arrangements with the governor of the island for Panterilla to return. The Bishop was obliged to give the uncle of the murdered man a large sum of money, I do not know the amount; but my Priest told me, that if Panterilla had not been a Priest, they would have committed him to the gallows. They both returned to the Island, and were living there when I left.* They persuaded two young ladies, who lived in Chatham-street, in New York, virtuous and poor, to accompany them to Havanna, promising to set them up in the Milliner's trade. Panterilla and B. C——, his Mistress, who speaks three languages fluently, and is very smart, accomplished, and rich, passed for a wedded pair. After a short residence in Havanna, the young ladies found themselves in a snare among strangers. They demanded to be returned to New York free of expense; and, in their distress, wrote to a friend, to whom one of the young ladies was betrothed in New York; and they also found friends in Havanna to bring the matter before the governor. He brought Miss B. C——, Panterilla's Mistress, before him, and obliged her to pay the returning expenses of the young ladies, and threatened her that in a case of this sort again, he would send her to the Castle. The young ladies returned, under the protection of the young man, to whom one was married on their arrival in New York. All these things were well known and commonly spoken of among the Americans in Havanna; but I do not remember the names of the young ladies, nor have I seen or heard of either of them, though often I have inquired after them, since I have been in New York.

My Priest told me, that the Bishop was going to send Panterilla to a Convent in Trinidad, because the robbery and murder had become so public, that it would be better both for him, and the rest of the Priests, if he went where

---

* The iniquity of the Roman Priest having burst out in an act of insufferable violence, even in Cuba, he was obliged to fly before the terrors of justice. He took refuge in New York, and amused himself with his pencil, in a private way, and publicly ministered at the Roman altars in this city. So it happens, that when their vices make them intolerable in Havanna, they can find unholy employment in New York, guiding the citizens of this free country in the ways of Rome.

he was not known ; and the Bishop did not wish to send him to Spain, or to the Pope ; because he had a father living in some part of Spain, who was a great Priest in a Convent ; and there were a number of Priests then living in Cuba, who were intimate friends of his father.*

I would wish to remark in particular, that I have often heard Manuel, and other Priests, say, they did not like the new governor so well as the former one, who left the island about a year before me. The present governor was more strict ; and I heard the *citizens* say he was a far better man than the former one. You could not bribe him to do any criminal act. After the old governor had made his fortune, he left the island for Spain.†

I will here relate, as near as I can, their mode of living in the Convents, where the Priests reside. I have been informed by Manuel, that their diet is principally soups of the richest kinds, poultry, eggs, and fish. They take claret wine, instead of coffee, for breakfast, dinner, and supper.‡ This must be of the best quality. Each Priest has his own plate, goblet, and knife and fork ; and, after a meal,

---

* I knew two Bishops in the United States to act in the same manner, in respect, however, to other crimes.—ED.

† In this simple manner Rosamond notices a fact most notorious at the present day, to all readers of the New York newspapers, to wit :— that the new governor of Cuba has introduced a new order of things in Havanna. She states what she had heard the Priests say on the one hand, and what the citizens said on the other. She does not affirm a word of her own knowledge about the new governor, but many things in the Narrative impeach the righteousness of the old governor. He would take bribes, and do all corresponding iniquity. Him the Priests liked. But they like not the new governor, because he is "more strict."

He is strict. A merchant of the first rank in this city, who has spent a short time in Havanna, observed of him :—" He is a most extraordinary man. He has abolished gambling. He has introduced a police that makes the life of a man almost as safe there, as in New York. Assassinations have almost ceased. And when formerly money would accomplish any thing in the way of a breach of the laws, now it is positively refused in every form, as a bribe to turn aside the execution of rigid justice." The same is the frequent testimony of the public prints, repeated for a year or two past; and this of Rosamond falls in with it, as the little rill with the mighty stream, bearing distinctive marks of its own in the current.

‡ This is the Clerical custom also in France.—ED.

each takes and washes his own utensils, and lays them aside, until he returns again to his meals. Their servants are not permitted to handle them, as they believe their hands are not holy enough.* When they sit down to meals, they Cross themselves in prayer ; and after prayers, on rising from their meals, they Cross themselves, and go to wash their dishes. On laying them aside, they Cross themselves again. I never knew my Priest enter, or leave my house, (that is, when I had my reason to know him,) without Crossing himself.† They never retire to their beds without chocolate, wine, and confectionary. I have never seen the Priests partake of their common Convent meals ; but while I was in the Convent with Manuel, his table was supplied with such, and he informed me that was their mode of living. He was always in the habit of taking supper in my house ; and then, he was not so particular about his knife and fork, and plate ; but would always Cross himself, and say a few words in Latin, when first seated at the table ; but I cannot say he was so particular at rising from table. He would always take care to have his bottle emptied.

Manuel used to make his call at my house, during the day, in his habit ; but in the evening, as soon as he entered my house, he would lay aside his habit, and put on the dress of a citizen ; and on leaving the house, put on his habit again. The alteration would be so great in him, when dressed as a citizen with his wig on, that he could pass by his intimate friends, and not be known by them. I am sure if I had first become acquainted with him in a Priest's habit, I never should have lived five years such a gloomy and wretched life as I did ; for when dressed in their habits, they do not look like natural beings on earth ; even their complexion changes. He was a fine-looking

* The reader will perceive a much better reason for this, in the natural fear that souls so abused with religious profession, and intolerable oppression, as the servants of the Priests in Cuba are, might have something in their hands, when they cleansed the dishes, more dangerous to the bodies, than unholy hands of the servants could possibly be to the souls of the Priests.

† [....] their custom every where.—Ed.

man, when dressed as a citizen, a little above the middle
stature, and was admired for his easy and polite manners
by his friends.   He and all the Priests have their pockets
in the wrist of the great sleeve of their habits.   Here they
always carry their money.   The Priests are very particular never to allow any perfume of any sort on their consecrated habits, or on their persons, while dressed in their
habits.   But the Spanish gentlemen and ladies make great
use of perfumes ; and the Priests, when they put on their
citizen's dress, indulge themselves freely in this common
luxury; wetting their heads, and hands, and handker-
chiefs with cologne.

Every morning Manuel would carefully wash his head,
to remove all the scent of the perfume, before he resumed
the Priests' habit.   I have often asked him why he was so
particular ; and what was the harm of the perfume to the
consecrated garments.   He would always exclaim : " O,
Rosettee !" (so he called me,) " Ka, ka, esta, esta, sta
mallo !"—This is a common expression for something
very bad and horrid.   Before I came to fear him so
much, I have often plagued him for my sport, by sprinkling cologne water on his habit, or on him when dressed
in his habit.   He would jump up as if *aquafortis* came
on his head ; and in evident distress, exclaim as above :
" O, ka, ka, esta, esta, sta mallo !" and tell me, if I knew
how wicked it was, I would never do it.   I have forced
him to grant me small favors, by holding up the cologne
bottle, and threatening to throw cologne on him ; and
when he had promised, I would make him seal it with a
hoorie, that is, a Priest's oath ; and then I would be satisfied, and lay down the cologne.   This word is spelt in
Champerra, *whoorie ;* and the act is done by placing the
thumb across the middle of its nearest finger, to form a
Cross, and then, touching the thumb nail to the lips.   In
making me *hoorie*, he was always very particular, to see
that I put my thumb across the *middle* of the finger, for
fear that I would cheat.

When going out with him, in the evening, to the "*Place
de Armos*," (that is, the place where the people resort for

amusement, and hearing music,) we used to meet with his friends, other Priests, who likewise would be dressed in disguise. They would converse together, and appear to enjoy themselves, as worldly men, in all kinds of intrigues and dissipation. I have been informed, that if the robbers, (of whom there are plenty,) attack any of the Priests, to rob them, while in disguise, by taking off their wigs, and showing the robbers that they are Priests, they will not hurt them.* The Priests say they have not the power; for they always keep the gospel-bag, and our Saviour's image, round their necks.

This place is open for amusement once a week, and it is customary for ten or fifteen Priests to agree at this place to meet at some one of their houses, with their Mistresse with them. Some would be French, some Spanish. I was the only American amongst them. There they would partake of a sumptuous supper, with wines of every description, and remain until three or four o'clock in the morning, eating, drinking, and playing cards; and singing and playing on the guitar. I always observed, that they were not so particular about Crossing themselves and saying prayers on these occasions, as they were said to be in the Convents; but they would, at times, Cross themselves. As they were so much in the habit of doing it, it became natural to them, and an almost involuntary movement. I know it to be true, that the next day, and, perhaps, but a few hours after their carousal of wickedness, they would go to the Convents, and would Confess to the head Father of the Convent, and then, they would be ready to go out on their sacred, spiritual, and religious duties, reading Masses, or hearing Confessions at the private Altars in the houses, or the Confessions of the dying. I have heard Manuel say, when he would be going from my house, that he was obliged to go that morning to such a lady, or man, who was dying; or, perhaps, to go to a house, where there was a corpse laid out, to say prayers over the body. When I first went to live with him, and

---

* Honor among thieves forbids them to plunder thieves.

he would tell me he was going to pray over the corpse of any one, I would laugh at him, and tell him he was wicked ; but when I had become better acquainted with him, all this freedom forsook me.

15

CHAPTER XV.

"It is the pirate's cursed bark!
The villains linger to decoy!
Thus bounding o'er the waters dark,
They seek to lure, and then destroy!"
                            Miss L. M. DAVIDSON.

Father Pies, and his Mistresses, and his lap-dog.—Seduces the wife of a wealthy citizen, and is betrayed by the barking of his lap-dog.—The husband rushes in upon them, and bites his wife's nose nearly off.—Father Pies' amorous and wicked letters now in the hands of the Authoress of this Narrative.—He was the Confessor of the public criminals.—A wealthy lady imprisoned under a false pretext in order to get her money.—What the diabolical pretext was.

I CAN inform you of a Priest, who belonged to St. O'Christo Convent, whom I knew well. He was about sixty years of age, small face, and sandy complexion. His name was Father Pies. He was chief Father Confessor to the criminals about to be executed. He wore a snuff-colored habit, with a leather belt round his waist, and would walk with a cane. His hat was of black straw, except on duty in a procession, when he wore no hat. He was always accompanied by a little white lap-dog, which he appeared almost to worship, when walking in the street. I have been informed by Manuel, and others, that he supports a great number of poor families, where there are daughters. He visits them, as his Mistresses, in their father's houses. They are from twelve to eighteen years of age, and are all living near his Convent. The other Priests give him the name of " Father *Dulce* ;" ("SWEETY.") They say he is such a favorite with the young girls, and wins their affections, and obtains the consent of their fathers. His little dog once caused him a good deal of trouble, by betraying him in one of his wicked intrigues with a married lady, to whose house he used to go daily, to hear her Confessions.

When they were both retired alone to a room, but not into her Holy Room of worship, where her Saints' images

THE REV^D FATHER'S RETREAT.

P. 1/9.

were, her husband unexpectedly came home. He was a wealthy man, but very dissipated. He was intoxicated at the time, and inquired of his little daughter, where her mother was.—The child said her mamma had gone with Father Pies, to tell the Virgin Mary how wicked he was. This excited him, as he was in liquor, and he searched for her. Finding her Sacred Room empty, he walked to another room, which he found fastened. Knocking at the door made the little dog bark. This caused him to break open the door ; and aiming his violence, first, at his wife, he bit her nose half off, which disfigured her in the face until this day, if she is living, and she was, when I left the island. I have seen the lady often since it happened. Father Pies made his escape from the house, while the husband and wife were at combat.

Their violence caused great alarm to the neighbors, who came to see what was the trouble. The husband made no ceremony about making public the whole truth of what had taken place between his wife and Father Pies. Father Pies sent Captain Antony, a Spanish officer of the army, to Don Varilla, (for that was his name,) to make some settlement. I don't know what amount he was obliged to give Don Varilla ; but Manuel said, "*that was a dear Confessing-day to Father Dulce.*" In the island of Cuba, occurrences similar to this take place so frequently among the Priests, that when another happens, the first soon dies way. I have often seen this Father Pies, when in the procession with poor criminals going to be executed, (which is a dreadful and horrid sight.) He always walked at the side of the criminal, with a candle in one hand, and a prayer-book in the other, talking and praying with them, until they arrived at the gallows. I have seen him, during the solemn scene, wink his eye, and smile at a female. At executions, he would be dressed in a white habit, with two or three yards of beads, and an image of our Saviour, and a Cross, hanging round him. I have often told my Priest, that if I was going to die, I would not wish Father Pies to pray for me ; and he

would say he was chosen by the Saints above for that
office, and he was a good man.

I have never known or heard so much of Father Pies'
cruelty, or wicked intrigues, to rob people of their money,
as I have of other Priests; but I have always heard about
his weakness, in falling in love with every female he saw.
I have some letters in my possession at this time of his
own handwriting, which I feel it my duty to spread out
to the world. They contain the sentiments of his own
wicked heart, penned by his own hand. The lady, to
whom he addressed them, was at that time living on the
island of Cuba; but is now living in New York.* I was
well acquainted with her at the time Father Pies was
writing to her, and my motive in making his letters public, is, to show the inward sentiments of his own heart,
and then for the world to decide, if he is a true and holy
Christian Priest, and one of the chosen servants of the
Saints above, as my Priest told me he was. It was his
duty to Confess the poor criminals who were sentenced to
be hung, and to instruct them in their last moments, how
to repent, and prepare their dying souls, to meet at the
Judgment Seat of Christ.

I lament much, losing my letters with my trunks, at
the time I lost them; as you will see in my Narrative,
how I lost them on my way from Philadelphia to this
city. I had letters written by my Priest's own hand,
which he sent me at the time I was living with him; and
if I had them to expose to the world, they would show a
great deal of the wickedness of different Priests.

Father Pies once called at my house with Manuel, to
take some refreshments, as they both had been to the
prison that day, to hear the Confession of a lady who
was put there by her husband; so that he could leave
her, and go to Spain, with all her property. My Priest
had been her Father-Confessor some years. Father Pies
had been to see some criminals, who were shortly to be
executed. I will inform you how this Spaniard managed

* See these letters in the introduction to this Narrative.

to get rid of his wife, and go off with her property. This Spanish gentleman's name was Don W—— L——. He was a native of Spain, and his wife was a Catalan Spaniard. They lived about three miles from the city. He was a dyer by trade, and had accumulated, with his wife's assistance, a good deal of money. She had a character for being a good and industrious woman. They had lived together about twelve years, and had three sons. Don W—— had treated his wife cruelly for some time, and had tried many schemes to prove she was not honest; and would appear to be jealous of her, for which, it was said, by those who knew her, that he had no cause. My Priest informed me, that in her Confessions to him, she told him she was afraid of her life with her husband. She used to have Masses said for him, and was always having the evil spirits burnt out with Holy Candles around her house; for which she was called a good and holy Christian by those I heard speak of her.

Don W—— succeeded, however, in effecting his wishes, at last, and possessed himself of her property in this way. He hired a Spaniard, a native of Cuba, no better than himself, but notorious for his dissoluteness, to come to his house at a time when Madam W—— was very unwell, and confined to her bed-room. He came, pretending to inquire for a servant-girl that he wanted to hire, as Don W—— kept servants to hire out by the month. He told the servants that he was acquainted with their mistress, and would walk into her bed-room, which he did, and drew a small bolt for an inside fastening of the door unperceived by Madam W——. The customs and habits on the island are so different from what they are here, she did not think it any harm for a man to come on business into her sick-room, as he wished to have one of her slaves.

Don W—— knew the precise time he would be there in her room, and he came home with three commissaries in company. In their presence he inquired of his servants where their mistress was. They told him she was in her bed-room, and that a gentleman was there with

15*

her. Don W—— went with the commissaries to the bed-room door, and finding it fastened, he directed them to break it open. The sudden alarm, and the strange voices outside the door, and the violent entrance of three strangers into her bed-room, frightened Madam W——, so that she knew not what she did; but she sprang from her bed, and flew to this man for protection, when the commissaries entered, and found them together. Madam W—— fainted. The family and neighbors, in alarm, came in to see what was the matter. Her fright made her appear guilty in the eyes of all, as this man, found with her, was well known for his vile habits. Don W—— had his wife taken by the commissaries, and put into the Cathedral, which is a prison. He then sold his house and slaves, and changed all his estate into money, and left the island with his three sons for some part of America. I have heard Manuel say he was here in New York; and Manuel was well acquainted with the Father-Confessor of Don W——.

This took place about a year before I left the island, and made a good deal of talk. But as Madam W—— was left poor and penniless, and had no rich friends to bribe the Alcades, or judges, or to fee the Priests, her situation was hopeless. When her money was all gone, the Priests were at no pains to comfort her blinded mind with Masses, and candles, and prayers, for her husband and dear children, which they would have been forward to do, if she had possessed money or rich friends. Then she might have had all the Priests on the island around her; and they would have kept her mind well employed with Masses, Confessions, penances, and burning candles; but she was deprived of all these comforts for the want of money; as Manuel, who was her Father-Confessor, told Father Pies at that time, he should not go to see her again, for he had told her long since to take what money she had, and leave him, and find another Confessor: that she had not taken his advice, and he should not trouble himself any further about her: and laughed, and said, " Don

W—— was no fool; he can have a fine choice in America; for he had a good store of money."

I asked Manuel if he thought it was right to leave Madam W——, when she was in trouble. The answer he made was, "*Ka sta mallo*," and, I cannot spend my time with her for nothing.

I saw a person that had seen Madam W—— in prison, and had conversed with her, just before the cholera broke out on the island, who told me that she had not, at that time, any prospect of ever being liberated from prison, as the laws of the island are such, that she must be in prison until her husband appears, and takes her out. It was said that her mind had become bewildered and childish.

CHAPTER XVI.

" Gold many hunted, sweat, and bled for gold !
Waked all the night, and laboured all the day ;
And what was this allurement, dost thou ask ?
A dust dug from the bowels of the earth,
Which being cast into the fire, came out
A shining thing that fools admired, and called
A God ; and in devout and humble plight
Before it kneeled, the greater to the loss.
And on its altar, sacrificed ease, peace,
Truth, faith, integrity ; good conscience, friends,
Love, charity, benevolence, and all
The sweet and tender sympathies of life ;
And to complete the horrid murderous rite,
And signalize their folly, offered up
Their souls, and an eternity of bliss."

                             POLLOK.

*Some description of Havanna.— The Priests afraid to trust their servants
in marketing.— The people drink wine out of their Priests' mouths.—
They think the food from his hands, is blessed.— The Priests become acquainted with domestic concerns through Confession.— It is the custom
for man and wife, to have their domestic disputes in the presence of their
relations.— To have Mass said, is the way to settle disputes.— The
Priests sell blessed Candles to perform conjuration or witchcraft.— Superstitious fear of the Priests.*

THE houses in Havanna are built of stone, mostly one
story, but they are very large and roomy. The parlours
and bed-rooms all extend on one level. The rooms are
very long and lofty, painted with landscapes, or flowers,
very showy. They have no glass in the windows, which
are large and high, extending nearly from the floor to the
ceiling. Instead of glass, they have iron bars arched outward, about five or six inches apart, to secure them from
robbers. They have strong shutters inside. Their furniture is very rich and beautiful, gilded very much, which
makes it appear very rich and tasty. They have no fire-
places in their houses, as the climate is warm. They
cook with furnaces in the yard. Their parlours and bed-
rooms are lighted with chandeliers ; and they make use
of no lamps or candlesticks. House-rent is high, from
eighty to a hundred dollars a month, for a comfortable,
decent house. You must buy all your water. It is car-

ried about from the public fountains, by negroes, in half-barrels on their heads, and sold two pails full for six cents. It is so poor, that it must be purified with a small piece of brimstone. This lies undissolved at the bottom of the jar, where the mud settles, and will purify for months. The markets are very filthy. Meat, poultry, and vegetables, are suffered to lie in market, on the ground. They have no stalls for them ; and they are high in price. Vegetables are in great variety, and good at all seasons of the year. Fish and poultry are good. Pork is thought to be better than beef. The Spaniards in Havanna are very fond of pork, which is commonly fried with plantain.

The Priests have their select places for market. They never trust their servants to go alone. One Priest will always go with them. Neither do they suffer their servants to cook their food alone. There is always a Priest to overlook them in the kitchen ; the same Priest who goes to market, also for that day oversees the kitchen, and this office they take in turn. They say it is to bless the food. I knew some Catholic families there, who were so superstitious and blind, that when the Priest called on them, and took wine, which it was customary to offer to them, he would take the wine into his own mouth, and after Crossing himself, his friend, or friends, they would take and drink it from his mouth. They believe it is then blessed and holy. I have seen it done myself; and my Priest has told me, that it is frequently done in high and respectable families. When sick, they also send for the Priest to come and feed them. They think the food from his hand is blessed.

When a gentleman is paying his addresses to a young lady, their courtship is mostly carried on in the presence of the family ; and when she gets married, if she has any property, it is settled upon her in her maiden name ; so that her husband cannot spend or make use of it without her consent, and she transacts all her business in her maiden name. The Priest knows all about their courtship from her Confession. I have often heard Manuel say, how such and such were going to be married. They generally marry distant relations, so that their property may remain in the family. A wife not only transacts business in her maiden name, but generally goes by it. The Priests always call them by their maiden name.

It is customary in the highest circle, among the nobility, for a married lady to have her gallant,* to escort her about to the amusements, and a man to have his Mistress. As I have said, there is not much virtue or moral principle possessed by them ; and if a husband becomes jealous of his wife, or a wife of her husband, they will have their disputes in the presence of all the family, or

---

* For a corroboration of this shameful Popish custom, we will give the following, from Sismondi's "History of the Italian Republics." We will observe, in regard to this author, that his "History of the Italian Republics," a work in 16 vols., is written with a good deal of candor, considering that he was a Papist, and that he published his elaborate work in Italy, immediately under the very eye of the Sovereign Pontiff. This work, for reasons which we have not room here to explain, has escaped the condemnation of the "Expurgatorial Index." We see that the "Catholic Miscellany" of Charleston, and other Popish papers in the United States, quote from this author as from good authority ; and it is to be presumed they will not refuse us the same privilege.

Sismondi describes the manners and customs of the Italians, and especially of the Clergy, in a manner calculated to excite both our pity and contempt.

The description which he gives of the gallants of married ladies, is as follows:—"One of the greatest public misfortunes, in Italy," (says he,) "and which affects almost every family, is the stain to the sacred bond of marriage, by another bond which is acknowledged, and considered as honorable, and which strangers in Italy always look upon with the same surprise, without comprehending it ; and this is the ' Cicisbei,' or ' Cavalieri Serventi.' This direful custom was introduced in the 17th century, by the example of the Court, and being placed under the protection of all the vanities, the peace of families was banished from all Italy.—No husband any longer regarded his wife as a faithful companion.—They could no longer seek counsel of her in doubts ; or support in adversity.—They found her no longer a saviour in danger, or a comforter in despair.—No father could be assured, that the children who bore his name, were his own ; and, in fine, every domestic relation was poisoned."

" These Cavalieries were gallants that, with the consent even of the husband, always escorted the lady out on her visits, walks, and shopping, and to the theatres, balls, &c., and back home again ; the husband attending to his business or pleasure elsewhere." Sismondi, Hist. Ital. T. XVI. p. 221.—Ed.

friends who may be present, and both sexes have jealous dispositions. Whenever they have settled a dispute, they will go to their Priests, and Confess, and have a Mass read. That seals the settlement. It is generally known that the Priests get a good deal of money for candles and Masses, to be burned and read in the Convents, from persons going to law, to bewilder and craze the mind of their adversary. I have known Manuel to perform this office, and he has given me money, which he said in the act of giving it, that he had received that day, for this sorcery of the Mass and red candles, to confound an adversary in the court of law. This is done in the higher classes among the rich people. The power of the Priests in this particular, is generally believed. I have seen so much of their wickedness, and conjuration, and malediction Priestcraft, that I could not help believing it. Each have their own Priest; the man his and the wife hers. My Priest has often told me, when a married lady came to him, to Confess, she would tell him all about their disputes, and what her feelings were towards her husband. In telling me, he generally sympathized with the wife. Whatever the Priest told her to do, to regain the affections of her husband, she would believe, and do. Her husband would likewise complain of her to his Priest, to subdue her by a curse to submission, when he could not persuade her by his love, and would have Mass said on her head.* I have known Manuel often to have this duty to perform. The wife will also buy candles of her Priest, to burn nine days, with nine Masses, upon her husband's head, but I never knew a man to buy the red candles. The Priest tells her, that he will bless them in such a way, that by her burning them nine days, and his reading of the nine Masses, her husband will become humble and submissive to her. She must pay the Priest for these candles and

---

* This "saying Mass on the head," is an idiomatic expression among the Papists in Cuba. The meaning of it is, not that the Mass is actually celebrated on the head of a person, but merely that it is celebrated or said with a view of being applied to some particular person and for some special object.— Ed.

Masses.* The Priests do sell candles to the people to perform conjuration or witchcraft, (or *malediction* as the
natives call it.) It may be thought to be my weakness,
but I tell the truth: I have bent my knees before Manuel,
and cried, and begged, that he would not do so; that he
would not say Masses, and burn candles on my head; and
that he never would make me crazy. One Sunday, in
particular, I felt very wretched, and when Manuel came
in, I told him, on my knees, I knew by my wretchedness,
that he had just been saying a Mass on my head, and
begged him not to do so. He sank into a chair, pale and
faint, so that I left caring for myself, and brought him the
cologne. He gave no explanations, but did not leave the
house again that day, except for evening oration in the
Convent; after which, as his custom was, he would put on
a citizen's dress, and go out to the public amusements.
Manuel has often told me, that no one had the power to
injure a Priest.

It will be seen in my Narrative, at the time I was living
in New Orleans, that I have gone myself to the Catholic
Priest, and bought candles, for which I gave a five dollar

---

* There are some Papists in the United States, who deny that money
is received by the Priests for saying Mass. And they have frequently
said, that if such could be proved to be the practice of the Church, they
would renounce it. To these, I say, it is the universal practice of
the Priests, acting according to the doctrine, and under the authority of
their church, not only to receive pay for Masses, but to *exact it.* This
is one of the principal sources of their revenue. I myself, who was
once a Popish Priest, was forbidden by a certain Bishop in the West,
from ever saying a Mass gratuitously for any one whomsoever, however poor and needy he might be.

For the proof of what is advanced, that is, that pay can be *exacted* for
the saying of Masses, I could refer to hundreds of Popish authorities.
From them all, it will be sufficient to select two who stand the highest,
and these are the Angelical St. Thomas, and St. Ligori. The former
says, speaking of Masses, " *Gratis tamen, &c.*"—"Spiritual favors having been previously bestowed, the fixed and customary *oblations,* and any
other proceeds whatsoever, *can be exacted* from those who are able and
unwilling to pay." Thom. Aquin. 2, 2 q. 100, A. 3.—St. Ligori says,
that "a Priest is allowed to take pay for Masses, *because* it is the com-
mon practice of the whole church, and, because every laborer, whether he
be rich or poor, is worthy of his hire." Ligor. de Euch. L. V. C. 3.
—ED.

note, a free-will offering, to burn on a gentleman's head, to gain him to buy me a valuable servant, and a Brussels carpet, and for other like purposes; and the Priest knew what I wanted them for. It was done in the same manner as you would go to a fortune-teller, or conjurer, to gain any thing by their black art. I know my wicked heart would not have been too good to have done the same at Cuba, if I had not been living with this Priest; for I was so blinded, I thought he had power with the Saints to prevent my doing any thing to him by sorcery. Seeing and hearing so much of their Priestcraft, my mind and feelings were eaten up with superstition and misery; as the minds of all are who fall under the blind guidance of the Roman Priests in the island of Cuba.

Their minds are all destroyed by superstition, and the Priests themselves are eaten up with it. Many ladies, who professed to be of the first respectability, when talking to me about living with this Priest, would say, that he could pray for the curses of the sin of our living together on my head; but made me promise not to tell him, as they believe that a Priest can go into any house, and leave a curse on any one, if he be displeased. They are so superstitious, that if one individual has any thing against another, and calls at his house, when he is gone, the householder will rise, and Cross himself, and sprinkle Holy Water after him; or, if one friend calls upon another, and is in trouble, or unfortunate, when he leaves the house, those in the house will burn incense, and sprinkle Holy Water round the house. This is done in the most respectable families; and I need not pretend to tell how much more superstition and Priestcraft is carried on among the lower and ignorant classes of the people.

16

CHAPTER XVII.

Though you, and all the kings of Christendom,
Are led so grossly by this meddling Priest,
And, by the merit of vile gold, dross, dust,
Purchase corrupted pardon of a man,
Who,.in that sale, sells pardon from himself;
Though you, and all the rest, so grossly led,
This juggling witchcraft with revenue cherish,
Yet I, alone, alone do me oppose
Against the Pope, and count his friends my foes.
                    SHAKSPEARE.

Scheme of a Priest to get possession of the estate of Poncheetee, one of their female devotees.—Her private chapel.—Mode of penance.—Becomes a mere skeleton.—Counting of the beads in the street.—She commits the unpardonable sin in judging the Holy Priest; for which she is enjoined a severe penance.

THERE was a poor woman, who was a strong and superstitious Catholic, a native of Old Spain, who had been living in Cuba fifteen years. I was in the habit of going to her house often. Her husband was a bad man. He died in Moro Castle, in Cuba, a number of years since. At the time I first knew her, she had been informed by some of her friends, that her uncle had died in Spain, and had left her property to the amount of a hundred thousand dollars, which, I believe, was true; for so, 'it was generally reported, and Manuel told me it was true. Immediately after she heard of it, she went to a Priest belonging to St. ——— Convent, which stands on the hill, back of St. Wanadou, to ask his counsel and advice. His name was Father *Francisco.* He advised her to employ a lawyer to send to Spain for the Will in writing, and to take, for her, the possession of the estate. Francisco himself engaged the lawyer to transact the business. The lady's name was *Poncheetee.* She was obliged to go with the lawyer and Priest, to the governor, to give her proofs, that she was a niece of the deceased, before they could send to Spain. I have seen the Priest and lawyer at her house on this business, and have drunk wine with them, for they never fail to offer the Priest wine. She, being a poor woman, had not wherewith to buy large images of the Saints, and the Virgin Mary, to decorate a private room for worship, but was obliged to have her images in her bed-room, which had nothing in it but a cot, and some old faded Saints, that had been given her. Neither was her Virgin Mary dressed in rich apparel, but looked as if she was forsaken, and had become poor, like her worshiper.

After they had it all arranged, the Priest, the lawyer, and the heiress, they sent to Spain. Her Priest was very attentive to her, in calling at her house every day. She then went under penance for a year, to gain a blessing on the arrangements which were made; wearing a coarse blue striped loose dress, with a leather belt round her waist, and her hair combed straight back, braided, and hanging down her back. She wore half sandals, and no stockings. She was not permitted to sit in a chair at table, or to use a knife and fork when eating; but would take her meals on a dressed morocco skin, on the stone floor, using her hands.*

---

* By this Roman discipline, the Priest placed Poncheetee in close confinement, and cut her off from the intercourse of society, without exciting a suspicion in her mind, that she was under bonds, stronger than iron chains, and was restrained by customs, higher and less penetrable than prison walls. How could she visit, or receive company, in her garb of penance, her leather-belt, her hair braided down her back, her naked feet in sandals! A few might approach her, such as were in like misery with her, under the Roman yoke; but no one able to expose the Priest's wrong, able to contend with *the oppressor*, "able to make war with *the Beast*," would be likely to visit so forlorn an object of Priestly deception.

By this power of inflicting penance, and by the true "*doctrine of devils*," that self-inflicted pains gain the Divine favor, the Roman Father Francisco shut up his victim, as effectually as ever a fly was taken in the toils of the spider's web; and he wore out her life in this confinement, with false hopes, suggested to the mind, and with severe hardships, exacted of the body; fasting, kneeling, watching, hoping, and obtaining nothing, but death at last.

" *Ye shall know them by their fruits.*"

Every Roman catholic must see that the forms of his church enable the Priests to impose in this manner on the people of their charge. And the history of the world, and the experience of mankind, show, that *power* always has been abused by Priests or magistrates, where the line of succession is formed by the rulers, and not by the people. The abuse of power is not peculiar to Roman catholics or to Priests; but it is common to those who have power, independent of the control of the people.

I have been at her house often, when she has been eating,
and have partaken of her fare with her off the floor. They
think it a sin to refuse, when asked, to eat or drink with
any one under penance. Her rule was, whenever she eat
or drank, to Cross herself, and call on the Virgin Mary
before sitting down; and as soon as her meals were finished, to go to her bed-room, where there were always
candles burning before the relic,* and the images of the
saints, and kneel down and pray to them. Her knees had
become callous by kneeling on them, bare, upon the hard
stony floor. She worshiped her images nine times a day:
at six o'clock, at nine, at eleven, twelve, three, five, seven,
ten, and eleven. Then she retired to bed, which would
be a bare cot, without a pillow, or any clothing.

Every Friday she would fast, and scarcely rise from
her knees. All Catholics fast, so far, as to abstain from
meat on Friday. When praying and Crossing herself,
she would strike on her breast with such force, that you
might hear her stomach ring, as she was nothing but skin

---

* Such is the veneration that the poor deluded Papists entertain for
relics, that "even the very hair that fell from Peter the hermit's mule,
was treasured up as a precious relic." So says their own historian
Guibert, L. II. C. VIII. This is the Peter who led on the Crusades
against the Holy Land.

Henricus, one of the Romish Divines, maintains, that the relics in the
form of ashes or dust, may, and ought to be adored, but not under the
form of vermin; but their great Vasquez rejects this scruple, and the
grounds of it, as vain and frivolous; and concludes they may be worshiped as well when they are vermin as when they are ashes. Vasq.
An. 34, in Spondon. Cap. Ulto. N. 113, 114.

It was, for ages, palmed upon the deluded Papists, that it was the real
blood of Christ that was exhibited in various churches in Europe, and
which they adored. But, afterwards, when the heretics, (so called,)
asked, "How this could be?" since the doctrine of the Romish church
is, "*quod semel assumpsit nunquam reliquit*,"—"THAT WHICH CHRIST ONCE
ASSUMED, HE NEVER LEFT."—To this the Angelical Doctor Thomas of
Aquin, gave the following answer :—"*Sanguis autem ille*," &c.—"The
blood which is preserved in certain churches, as a relic of Christ, did
not flow from the side of Christ, but is said to have *flowed*, in a miraculous manner, *from a certain image of Christ that was struck*." Thom.
Aquin. III. Ques. 54, Art. 2, ad 3.

Valla, a person of great learning and eminence among the Papists,
says, that "at Rome there are ten thousand different sorts of relics."
Valla de Constant. Donat.—ED.

and bone. She would pray, and talk with the Saints'
images, as if they were actually human beings before her.[*]
At this time, she was not pleading with them to forgive
her sins, but praying for this money, sometimes the tears
streaming down her cheeks, and sometimes getting angry

[*] "How have we renounced the devil and his angels, (says Tertullian,) if we make images? (simulachrum.) How can we be said to re-
pudiate those things not only *with* which, but *by* which we live?—Can
we deny with our *tongues* what we confess by our *hands?*—Destroy by
our words what we confirm by our deeds ?—Can those who have many
gods preach that there is but one God ?—I make the images, some will
say, but I do not worship them.—Wherefore, then, do they make them,
if it is not right to worship them?—Verily, they worship them, who
make them that they can be worshiped.—If honor is due to an image,
doubtless the honor to the image is idolatry.

"We are to render unto Cæsar what belongs to Cæsar, and to God
what belongs to God; that is, the image of Cæsar, to Cæsar, which is
upon the coin ; and the image of God, to God, which is *in man.*—To
Cæsar, indeed,' the money belongs, but you belong to God ;—otherwise
what would be for God, if all belongs to Cæsar ?" Tertul. de Idololat.

Jerom, whom the Papists claim as their own great Saint, settles the
controversy between us and the church of Rome at once, in respect to
what constitutes idols. His words are as follows :—"Idola intelligi-
mus imagines mortuorum."—"By idols we mean the images of the
dead." Hier. Com. in Isa. C. 37.

Tertullian confirms the above, when, he says, " *Quid enim,*" &c.—
"What is there so worthy of God, as that which is so unworthy of
being an idol?—And what is there so worthy of being an idol as that
which is dead ?" Tertul. Corona Militis.

The Popish historian, Mariana, speaking of the multitude of miracles believed in Spain, exclaimed, after having described some of
them, " Methinks I am writing Fables or Romances ; but many of this
nature are recounted in the Chronicles of Spain, which I will neither
condemn nor approve of." Marian. His. Esp. L. VIII. C. 10.

He dared not openly condemn them for fear of the Inquisition ; and
he could not approve of them for conscience' sake.

So completely infatuated is the Popish church, and her devotees
upon the subject of miracles, that they will have them to be performed
even in confirmation of a lie. In proof of this I will give an example
from Mariana's History of Spain, which is now before me.

"Casilda; the daughter of the king of Toledo, and Zaida, of the king
of Seville, whose fathers were Moors, were converted to the faith by
the following incident:—Casilda was very compassionate, and frequently used to relieve the captive Christians. These acts of benevolence offended her father, who met her, one day, carrying meat to them.
He asked her what it was ?—she replied, ' they were roses;' and, un-
covering it, they found the meat converted into those flowers. This
miracle moved them to embrace Christianity." Marian. Hist. Esp. L.
IX. C. 3.—ED:.

and out of patience with them. She was upwards of fifty years of age, and very thin.

Every month on the island there are issued from the Press, Saints, with prayers under them, (a few words in Latin,) printed on an octavo page of paper, and carried about the streets for sale, at twelve and a half cents apiece. These are sold by boys and the servants of the Priests for the benefit of the Priests. She had her bed-room papered over with these prints of different Saints, which she had bought. She was still obliged to continue paying the Priest for Masses, which he read, to make the Saints propitious to her claim to the deceased uncle's estate, with money which she begged her friends to give her. I have given her money, when I knew what she wanted it for, until Manuel found it out, and said :— Father Francisco had more money than he had, and I must give her no more. He then told me that Poncheetee never would get any of the money left by her uncle; that Father Francisco had the deed of the property already in his possession. This he charged me not to mention at the price of my life; for he said it would do more good to the Convent, than to her. Manuel did not feel unwilling to have me visit Poncheetee. We loved to talk over our mutual troubles together.

I often met this Priest, Francisco, in her house, with a prayer-book in his hand, after I was informed that he had got possession of the estate, and he would still be encouraging her to believe that she would, sometime, get the money from Spain; and, if not, it would be, because she was not faithful in her prayers. This made her scarcely give herself time to eat; and whenever any lady called to see her, (which I often did, for I pitied her, and in her misery found company,) if it was prayer time, she would ask her into her bed-room, when she would be obliged to kneel, or sit down on the floor, until Poncheetee had gone through her ceremony. She would plead and pray for the Saints, *to fix a time*, when she should get her money. For the Catholics do not mind praying before any one, and you will see the females praying to their Saints, and counting their beads, when they are going along the streets to church.*

When I left the island, Poncheetee was laboring under the same state of mind she had been in, for two years, since she first heard of the money being left her in Spain, and she was a perfect skeleton. When I saw her last, which was after the cholera broke out, and but a few days before I left the island, some one had hinted to her, that the Priest would wrong her out of this money, and she had asked several Priests about it; but they all rejected the idea; and Manuel told her before me, that she had committed an unpardonable sin, and she must Confess to her Priest, and go under a deep penance, for harboring such a thought against her Father-Confessor. She appeared to be very much distressed, and I have no doubt she was. I am sure, if they put her under some penances I have known them to impose on others, she would never live through it.

---

* *Use not vain repetitions, as the heathen do; for they think that they shall be heard for their much speaking.*" Matt. vi. 7.

CHAPTER XVIII.

" Come, thick night,
And pall thee in the dunnest smoke of hell!
That my keen knife see not the wound it makes,
Nor heaven peep through the blanket of the dark,
To cry Hold! hold! "
                                    SHAKSPEARE.

The executions of negroes for the killing of negroes, and making sausages of their bodies.—By bribing the Priests, some of them are reprieved.—People rendered crazy by the malediction of the Priests.—The wealth of the Priests in proportion to their wickedness.—The wickedness she witnesses, too horrible to be described.—The Virgin can pardon all sins.—Avarice of the Priests.—When the Priests fall in love with a female, they induce her to enter into a Convent.—Priestly stratagems for seduction.—Females secretly armed with the Spanish knife.—Priestly abominations too shocking and immodest to be related.

FATHER FRANCISCO, who was the Confessor of Poncheetee, was the Priest who obtained the reprieve of some of the robbers who were condemned for killing black people, and making sausages of them. This occurred just before, and at the time of my first coming to Havanna, about eight years ago. They were Spaniards, Frenchmen, Italians, and Portuguese, who belonged to the gang. They had their trial while I lived on the island, and were condemned. I saw twelve of them hung. There were about fifty belonging to the gang. Some were sent to the Spanish mines. Of those who were reprieved was the captain. He had a great deal of money; and with the former governor, and the Priests, money would save any person's life from the gallows.* I have frequently heard people say, that they carried on their robberies two years before they were detected. They lived about two miles

* Captain J. E. Alexander, in his tour through the West India islands, tells us that, " If a criminal has money, he may put off capital punishment for years, even after sentence is passed upon him; but he who is friendless and penniless, mounts the scaffold immediately after he has been found guilty of a capital offence." Alexander's TRANSATLANTIC SKETCHES, Vol. I. p. 357.—Ed.

out of the city, by the Montscrat gate. They used to
seek out the young, and fat negroes, to make up the sausages. Those who bought and eat them, said they were
the best they ever eat. They called them French sausages; and people far and near would buy them. They
were detected by two young negresses, who were sent out
according to the custom of the city, with dry goods, and
other articles for sale, in the streets, as is customary. One
of them was fat and young. They called her into the
house, pretending to want some of her goods; and told
the other to go along and sell. She waited opposite the
house sometime, for her companion to come out, until she
was tired; and then went to the door, to ask for her.
They told her she had gone out at the back door some
time since, which alarmed her, lest they had robbed her
of some of her goods, as it is not uncommon for the natives to call in those Mashons, who sell goods, to pilfer
them; and then the poor slaves are punished by their
master or mistress most cruelly for the loss. If they die
in consequence of their punishment, there is no law to
inquire how they come by their death.

The negress returned immediately to her mistress, and
told her about her companion's going into the house, and
not coming out again; and she took the commissaries,
together with the soldiers, who guard the city, and went
to the house, to demand her slave, without thinking she
was murdered. The commissaries saw all was not right,
and sent for more soldiers to help them. When they
reached the place, they found the girl in their slaughter-
room, with her head cut off, and a number of other dead
bodies, which they were cutting up. They took, at that
time, eighteen of the murderers, and confined them in
Moro castle; and numbers of the others were taken afterwards, and confined in this prison.

Father Francisco was one of the influential Priests,
who signed the request which was sent to Puerto Principe, and to the king of Spain, in order to obtain the reprieve of part of them. Those who were reprieved gave
immense sums of money to those that obtained their par-

don. The way I learned that Father Francisco had be-
friended them, was through Manuel. When he told me
that Francisco had got the power, and the will of Poncheetee's money, he added, that he was always fortunate
in getting hold of persons who had money, and mentioned
this instance of his befriending the cannibals in proof of
it. Father Francisco had been living with a Spanish
woman a great many years, and had a number of children
by her. Some of them were grown up, but their mother
had been crazy a number of years. I have heard the
Catholic ladies say, he had prayed all the curses of his
sin on her head, and that this was the cause of her being
crazy. I never saw the woman, although I often passed
their house; but I have seen the children. They lived
opposite St. Wanadou's Convent; and Father Francisco
was a great friend of Father P———, who was suspected
of murder, and was obliged to come to New-York, to remain until the Priests, his friends, had arranged for him
to return. Those Priests who had the most money, were
those who had the most influence and power; and those
who were the most wicked, obtained the most money.
I have heard that the former Bishop, who was deceased
about two years before I left the island, was in the habit
of signing papers, to favor the worst of criminals; but
when the latter Bishop came, who died of the cholera, it
was thought he would not be so favorable. I have heard
Manuel say, that the Priests generally did not like him so
well as the one deceased. He had been appointed Bishop
but a few months, before he died of the cholera. His
death occurred before my escape from Cuba.

I have witnessed, and gone through most horrid and
awful scenes, while living on the island, such as I dare
not and can not bring my mind to inform the world of.
The remembrance of them brings me to loathe myself,
and my past life, and brings me to feel what obligations I
am under to God, for sparing my life, and forbearing with
me, when I also was living in rebellion against him. Oh,
how plain I can see and feel his loving mercies, that he
has had for my poor immortal soul, in not cutting me off,

and sending my soul to everlasting wo; and in bringing me out from among them, and placing me among his chosen people in this Christian country; and in opening my blind eyes to see and seek the right way to save my poor immortal soul! Oh, that I may always have death, judgment, and eternity in my view! I know it cannot be long, (as this poor frail body is in a decline,) before my soul will go to Jesus. I have that faith, hope, and comfort, that when it is the Lord's will to call me, Blessed Jesus will guard my soul through the dark valley of death.

> When on my dying bed I lay,
> Lord! give me strength to sing and pray,
> And praise thee with my latest breath,
> Until my voice is lost in death.

Oh! that serious thought,—the Judgment-seat,—where my soul must shortly appear before a holy and just God; there to have all my wicked pilgrimage exposed, with all the wicked deeds that I have nourished and cherished in my wicked heart all my life! But now I cannot see God wronged, or the Blessed Jesus wounded, but my heart melts within me.

While I am writing an account of my dark and wicked pilgrimage, to be read aloud to this evil and gloomy world, it brings me to see and feel more clearly what a sinner I have been: and how merciful the Lord has been to me. Yes,—I can now look back, and see when I was in misery, in trials, and troubles, in a far and wicked country, I brought them upon myself. And I can see the blessed Lord was by me, and kept me from slipping down into the gulf of wo. I did not think so then. I saw many Crosses, and images of the Virgin Mary and the Saints, but it looked to me all like a show, until I was brought by the Lord to this Christian land.

While I was in Cuba I heard much about Purgatory and hell, and I felt sure they must all go there, when they died, for I could see, that instead of trying to save the people, they were encouraging them to go on in the broad road to destruction; and I felt, that if I died on the island with this Priest, I should certainly go with them. I felt as if I wanted to be a Christian, but did not know how. There was no Christian friend there, to take me by the hand, and show me the way to the Blessed Jesus. I was living with a man, who was leading me with himself, and all his people, down to the pit of wo.

As I have said, you may murder, steal, or lie, according to their doctrine, if, at the time, you have your heart fixed on the Virgin Mary, and go immediately to some Priest to Confess, and hear Mass read. Thus the criminal is set free, until he is detected by the law; and I have said it is not uncommon to hear, in the confession of a criminal who is to be hung, that he has taken the lives of many persons before he was detected. Manuel has often come home, during the day, and counted over the money he had gained by Confessing, and reading Masses for the dying. If any one had murdered or robbed, he would appear to rejoice in it, for the gain it brought him, and would say : " This has been a lucky day;—I have never seen so many Priests out Confessing as I have to-day."—And at other times, when their wicked duty was dull amongst them, he would say : " he wished the Bishop would send him to some other place, where there was more money to be made."—Many of the other Priests wanted to leave the island ; some wished to go to one part of America, and some to another ; and many to the Valley of the Mississippi.

Some appeared to have a greater desire to go to America, than to some of the Spanish islands, for they say they are very partial to the American females ; as you will see in Father Pies' letters, which he wrote to the American lady at the time she was living at Cuba. If I had those letters which I lost in my trunks, in coming here, they would show the same thing. These letters were written to me by different Priests while I was in Cuba, begging me to be their friend, and to take them to some lady ; perhaps to a married lady, or to a young and beautiful female, they had fallen in love with at church ; but I can appeal to my conscience, to my comfort, that I never did comply with their request. I used to hide their letters for the ladies, and lock them up; but I have often said to the Priests, that I had delivered them to the maiden, or married ladies, to whom they were addressed, when I had not.

While I am writing an account of my wicked pilgrimage, I can say, that the sin of leading or encouraging any of my own sex from the paths of virtue, I never have been guilty of. Whenever I was placed in snares of that kind, it would come to my mind, that I had a dear young sister, whom I had left behind.

I often told the Priests falsehoods, how the ladies received their affectionate notes; for they plagued me so much, I was obliged to do it; sometimes, to get rid of them; and, sometimes, to flatter them. I feel the loss of those letters, and some other writings, which were in my trunks; for, I have a great desire to convince this Christian land, how wicked those Priests truly are. I have heard Manuel and others say, in our social circles, and boast of it, that, whenever they put their eye on a handsome female, they wanted the power to get her, and gain their purposes; and to persuade her to go into the Convent, and take the veil.

I know many forms and ways they use, to effect their object, in destroying the innocence of virtuous females. One way they use, is to put young females on penances, unknown to their parents, in order to subdue them to their will. Delicacy must prevent my exposing all their intrigues of wickedness; one thing I will say, that these snares are laid for young girls of the first families. What would a mother think of a minister, to whom she was looking for instruction, who would tell her tales to obtain the ruin of a young and beautiful daughter, perhaps only twelve years of age?—for, among the poorer class of people, when the wicked Priest sees a young and beautiful girl, he will tell her mother, that he has a foresight and warning from the Saints, that so many crosses lie before her, and snares which she is to fall into, that she must immediately be given under his holy care. They will also

17

say, that these misfortunes will happen in such a year ; and at such a time they will be murdered, or will attempt to commit murder, or to rob, or something similar. Some of the females, especially the natives, from the highest to the lowest, will carry a knife in their stockings. The mother will then deliver her daughter up to the Priest, to look after her. She will be trained up by him ; and he will place Beads, and three Crosses, and the Gospel round her ;* and will be liberal towards the support of the whole family, until she is old enough to become his prey.†

* This Gospel-bag is a certain talisman or charm worn, suspended to a string or chain, around the neck. It consists of some verse of Scripture rolled up, and sewed in the bag. It is, indeed, a fair representation of the Gospel in the hands of Papists :—"*it is hidden :*—it is " *a book sealed.*"

There is another species of charm worn by almost every Papist, called the Scapular. This consists of two small pieces of cloth, which is also suspended to a string, and is worn around the neck. This is to protect them from all the accidents of life, from sudden death, from the power of the devil, and from hell. They are taught to believe, that the Scapular is a part of the Virgin Mary's dress, which, it is related, was actually presented by the Virgin herself, to one Simon Stock, on Mount Carmel. It is said, that the Virgin commanded him to establish a Monastery in her honor, and that she assured him, that whosoever should be found with a piece of that garment about him at the hour of death, should never go to hell, and that they should be delivered out of Purgatory on the first Friday after their decease. The Order was accordingly established, and it still subsists under the title of the Order of the Carmelites.

In order, however, to reap the highest benefits to be derived from this charm, they are taught, that if they are not addicted to mortal sins, and have no habitual attachment to venial sins, their souls will be received into heaven, by the Virgin, immediately after death, without being detained at all in Purgatory. To gain this Indulgence, however, they are bound daily to recite a certain number of prayers to the Virgin ; otherwise, they would still have to suffer in Purgatory until Friday.

For the proof that such, and precisely such, is the doctrine of the Romish church, on the subject of the Scapular, I refer to the " HISTORY OF THE SCAPULAR," which they all have in their own hands. I point to no one in particular, but to any one whatsoever, since they are all substantially alike.

It is very apropos, while we are on this subject, to state, that I was once, while a Papist, dupe enough to believe all the absurdities of the doctrine respecting the Scapular. I wore it constantly during many years ; and I was firmly persuaded that, if I died with it about me, I should not be lost ; and that I would infallibly be delivered from Purgatory on the first Friday after my decease.—ED.

† The Popish Priests, if their church is the infallible church, cannot

I was well acquainted with a little girl of sixteen, that my Priest had plunged into vice by measures of this kind,

consistently be blamed either by any of their Bishops, their Popes, or their people, for having, at least, one fair object in the place of a lawful wife. They cannot consistently blame them, I say, since, by their own Council of Toledo, in the 17th Canon, it was declared, that any person, Clergyman or layman, who has not a wife, but a concubine, is not to be repelled from the Communion, if he be content with one. "Christiano habere licitum est unam tantum aut uxorem aut certe loco uxoris, concubinam." Pithou, 47. Bin. 1, 739, 740. Crabb, 1, 449. Gian. V. 5. Dachery, 1, 528. Canis. 2. 111. The Bishops, indeed, would not allow two women to one man, but any one might keep either a wife or a Mistress. This liberality of the Council of Toledo, was afterwards confirmed by the Head of the church, Pope Leo. Bin. I. 737.

This indulgence of the Council, and the Pope, has been inserted in the Canon Law of the Romish church, edited by Gratian and Pithou. Gratian's compilation of the Canon Law, it is true, was a private production, unauthenticated by any Pope; but that of Pithou was published by the command of Gregory XIII., whose work contains the Canon Law as acknowledged by the Romish church. Dist. 34. C. 4. Pithou, 47. Thus, we see, that fornication is sanctioned by a Spanish Council, a Roman Pontiff, and the Canon Law.

Fornication, in this manner, was, in the Clergy, not only tolerated, but also preferred to matrimony. Many of the Popish casuists, such as Costerus, Pigius, Hosius, Campeggio, and those reported by Agrippa, raised whoredom above wedlock in the Hierarchy. Costerus admits, that a Clergyman sins, if he commits fornication; but more heinously if he marry. Concubinage, this Jesuit grants, is sinful, but less aggravated, he maintains, than marriage. Costerus was followed by Pigius and Hosius. Campeggio proceeded to still greater extravagancy. He represented a Priest, who became a husband, as committing a more grievous transgression, than if he should keep many domestic harlots. "Gravius peccat si contrahat matrimonium." Cost. C. 15. The Cardinal gives an odd reason for his theory. The Clergyman, he affirms, who perpetrates whoredom, acts from a persuasion of its rectitude or legality; while the other knows, and acknowledges, his criminality. "Quod sacerdotes fiant mariti multo esse gravius peccatum quam si plurimas domi meretrices alunt. Nam illos habere persuasum quasi recte faciant, hos autem scire et peccatum agnoscere." Campeg. in Sleidan, 96. Edgar.

We learn also from Agrippa, "that the Clergy who married, were dismissed from the exercise of the sacred functions; while the Sacerdotal fornicators, who violated the laws of God and man, were allowed to retain the holy ministry." Agrippa in Bayle, I. 111.

Thuanus, the famous Popish historian, writing on this subject, says, that "it is absurd indeed, that Priests should be suspended from the exercise of their functions on account of getting married, while whoremongers, who violate both the laws of God and man, are tolerated." Thuan. 2, 417.—ED.

before I knew her. About a year after he had ruined her, she took the small-pox, which disfigured her, and he left her. Father Hosa, who went to the Valley of the Mississippi, as you will see in my Narrative, was guilty of the crime of ruining a young girl of fourteen, by gaining the consent of her parents to his training her up. She died in child-birth, about two years after. I have heard him talk about her, and say, if the child had lived, and been a girl, what he would have done for her. I have seen her mother often at Poncheetee's house, where she would mourn much about her, and say, she never could rest, her child was always before her. She was continually having Masses read, candles burning, and the body of her child laid by some Priest. She was a superstitious Catholic, like Poncheetee, her friend. I could relate a number of circumstances of this kind, which I have been eye-witness of, and of others my Priest has told me, but their cruelty and immodesty are such, as to make me cover them from the public eye: they would hardly be believed, and they cannot be told.*

* "How many soever of the members of the Church be dead and impious," (say the Popish divines,) "so long as there is any one man that retains holiness, the Church must be called holy." Costerus, Enchirid. L. III. C. 7.

Therefore, the Romish church is holy, notwithstanding all the filth she contains :—is true, in spite of all the errors which she propagates : —is a Dove, although every Pastor of her flock is a ravenous Vulture : —provided, however, that "*one man* can be found that retains holiness."—ED.

CHAPTER XIX.

"There's not a hollow cave, nor lurking place,
No vast obscurity, or misty vale,
Where bloody murder, or detested rape,
Can couch for fear, but I will find them out;
And in their ear tell them my dreadful name,
Revenge, which makes the foul offenders quake."

SHAKSPEARE.

*The " Groting," or public execution of a lady twenty-one years of age.—
The Priests get her money.— The burning of red candles on her husband's head.— The relation of her extraordinary case.— She kills her
husband, cuts up his body, and packs it in a barrel.— Is betrayed by her
god-mother.—A Priest attends at her execution: his singular costume.—
The Priest terrified by a black cat.*

Now I will inform you about a married lady, twenty-
one years of age, whom I saw "*groted*," while I was living on the island. They do not hang white convicts,
but they are placed on a scaffold, in a chair, and strangled
by an iron collar put round their necks.* This law was
made by the queen of Spain, to distinguish the whites
from the blacks. Sometimes a rich man will commit murder; in this case the Priests will fare well; for they will
get money from the criminal for candles, Masses, and
praying his soul out of Purgatory. They think it is not
so much disgrace to be *groted*, as to be hung.

This lady was born and educated in Havanna. Her
parents were very wealthy, and natives of Old Spain.
Her name was Mariettee. Her parents compelled her to
marry a Catalan Spaniard against her will; for she wanted
to marry a Spanish officer. The Catalan Spaniard had a
very dark complexion, his name was Roupee, and he was
very rich. Before this young lady would marry him, she
was put under heavy penances by a Capuchin Friar of

---

* The convict sets upright in the chair. A board runs up behind his
back, to a height above his head. The iron collar runs through the
board and round his neck. The pressure is applied by means of a
screw in the iron collar behind the board: as the screw is pressed home
the collar tightens, and strangles the criminal.

17*

the name of Father Sobrisco. Manuel did not tell me what those penances were ; but I have heard, in cases of this kind, they are very cruel, and sometimes death. Mariettee lived a dreadful life with her husband three years ; for she loved this officer, and was in the habit of seeing him often, and her husband knew of it. She was in the habit of having Masses read by different Priests, and having red candles burning upon her husband's head. Manuel told me she had been a number of times to him for Masses and candles ; and that it was expected, by a number of Priests, she would destroy her husband in some way.

It was said this officer had agreed to help her to murder him ; and the night was appointed for him to be there. During the day, she put laudanum into her husband's wine, to make him sleepy ; and when night came, he was quite stupid from the effect of the laudanum and wine ; and went to bed. The officer went to her house, and she got all arranged for the murder ; but he would not stay, and went away, promising to return shortly. She waited ;—and as he did not come, she, being alone, with the servants asleep in a back room, thought it was the only time, and stabbed him with a knife in several places, as he was asleep, stupified with the laudanum. He made no noise, and after she had killed him, she cut him up, and put him into a barrel, as had been agreed on by the officer and herself ; and he was to send some soldiers, who were to take the barrel outside the walls, and cast it into the sea. But he did not send ; and she waited till day-light, and then went to her god-mother, and told her what she had done ; and begged her to send some of her servants, to put it into the sea for her ; which her god-mother told her she would do. She then told her to go home, and not to Confess to any Priest. Her god-mother, in the meantime, sent to the commissaries, and told them what she had heard, and they went to the house, and found her smoking a cigar in the bed-room. They found no blood in the room, but the barrel was there, with her husband cut up in it.

She immediately confessed all to the commissaries; and was taken and put into prison. All the Priests fared well for Masses and candles, as she had a great many rich friends. The Priests got a good deal of money from them, as well as from her. It was commonly said by the Priests, that she would not be *groted,* she had so many rich friends; and there were petitions sent to the king and queen of Spain, to have her reprieved, or transported to some part of Spain, signed by the Bishop, Priests, and natives of Cuba, as her friends. The ladies of the nobility thought it would be a disgrace, to have her publicly executed, she being a native of Cuba. Her friends gave a great deal of money to the Priests, and to some of the civil officers. But the queen would not reprieve her, and she was *groted.*

I saw her in the procession, which was an awful scene to witness. She was placed in the chair, which was to be set on the scaffold, dressed in white; and appeared to be lifeless. Father Pies was walking close by her side, dressed in a white habit with Beads, Crosses, and an image representing our Saviour, hung about him: a prayer-book in one hand; and in the other, a long gilded pole, with a large Cross, and a candle burning at the end. The pole and Cross were trimmed with black crape; and Father Pies was saying prayers for her. In processions of this kind, there are always about fifty men, who live in the Convents, as waiters to the Priests, dressed in black habits, and a kind of turban of black crape on the head, with poles, and Crosses, and candles, carried in their hands before them. When the procession passes outside the walls of the city, at the Pontra gate, where there are soldiers stationed, sometimes there will be a table placed there, covered with white, having death-candles burning, and Crosses laid upon it; and sometimes a Virgin Mary is seated at this table, dressed in black. This is when the person to be hung is rich, or has rich friends.

In bringing this most horrible scene to my mind, it makes me feel more sensible of its horrors, than when I witnessed it; for when you live in a country, where there are so many scenes and crimes of this kind, you get hardened to them. I have been laughed at by Manuel and others, for the effect it would have upon me; and they would say, they did not think before this, that a Protestant had any feeling. I did not then know what they meant by insisting that I was a Protestant. I have often been persecuted by my Priest, because he said I knew, and would not own of what religion I was. The friends of Mariettee gave what property she and her husband had, to the Capuchins of St. Philippee Convent, which I was told by my Priest, was to pay the Priests for praying their souls out of Purgatory. I never heard that the officer was taken, or done any thing with.

As all these dreadful scenes are now before my mind, I will tell you what took place at my house, the night after I saw her *groted*. Several Priests had been at my house that night, to supper. They talked a great deal about Mariettee, and of her guilt, and other crimes of a similar kind. Being drowned in superstition, in the belief of forerunners, and ghosts, and Purgatory, I was afraid of myself, and of every body about me. After they had gone, about twelve o'clock at night, I was waked up by a large black cat, which had got into the house in some way. Manuel would have some candles always burning in the bedroom, above which candles, he placed an image representing our Saviour, hung on a string of beads, and the Gospel-bag, and a prayer book on the table. He would also put his knife under his pillow, to defend himself from robbers; for, in a citizen's dress, he would always fear them; but he was not afraid, when dressed in his Holy Habit. As the room was light, when I heard the noise, I looked up, and saw the black cat by my bed side, and I cried out to my Priest for help; but he was speechless from fright. I really thought it was the Old Adversary himself, come to take us both off. We both remained in this awful condition, till day-light. Sometimes the cat would be in my room, and sometimes in the parlor, making a most horrid cry. I never knew, till then, how much Priests feared and hated cats. Manuel informed me, that the Priests dislike cats ; and what a time it used to make, if a cat got into the Convents ;* and how they would instantly drive them out, and sprinkle the Convent with Holy Water, lest death would follow. They do not dislike dogs ; but are generally very fond of them.

I have mentioned this occurrence, to show what a superstitious state of feelings, both his and mine was. The fright actually made him sick for a number of days ; and he never went to bed, another night, without a good look out that there were no cats in the house.

---

* The aversion to black cats is not peculiar to the Roman Priesthood of Cuba. From a relation given by the author of SHIP AND SHORE, we find that sailors also are somewhat affected with odd notions about black cats. Speaking on this subject, he says, "This restless domestic is looked upon by the sailor, especially when afflicted with a black visage, with no kindly or tolerant feelings. There is no bad luck about the ship, which is not ascribed to some evil influence, which she is supposed to exercise. Hence, in a storm, or dead calm, poor tab has a tremendous responsibility. Our unfortunate puss had been taken on board at Malaga, and since her embarkation we had not been visited by one favorable breeze. This calamity was attributed to her universally among the crew. There needed no language to tell what their sentiments were, for as poor puss came upon deck, so far from being petted, she encountered every where looks of the most threatening aversion. 'Never,' said an old tar to me, 'did any good come to a ship that had a black cat in its concern. I have sailed,' he continued, ' on every sea, and in every kind of craft, and I never yet knew a ship make a good voyage, that went to sea on Friday, or had on board one of these black imps. These are facts, sir ; land lubbers may laugh at them, but they are facts, and true as my name is John Wilkins.' It was no use to question the convictions of the seaman's experience ; he was as confident and deeply earnest as a man testifying to the indisputable evidence of his senses. So poor tab went overboard."—ED.

CHAPTER XX.

———————— " He strewed
The path that led to hell with tempting flowers,
And in the ear of sinners, as they took
The way of death, he whispered. peace ! he swore
Away all love of lucre, all desire
Of earthly pomp; and yet a princely seat
He liked, and to the clink of Mammon's box
Gave most rapacious ear."

POLLOK.

Manner of the Priests' begging for the Convents.—Money stolen to pay for Masses.—The Priest gives his Mistress the money, which had been stolen to pay for a Mass.—Jealousy about the fees for Confession.—Various benedictions, and their prices.—Funeral, and other prayers, with their prices.—The Priest's money is considered blessed.—Sin to pay money without Crossing one's self.—Every action to be consecrated by Crossing one's self.—The Priests change their dress to gallant the females.—Two of the Priests sent as criminals to Spain.—The sudden and suspicious death of the Bishop.

I WILL here mention the way the Priests beg for their Convents, and churches. Men are continually passing and repassing, from eight o'clock in the morning, till six in the evening, every day, dressed in the Priests' old habits, with a small box, carried in the hand; on the front of which box the Virgin Mary is drawn on paper, and decorated with artificial flowers. They beg in this way, for money for the church :* or if any Priest is dangerously sick in the Convent, his likeness will be drawn, lying on a cot-bed, and placed on the box. The money given into the box, is to pay for ·Masses and candles for the sick Priest. The money is dropped into the box through a narrow hole; and the Priests keep the key. If a person has no money, he must take the box, Cross him-

---

* Cicero, in his book of laws, restrains this practice of begging, or gathering alms, to one particular order of Pagan Priests; and he allows it only on certain days; because, as he says, "it propagates superstition, and impoverishes families." Cicero de Legibus, Lib. 2. 8. 16;—which, by the way, shows us the policy of the church of Rome in the great care they have taken to multiply their begging orders; which, in Europe, are numerous.—ED.

XX.]

self, and kiss the image of the Virgin on the box. If he gives money, he must Cross himself, and kiss the image, after he drops the money in.

There is also a man out three days before any one is hung, or *groted*, begging for money, in charity, to give the Priests for Masses and candles, to be read and burned for the saving of the criminal's soul. The beggar is dressed in a black habit, with a small pole about five feet long, with a large silver Cross at the end, and a large silver plate in his hand. If it is a white man that is to suffer death, the pole is painted white; and black, if a black man. It is a white man that begs for a white man; and a colored, for a colored man. In either case the beggar is always accompanied by a Priest. When they give, they believe the Priest can pray the criminal's soul out of Purgatory, or, that they have such influence with the Saints, and the Virgin Mary, that their sufferings will be light. When begging is made for the Priests, no Priest goes along; for the boxes are made in such a way, that the beggar cannot take any money out, neither must he receive any; but the giver must Cross himself, and drop it into the box. Sometimes, however, the beggar never returns to the Convent with the box. But when they beg for a convict, the money is put into the plate, and the Priest is by to watch it. They have from fifteen to twenty men, begging every day, for each Convent. The money, they say, is to pay for the Holy Candles they burn in the Convent. The lowest prices for Masses and Confessing, for white people, is one dollar; fifty cents for colored persons. They cannot receive less than that, or its value.

When Manuel saw any change lying loose about my room, he would caution me, and say, " my servant would take it, and think it no sin, if she went to some Priest and Confessed."

When I told him I did not believe my servant would take any thing, he would tell me not to be too sure; for if she did, and came to him to Confess, he would not tell me of it, or injure the girl. I lost a very costly belt-buckle, set round with diamonds, which was given me by a

Marquis' lady, shortly after I was robbed, which I valued much; but never thought my girl took it. I had several presents sent me after I was robbed, by very wealthy ladies, some of whom I never saw. One gave me a set of diamond ear-rings, which were in my trunk, which I lost in coming from Philadelphia to New York. This present was, probably, because she heard my ear-rings were violently torn out by the robbers. Another sent me a doubloon wrapped up in a piece of paper.

There were two large leather covered trunks, marked with brass nails, one A. G. the other R. C. In the trunks were a number of letters, some of which were for persons in New York; and many of them were old letters addressed to me. Fine linen, and costly dresses, filled the trunks; such as are common among the wealthy of Havanna, but are very rare in this country. I note these facts in hopes that some of the contents of those trunks may yet be found, to confirm the accuracy of this Narrative, and to throw further light upon the works of Roman darkness and Priestcraft. I then told him I believed the girl had taken it, and given it to him for Masses. I did not believe it; but I was angry at the loss of the buckle, and at him, for telling me, that if she had stolen any thing from me, and she should Confess it to him, he would not tell me. Then he called the girl, and asked her who was her Father-Confessor. She replied, Father Antonia, of St. Augustine's Convent. Manuel knew him, and went and asked him, and learned that he had had it at one time, in his possession, and that my girl had given it to him for a Mass; but he had given it to his Mistress. Manuel made me promise never to mention it to the girl; and said Father Antonia would charge her never to take any thing from me again. When I asked him, why he did not wish me to mention it to the girl, he said, Father Antonia was a friend of his, and the girl would then go to some other Priest to Confess, and Antonia would lose the fees of Confession. For the Priests think as much of having a large number of penitents on their Confession list, as any newspaper publisher thinks of having a long list of subscribers. The Priests are very jealous of one another. The honorable among them, are particularly careful to do nothing that seems like taking from another Father-Confessor, his penitents. I was obliged to submit to this : and never said a word to the girl about it, but kept her. trusting more to the charge of Father Antonia, never to take any thing from me again, than to her honesty.

The price for blessing a house you are going to move into, or a new house, that is, to sprinkle Holy Water, with prayer, and read a Mass in every room, is one *ounce*, or seventeen dollars :—for saying a few words in Latin over a corpse, two dollars :—for going to a house to bless the sick or well, (they Cross them on the stomach, sprinkle them with Holy Water, and say Mass,) four dollars :—for going to burn out evil spirits from a house, (that is, to burn incense with prayer and a Mass, and Holy Water in every room,) four dollars. Nothing less can be taken for these blessings: but the rich always give more. When I have been paying money for any little thing to poor people, who knew with whom I was living, they would say they liked to take money from me, *for it was blessed ;* and when they took it, they would Cross themselves, and put it by itself. Manuel would tell me it was a sin to pay money without Crossing one's self. I never knew him to give away money, or any thing else, without Crossing himself, and saying some word in Latin. When I first went to live with him, I laughed at his rules, until he brought me into fear of him. A Priest or Catholic never enters or leaves a house, without Crossing himself ; and when gaping, he Crosses his mouth. Manuel would never put on, or take off his habit, without Crossing himself ; but he was never so particular with his citizen's dress.

The rule is for them, never to wear a citizen's dress. when they have once taken the habit ; also, never to ride in a carriage with any lady, or walk with one in the streets. When they once take their habits, they vow never to leave them ; but they are not particular, when they have broken their rules by putting on a citizen's dress, to break it again by riding or walking with a lady in the

18

streets. Manuel has often reproved me for not Crossing myself, when paying, or receiving any thing, or gaping; which practice through fear I learned, and got such a habit of it, that it was some time after I came to this Christian country, before I could break myself of it. How many lonely hours have I reflected on these past scenes! and how I have been brought through, seeing and hearing all these superstitious and wicked rules! You will see, in some after part of my Narrative, how the Cross which the Capuchin Priest put round my neck, at the time he christened me, worried me at the time I was under deep conviction.

I feel as if I had a right and privilege, to express my thoughts about the conduct and principles of the Priests, then living on the island of Cuba. Whatever the result may be to Manuel Canto, the Priest I lived with, when my Narrative comes out, to be read to the world; (it has already been read in heaven, where I must shortly appear at the judgment seat; and it will all be presented before me,) I think, from what I know about them, the result will be this;—he will be privately sent to Spain, or to the Pope; not but what all the Priests know themselves to be just as wicked; and, I believe, some are more wicked, although they may not have acted exactly as he has done: but some are deeper in seductions, and other snares and traps of wickedness. The only difference I think there is in the case, is, that Manuel is the individual through whom the information comes out. He has not only exposed his own wickedness, under the cloak of a Holy Habit, but theirs also. Oh, how little have I been able to expose the many dark and gloomy places and corners which they have in the Convents, that I know nothing about, except what they themselves have told me!— They are all, however, known to God.

During the time I was living with this Priest on the island, there were two Priests sent privately away to Spain. I never learned exactly all the particulars of what they had done to their religion, in exposing it; but they had done something of this kind, and they were kept prisoners in the Convents several months, before they were sent to Spain.* They were confined in some cells, to which no communication could be had, but by the Superior of the Convent. One belonged to St. Francisco Convent, of the name of Ferdinand; the other belonged to St. Domingo Convent, whose name I did not know, or have forgotten it. I used to hear my Priest lament, and say rash things about the old Bishop, and some Priests who were the Superiors of other Convents. Before they were sent away, neither the Priests, the prisoners, nor any one, except the Bishop and the head Priests of the Convents, knew that they were going to be sent away to Spain, until the very hour of the day the vessel was to sail; and, when they were taken on board by soldiers, as criminals, they did not wish to have it known. I asked my Priest what they would do with them, when they were in Spain. He said he did not know, but I could see by his countenance, he dreaded something horrible. He often spoke about them in conversation with the other Priests, who came to my house; and he informed me, with regret, the very day they were sent away, charging me not to mention it to any one.

How much more of their wickedness I could have learned from Manuel, if, at that time, I had any desire to

* To such a notorious pitch of licentiousness the Popish Clergy had arrived, at the time when Pope Benedict XIV. sat upon the throne, that this Sovereign Pontiff, (as St. Ligori himself tells us,) was under the necessity of issuing a Decree, in order to put a check to the continual and multiplied accusations which were laid by the people against the Clergy. The Decree ends as follows:—" If any one soever dare to infringe or disobey this our will and command, let him know that he will incur the wrath of Almighty God, and of the blessed Apostles, Peter and Paul.—Given at Rome, in the church of Holy Mary the Great, in the year of the Incarnation of the Lord, 1741." Ligor. Theol. de Rom. Pont. Dec. C. II. Dec. 1.

Such was the fixed determination of the *Holy Father*, that the people should not accuse the Clergy of their nefarious deeds, that he forbids " any Priest whatsoever to give them absolution, except in the article of death." Id. ib.

" The Clergy are by no means subject to the civil law," says the same Saint. Ligor. Theol. de Privilegies, C. II. N. 18. The Canon Law, St. Thomas Aquin, Bellarmine, Dens, and all the Popish Divines, without exception, teach the same doctrine.—ED.

know, cannot be told now.   When he brought his friends, among the other Priests, to the house, I have heard them consult about the affairs of different Priests, in the Convents, and about their late Bishop, who died of the cholera.   He was appointed but a short time before he died, but, as I said, it is all known to God.   The Bishop who died of the cholera did not suit the Priests at all. They were sure he would not continue long in his office. He died unexpectedly to the people, and was buried privately, which led the people to talk much about it, when they compared his unknown burial with the funeral of the old Bishop, which was so splendid.

CHAPTER XXI.

"He was a wolf in clothing of the lamb,
That stole into the fold of God, and on
The blood of souls, which he did sell to death,
Grew fat; and yet, when any would have turned
Him out, he cried, 'Touch not the Priest of God.'"
                                        POLLOK.

The Priest in disguise.—The Convents a harbor for robbers and murderers.—The criminal refugees in the Convents cannot be apprehended by the officers of the civil law.—By day, the criminals lie concealed in the Convents, and by night, prowl the streets.— The Priests are well paid for screening criminals in the Convents.— The Priests rob one another even when dying.—An account of a Priest and his chest of Money.— Suspicious exit of inmates of the Convents.—Robbing a Priest synonymous with robbing the Church.— The Priests, when superannuated by vice and dissipation, are employed in the Convents as domestics.— To be good, in Spanish Popery, signifies to be wealthy.— The effects of Priestly vice conspicuous in the disfiguration of their faces.—Priest testifies against Priest, that he is possessed of the devil.—Priest turned fortune-teller ; he makes the people kiss his frogs, scorpions, and devils.— The Bouquet or picture to frighten profligate Priests into virtuous ones.— The awful impressions made by seeing the Bouquet, made instrumental in determining Rosamond to escape from Cuba.

I WILL mention here, that they have a Catholic Priest living in Havanna, and one in Matanzas, who are of Irish descent.   Their duty is to Confess, and instruct their own country people, or any foreigners, who live in Havanna. The one in Havanna does not live in a Convent with the other Priests ; but in a house alone ; neither does he wear a habit, nor have his head shaved.   The only thing by which you can know him to be a Priest, when you meet him in the street, is the stock he wears, made of different colors, either blue or white, in stripes.   His name is Father Bailey.

I have seen him, but had no acquaintance with him. I am not afraid to say, from what I have heard from the Priests, that their Convents harbor gentlemen, and sons of the nobility, who have robbed or stabbed any one, or done something of this kind.   Their parents or friends can put them into the Convent, to remain ; so that they

18*

are not taken by the officers of the civil law ;* and they will come out at night, in disguise, to see their friends, and remain all the day in the Convents. I mention this to let you know, what the Priests will do for money. I have heard from some of the Priests, that they will even rob each other of money.†

There was a Priest, who died in St. Francisco Convent, at the time I was living on the island, an elderly man, of the name of Father Sedoha, who died in a consumption, after an illness of about two years. He had a large sum of money, which he kept in an iron chest. I do not know the amount of his money, but my Priest said it was a large amount. He kept it by the side of his bed, and, for several months before he died, he used to count it over, for fear some one had robbed him. A few weeks before he died, he became delirious; and he still continued counting it over. When he died, it was all missing.

---

* In Popish countries, the churches, Monasteries, and Cardinal's palaces, are a sure refuge from the law. " A man guilty of the greatest crimes," (says Petrarch,) "had only to take refuge in the court of a Cardinal's palace, and he could not be pursued by justice." Dob. Petrarch, L. VI. P. 451.

Middleton, in his " LETTERS FROM ROME," writes as follows:—" The Popish Asylums are continually open, not to receive strangers, but to shelter villains; so that it may literally be said of these, what our Saviour said of the Jewish temple, ' That they have turned the House of prayer into a den of thieves.'" Matt. xxi. 13.—Middleton's Letters, 215. —ED.

† This Priestly trait of robbing or stealing from one another, is by no means to be limited to the island of Cuba. Such conduct I have frequently witnessed among them in the United States. They stole from me, when I was one of their number, and I have known them frequently to steal from one another. One of them, a certain Rev. Mr. K——, with a false key, entered the room of one of his comrade Priests, during his absence on a missionary tour, broke open several of his trunks and boxes, and robbed him of various articles to a considerable amount. The Priest returned, missed the articles that were stolen, suspicion fell upon the guilty, search was made, and some of the things stolen were found in the possession of his Reverence Mr. K——. I, myself, was one of those who made the search; therefore, I can personally testify to the truth of what I state.

For a fuller detail of this transaction, I refer to the 52d Number of the 1st Volume, and to the 1st Number of the 2d Volume of the " DOWN-FALL OF BABYLON," a weekly paper, published by myself, in the city of New York.—ED.

The Superiors of the Convent made a great stir about it, and a number of Priests were suspected of having taken it, and Manuel among the number. At this time, Manuel told me, that occasions of this kind frequently took place in the Convents. They would rob from each other even when dying. They never are robbed by their servants; for when they are sick, their servants are not allowed to wait on them. The Priests wait on each other.

I believe, from what I have heard and seen amongst them, that many a poor man whom the Priests will get into the Convents, to be their servant, will be suddenly missing, without any one but the Priests knowing where he is, or what has become of him; but it is known to God. A servant, who attends the Priests, is more obedient and humble, than a poor slave, in serving and aiding them in all their wickedness. I have been eye-witness of some of the wickedness of their servants; but they appear to do it in fear. Sometimes the Priests are robbed by their *Alcowaters* of their citizen's clothes, when they are taking them to, or bringing them from their houses. The Priest cannot leave the Convent in a citizen's dress. When they have robbed a Priest in this way, and the Priests pursue them, they do not tell what they have been robbed of, but will say, the *Alcowaters* have robbed the Church; and when they are taken, they punish them cruelly.*

I will mention here what I know of some of the old Priests, who were living in the Convents, and who had formerly been Priests of high standing in their churches; but through dissipation and wicked vices, were laid aside.†

---

* This is striking,—and shows how well the Authoress was versed in the technical quaintness of Jesuitism. She was thoroughly initiated into the mysterious subtleties of Priestcraft, or this idea would never have glanced across her mind.—How simple; how unaffected; and yet how wonderfully varied are the facts which she discloses!—ED.

† Cardinal Bellarmine, describing the degeneracy of the Priesthood, in the days in which he lived, the 17th century, and contrasting it with the holiness of the primitive times, represents the answer they would be wont to make him, as follows:—"But we are no longer in those days," (some of you will say,) ' and things are entirely changed.'—I grant that

They were still maintained in the Convent. Some of them were employed as door-keepers; others, in keeping the Convent clean, and various other offices, as they were old and decrepit. They were permitted to wear the old habits. I have heard it remarked of them, by Catholics of good standing, when seeing them pass in the street, as they go on commissions for the Superior Priests, (and you can tell them by their old and faded habits, they look poor and forsaken,) it would be remarked: "Look at that poor Father! but a short time since, *he was* a good man!"*

time has effected great changes, both in discipline and morals; but the obligation is always the same.

"The little circumspection, and the great facility with which *Holy Orders!* are now-a-days conferred, is the reason why the Clergy is crowded with those who aspire to be Priests; not, that God alone may be their portion; but for the sake of placing themselves *above the control of the civil jurisdiction;* or in order to have wherewithal to live upon; or in the hope of being promoted to the dignities of the Church.

"Hence it is, that we see Priests reduced to a shameful state of beggary, and going from door to door, seeking for sustenance. Others, again, we see, who by their enormous crimes, dishonor their character, and oblige the civil authorities to condemn them, some to the galleys, and others to perpetual imprisonment. Let us beg of God, said St. Gregory, the tears of Jeremiah; and exclaim with grief, '*How has the gold lost its lustre!*'

"In ancient times, public penances were not laid upon the Priests, whatever might have been their crimes, for fear of tarnishing in the least degree, the glory of the Priesthood. If they deserved some signal punishment, their resource was *to confine them in the Monasteries*, that they might there expiate their faults. But now we find them among the most abandoned villains, in the dungeons, and the galleys." Bellarm. 3 Opusc. Lib. II. C. 5.—Ed.

* This reminds me of something I observed when I was in France, which may very appropriately be introduced here, by way of illustration. The Papists, in that country, are so habitually trained to connect the idea of holiness with that of levity, frivolity, and dissipation, that, when they wish to express,—a man is good or holy,—they say, "*Il est gaie*,"—"HE IS LIVELY."—This levity, and frivolity of disposition, which is so peculiarly characteristic of the French, is to them the only criterion by which to judge of a man's piety.—If he is not "*gay*," as they call it, he cannot be pious, let him, in other respects, be what he may. Lost indeed, and Priest-ridden, must be a people whose sentiments can be so warped as to substitute frivolity and dissipation for true piety! Well did Addison, alluding to Popish France, exclaim; "that trifling nation!"—

In France, then, to be gay and trifling, is to be pious.—
Among the Spaniards, to be pious, is to be wealthy.—

And another would say:—"Why, I know him;—I have gone to him to Confess, and to have Masses read!"—The people would sometimes call them in, and treat them with wine and cigars; and give them money. They would appear to feel very sorry for them, and to pity them; but not to feel as if they were wicked and had done wrong.

I was spending the day in a Spanish family, when an elderly Priest, about sixty years of age, came in. He belonged to St. Wanadou Convent. They called him Father Antonia. I was informed by this family, that he had been a Priest, beloved and worshiped by his people. The lady told me she had known him many years, when he stood high, and she had often gone to him for Masses and to Confess; but through dissipation, and other vices, he was laid aside. He was a dreadful object to look at, both on account of the old age, and a disease he was labouring under which disfigured his face. From the time he entered the house, until he left, he never spoke on any subject without Crossing himself. In talking over former days, when he stood, as a Priest, respected and worshiped by his people, he mourned, and appeared to feel deeply his fallen situation.—He cried like a child.—But I do not know whether he was mourning for his sins, or for the loss of his character, and the confidence of the people. Often, when any of the Priests asked my Priest, if he knew Father Antonia, of St. Wanadou Convent, he would reply that he did; and that he was a wicked man; and he believed he had made a league with the devil, and could put a spell and a curse on any one. The Priests were all afraid to displease him, and were obliged to give

In China, Popish piety is interwoven with heathenish idolatry, and the Virgin, their "*Regina cœlorum*," is rolled along upon a car, and worshiped, in order to reconcile Christianity with Pagan superstition.—Popery is every thing, or any thing;—truth and piety excepted.

Middleton, in his "LETTERS FROM ROME," observes, that "the toleration of Pagan prejudices, and mixing Christ with it by the policy of the Papists, however useful, at first, the Papists might pretend it was for reconciling Heathens to Christianity, seems, now, to be the readiest way to drive Christians back again to Paganism." Middleton's Letters, p. 223.—ED.

him any little thing he asked for in the Convent. His living was of the best that could be procured in St. Wanadou. Neither would he eat, but in a room by himself. Manuel also told me this Father Antonia had, at one time, an immense amount of money left to him, by different individuals, who died, and left their property to have their souls prayed out of Purgatory; but, he became acquainted with a French lady, who had ruined him, and made him poor. He told me, too, that he believed, he had left the religion of the Holy Catholic Church, and had made a league with the devil. He spoke with all sincerity; and no doubt, believed in the truth of what he said.

I knew another Priest, who was called Father Gosha, of St. Domingo Convent, who was once a Priest of high standing, and was almost worshiped by his people. Through the effects of dissipation, and other vices, which disfigured his features, he was laid aside, but was still supported in the Convent. He used to tell fortunes, and to sell things to conjure with. He is known all over the city and the country. People, far and near, would send for him, to have their fortunes told; and he made money by it. He was a very elderly man, and walked with a crutch. I have sent for him to tell my fortune, at a friend's house, as I dare not admit him to my own, because he was so well known by all the Priests. He carried with him a box containing Crosses, images representing our Saviour, and the devil, made of brass, and live lizards, and scorpions; and small frogs, in vials; all mixed up in the box together. These he would oblige you to kiss, and make you Cross yourself, before he would commence telling your fortune. He would still wear an old Priest's habit; but was not permitted to shave his head, as formerly. I mention this to shew, what wickedness has brought these poor Priests to in their old age; as well as the wickedness they do in their old age. They are not laid aside, until they become disfigured with disease.

They are always permitted to return to duty in their Priestly office, so long as they can be cured of disease,

PRIEST TURNED FORTUNE-TELLER.

without the loss of any feature. And I have often heard Manuel say; "such and such a Priest will receive his *bouquet* to-day;"—or, that he had been to see such a Priest, or such a Priest, who was confined by disease; and that, among other things, he said to him; "Be patient;—to-morrow, or in a day or two, you will receive your *bouquet*."—Every Convent is said to have a room set apart to sufferers of this unhappy description;—and its inmates are not allowed to put on their habits until they have received the *bouquet*.

I never saw but one *bouquet;*—and that, Manuel was sorry for having showed me, because it filled me with such awful impressions of my own doom. A friend of his loaned him one that he had from the Superior of the Convent, on Confession, and for a remembrance to re strain his passions. It was a drawing representing the countenance of the Priest getting well, on a body, gouty, swelled, and disfigured. Cherubs guarded the gouty Priest's head. Before him stood the representation of a beautiful female dressed in the highest fashion, at whom he sorrowfully gazed. She seemed to be returning his repentant look, with bewitching smiles. But, behind her, and above her, was the arm of the Prince of Darkness, reaching from darkness, and grasping the severed head of a lady by the crown, and drawing its ghastly features away in a black cloud. There were, I should think, two quarto pages of poetry in Spanish, underneath the drawing. Manuel would not suffer me to read it.

When I saw it, the whole came home to my heart. I felt as if there was no hope for me. It was my own self that had no cherubs to flutter around my head; no angels to defend me from the Old Adversary; but there the Wicked One seemed to have me by the crown, bearing me away to perdition, for living with a Priest. It distressed me exceedingly; and Manuel, in the last year of my residence with him, in order to break my spirit, often alluded to this grasp of the Great Enemy on the crown of my head: and the allusion never failed to do it. I would then retire, and fall before the image of the Virgin Mary, and pouring out my grief to her, I felt some relief. My confidence in the Virgin was strengthening every day in Cuba, from the relief I experienced in communing with her image.

The Priests have a separate room in their Convents for the blind people, of whom there are a great many living on the island. I have frequently been in the room in St. Francisco Convent on a Sabbath morning, and saw them kneeling down, praying to our Saviour, and the Virgin Mary. In this room they go to Confess, and have Masses read, for which they are obliged to pay the Priests. They are let out every Friday, and then only to beg for the Priests.

Two things I have heard said, which I will mention here.—Manuel and others have boasted in my hearing, that, whatever else had overtaken them, they never had a *bouquet.*

Again, when the Priests are confined by sickness, the ladies often send them little refreshments and presents suitable for the sick; and when it has happened to them, to be so favored in this particular room, I have heard Manuel and others laugh and say, " the sick Priest would not have received this kindness, if the lady had known what ailed him."

The sight of the *bouquet* did me a great deal of good. I had no idea how wicked I was, like that which this drawing impressed upon me. It quickened and strengthened my resolution to forsake the life I was leading, and to escape both from Cuba and the Priest, and the hand of the Evil One. Through the Lord's mercies this painful drawing, which was shown to me to impress me with the Priests' superior interest in the Divine favor, was made instrumental of leading me heartily to seek the forgiveness of God, and an interest in the Lord Jesus Christ; in the possession of which, I am sometimes ready to rejoice, that I ever went to Cuba, and suffered many sorrows there; for, through them I have been led, as by a way I knew

THE BOUQUET. P. 214.

not, to an acquaintance with my blessed Saviour. My anguish there was great; but it was for a little season; and it was blessed to the saving of my body and soul, I humbly trust, from the worm that never dies, and the fire that shall never be quenched.

CHAPTER XXII.

"Faults in the life breed errors in the brain,
And these reciprocally, those again,
The mind and conduct mutually imprint,
And stamp their image in each other's mint:
Each sire and dam, of an infernal race,
Begetting and conceiving all that's base."
COWPER.

Manuel's evening ride with Rosamond.—Extraordinary occurrence at sup-per-table.—Its effects on Manuel.—The king of Spain abrogates the cus-tom of criminals finding refuge in Churches and Convents.—The Priests act the part of Inquisitors: gamble and fight.—Criminal Priests con-fined in the " Expulsion Room:"—their grief for the loss of their fees.—Sin is no sin if committed trusting to the Virgin Mary.—Two dollars for robbing or murdering.—Money and the Priests are the gods of the people.—Escapes from Havanna, and arrives in New York.

In Havanna, the rainy season is very gloomy; and af-ter a succession of rains the nights are usually dark as well as damp; and most people keep in-doors, and shut up close, on account of the robbers.

On an evening, dark, rainy, and foggy, Manuel came without any previous intimation of his wish, driving up to my door in a *volante* or chaise, after evening oration; and wanted me to ride with him. I said he was crazy; but he insisted; and as he had been very unhappy for several days, weeping with wretchedness, I threw on my mantle, and went with him. People may not believe the Priests are so wretched, but they are the most unhappy beings in the world. I had more than once asked Manuel in his tears, why he wept—He replied, that it was at see-ing me so unhappy. This was after I had been in the Convent, during last year, on the island.

The *volante* was so closed that I do not know where we went; but we made several turns, and did not go out-side of the gates. It was by the side of the city walls where we got out; and it rained while we rode. We en-tered an ancient built and furnished house; and Manuel introduced me to his *commarthra*, a lady upwards of forty.

ATTEMPT AT POISONING. P. 219

Commarthra is an affectionate term, answering to *good mother*. No other person appeared about the house, except slaves. Wherever I went, Manuel's friends used to make a great deal of me, as all do of a foreigner; but this woman was cold and unfriendly; the very reverse of what Spaniards usually are to a guest.

After sitting a short time, in which Manuel had very little to say, (for generally when the Priests enter a house, their tongues can hardly go fast enough for the gay spirits,) we were invited to go and partake of refreshments. We passed through a hall into the back piazza, where a table was spread with cold ham, lettuce, almonds, bread, and claret-wine. There were two bottles of wine; and Manuel filled three tumblers from the same bottle.

We had gone through the usual ceremony of saying *"Bon santè"*—" your good health," and touching glasses;* and I brought mine towards me to drink; when, suddenly Manuel put forth his hand and seized my tumbler; exclaiming with horror, *"Ka! Rosetta!"*—which signifies, " Oh! Rosamond !"—And he laid down the tumbler he had taken from me, and fell back, and fainted.

The lady of the house did not appear surprised. I believe, before he got the tumbler out of my hands, the whole thing came to my mind at once. We sprang up.—The lady threw cold water in Manuel's face, and rubbed his temples. When he came to himself, he said he was very unwell.—We all left the table without having tasted a mouthful of any thing, as it is the custom to drink before eating;—and Manuel and I soon after went home.

I never knew the name of the lady; nor did I hear a word of explanation between Manuel and her; nor did I ever ask any explanation of the matter of Manuel, or even allude to it. I felt so thankful for my escape, that I would not trouble him about it. I knew that I owed my life to him; that he was set to do this deed by the Superior of the Convent, and the other Priests; and I thought I was safer never to let him know that I understood how

---

* The custom prevails in France.—ED.

near I was to death. 1 feared that if he found out I knew it, he would put me to death at once.

He drove in silence home.—It rained very hard.—1 was so overcome with fear that 1 would not speak.—We passed a dreadful night.—He walked in anguish to and fro;—said he was sick;—he wished the Bishop would send him to Spain. He sighed and exclaimed "*Mon Dieu!*" incessantly, and had a high fever and headache all night.—I bathed his head, and comforted him as well as I could. He left me in the morning more affectionately than he had done for some time previous. About eleven o'clock of that day he sent to me by his *Alcowater*, two silver forks, and two silver table-spoons, of uncommonly thick plate.

After evening oration, when he came in, I admired the thick plate of his rich present; and though sorrowful, he was more cheerful than he had been for several days.

No doubt his plan was to poison me, in order to rid himself and the other Priests of the presence of one whom they were afraid to dismiss, or to suffer to escape; and whose presence had, of late, been to them a source of much mortification. They had arranged every thing, but Manuel's strength failed in the execution of the plan. The Lord did not give him strength to complete his design. Seeing how freely I received the cup, he had himself poured out for me, his conscience smote him; his purpose failed; and he fainted in the conflict of his strong passions. The Lord took away his strength, and defeated his treacherous design.

While I resided on the island, many communications passed between Rome and Havanna, respecting a change of the Priests' residence, proposing to remove those on the island, and to replace them with others from Spain. There was much uneasiness among the Priests about it. They are like soldiers, and must go where they are commanded by the Pope and the Bishop. I used to hear them say, they did not care about being removed to the Valley of the Mississippi; but they were unwilling to be transported to any other of the West India islands.

I asked Manuel what this was for, and why they wished

to send away the Priests that were there, and to send others in their place.—" O," said he, " there are so many Priests and Friars in Spain, they do not know what to do with them. There are in some Convents there, two or three hundred of them." Shortly after, other news would come that used to revive the spirits of the Priests ; and they would all rejoice together in the hope of continuing on the island. So they were subject to hopes and fears, depending on the news from Rome. But, finally, they warded off the blow that was aimed at their places ; and the Priests of Old Spain were left to their own fate in Spain, and the Priests of Cuba to the enjoyment of their pleasures.

Before the new Constitution made by the king of Spain, any criminal guilty of murder, or of any other breach of the laws, if he could escape to any of the Convents, and touch or place his finger on any part of the Holy Convents, by that means he was made free from the penalty of the law ; so that no man could take or hurt him, while he remained under the protection of the walls of the Convent and of the Priests.* So I was told by Manuel.

I asked Manuel if there were not more murders committed before the Constitution, than now. He said, no ; that there was more robbery and more murder committed since the Constitution than before ; for now, when the robbers attack a man, he would not give up his money so deliberately and freely as was usual previous to the laws under the Constitution.

And further, I have heard Manuel and others say, that before the Constitution, the Priests could and would go to any gentleman's house, at any hour of the night, and enter it, and take any one, the husband from his wife, or the wife from her husband, or the son, or the daughter, from their parents, and confine them in the Convent for any thing they might have said or done against the Priests or the Holy Church. And I have heard it said that if the Priests had other motives, they would lay false charges

19 *

* See note on Chap. XXI. p. 210.

against any one they wished to capture, and so would make a prey of the innocent, and drag the protector of the family from the guardianship of his lambs, that the wolves might have easy entrance.

Manuel has told me that the Priests all liked the state of things before the Constitution better than they do now ; because they received more money, and fared more sumptuously, and were more respected, and the people were more humble and submissive. For then a parent would not dare permit his son to come to America, to travel in any part of the United States, as the Priests would not consent ; because they said it made the young men disobedient and wicked ; and they were never the same after returning, in respect to the forms of the Holy Church, and obedience to the Priests.

I have heard Manuel and other Priests say, that Cuba was getting more and more wicked every year, with the Priests, and the Convents, and the people. I can inform you what led the Priests to make this remark on themselves, and on their Convents. That night several Priests were at my house to take supper. A Priest by the name of Father Fortinner, of St. Domingo Convent, a friend of theirs, had been, the night previous, gambling in his Convent with some other Priests, who had been unfortunate, and had lost a great deal of money, and thought they lost it wrongfully, and had been cheated by another of the Priests. This caused a dispute, so that words came to blows, and Father Fortinner took a door-bar, (as I was informed by Manuel,) and struck his antagonist, and broke his arm. For this he was taken by the orders of the Superior of the Convent, and put into a room of the Convent, such as all Convents have, called the *Expulsion-room*, and was confined. The criminal Priest is confined here, during the pleasure of his Superior, or of the Bishop ; and is suspended during the time from all his duties.

Manuel was put into this room twice, during the five years I lived with him ; but he was confined only a few days each time. I recollect he was in five days at one time. He would not tell me what he had done; but I have heard them say, that they do not go in for trifles. I remember hearing him say, after he came out at that time, that he had lost a good deal of money a short time previous in this way; he had been engaged by some new subjects, who had chosen him for their Father Confessor, and also had been engaged to christen several houses; and he was afraid *some other Priest had taken the bargain out of his hands*, or had robbed him of the job. This appeared to bear on his mind more than the crime he had committed, for which he had been confined in the *Expulsion-room*, whatever that crime was; for he never would tell me what it was. But, as I have said, they do not enter there for a light offence; nor do their people know when they are in that room; for whenever their people, or any one of them, sends to the Convent for their Father Confessor, on any occasion, when he happens to be confined in the *Expulsion-room*, orders are given by the Superior, to say that the Priest is indisposed; and that probably he will be out in a few days. I have been informed by Manuel that the Superior usually sends another Priest, as a substitute for the one confined in the *Expulsion-room*, to punish him still more. The loss of his fees adds much to his vexation for the loss of his liberty.

All the people are led to believe by the Priests, that whatever they do in the way of crime, they commit no sin if they have not the heart and mind upon the crime, but upon the Virgin Mary, and go away immediately and Confess it to some Priest, and obtain pardon. But the Priest cannot pardon without money.

You may get any one marked in the face with an ugly scar, or robbed, or murdered, for two dollars.* This may appear unnatural and incredible to many; but not to those

---

* Captain J. E. Alexander, describing the manners and customs of the Papists in the West India islands, tells us that 'Murders are common almost every day. Some time ago no fewer than seven white people were murdered in different parts of the city of Havanna. People are here robbed in open day.' Transatlantic Sketches, Vol. I. p. 253.— ED.

who have lived on the island, and know something about the people. Almost every one you meet is marked with some scar or gash in his face. Even females are often made in this way to feel the envy of a rival beauty, and even while sitting at the window, they sometimes receive a blow from the passing assassin.

If any one, citizen or stranger, has business to transact on the island, or wishes to make any speculation, or to smuggle goods to any amount past the customhouse, or leave the island without a regular passport, and many other things of the same dishonest principle, he can bribe, with a small sum of money, either the commissaries, the *alcades*, or judges, or the customhouse officers : for money and the Priests are their gods, if I have any right view and knowledge of them, after living among them five years, and in the heart of their vile and wicked ways.

CHAPTER XXIII.

"And lo ! another angel stood in heaven,
Crying aloud with mighty voice, ' Fallen, fallen,
Is Babylon the Great, to rise no more.
Rejoice, ye prophets ! over her rejoice,
Apostles ! holy men, all saints, rejoice !
And glory give to God, and to the Lamb.
And all the armies of disburdened earth.
As voice of many waters, and as voice
Of thunderings, and voice of multitudes,
Answered, Amen.—And every hill and rock
And sea and every beast, answered, Amen.
Europe answered, and the farthest bound
Of woody Chili, Asia's fertile coasts,
And Afric's burning wastes, answered, Amen.
And Heaven, rejoicing, answered back, Amen."

POLLOK.

*Manner of laying out the dead.— The American and Popish grave-yards.
—Death of Mary Stewart — The Priests get her money.—Rosamond escapes from Cuba, and arrives in New York.*

I WILL describe as near as I can, the mode of laying out the dead. First, after a person dies, he is removed out of the room where his death happened, and all the furniture is also removed. The Priest then comes and blesses it; after this, he returns to his Convent and brings his Holy death articles, accompanied with attendants, to wait upon him. A Holy Brussels carpet is then spread upon the floor, and the room is hung round with silk velvet, or black damask lining. Then four sculls are placed in different parts of the room, with the Cross on the tops of each one of them, and with candles burning under them. The death-table, which is also brought from the Convent, is placed in the centre of the room. This is dressed in deep mourning for a man, but for a lady it is dressed in white. Four large death-candles are burning at each corner of the table, with the Cross lying by the side of each candle. The corpse is dressed in a new suit of clothes, and laid out on the table. The room is then sprinkled with Holy Water. An image of the Virgin Mary, as large as life, is placed at the head of the corpse.

She is generally placed in such an attitude as to appear to be weeping over it; and a number of candles are lighted up round about her, with a large silver Cross with an image of our Saviour on it.   When a female is laid out, her death-table is dressed in white, and ornamented with green or orange leaves and flowers.   The corpse is dressed in black silk or satin; that of a young maid or babe, has the head set off with flowers, and the face painted.

The people go more for the sake of seeing how the room is ornamented, and the corpses laid out, than they do to see the corpse, which looks more like the living than the dead; so much would they be laid out in disguise by their friends and the Priests.   The Priests disguise and dress the death-rooms, and the relations and friends dress the corpses.

In this death-room there will be a man, in the capacity of a clerk, to receive the gifts or fees which the people always bring on these occasions for the prayers they say over the corpses; this fee is two dollars and a half.   The ceremony which the Priest performs, is to Cross himself, and say a few words in Latin.   After he has performed the ceremony, he will go up to the clerk and get his fee. If the deceased be a rich person, you will see the Priests from all the Convents in the death-room.   In this case, you will see a table set out with different kinds of wine, confectionaries, and cigars.   It is not customary for the Priests to leave the room without taking some wine and cigars as a Blessing.   You will see too, in this room or in the adjoining one, ladies and gentlemen talking and laughing, smoking and drinking wine, playing cards, and playing on the guitars, as they think it is a sin to mourn, until the soul of the deceased is prayed out of Purgatory; and, they believe, that this is done by the prayers of the Priests.

When the corpse is removed to be interred, one of the Priests remains to have the Holy Ornaments conveyed back to the Convent, or to some other death-room, which, perhaps, may be waiting to be dressed.   The Priests always take the fee from the poor before they leave the house. The price varies from an ounce to four or six ounces, according to the circumstances of the relatives of the deceased.

When I reflect and bring up to my mind how merciful the Lord has been to me in sparing my life, and bringing me out from among those wicked people, and placing me here where I can see how wicked I was, I feel overcome with gratitude; and I hope and trust, that this wicked heart of mine has been melted down to that *"repentance which needs not to be repented of."* I know there is no one to blame but myself, for all the misery I have suffered. I know that from the time I left the path of virtue, my life was gloomy, wicked, and full of thorns; that my heart was never easy, and my mind was always like the waving ocean tossed to and fro. O, that I could then have said, and believed, that *"the way of the transgressor is hard!"* and *"the wages of sin is death!"*—But no,— that blessed Bible was a sealed book to me.—As soon as I was baptized by Satan, I can truly say, that I always found him to be a hard master. Many are the scenes of guilt, misery, and unmixed sorrow, that I have sketched in my wandering and wicked pilgrimage, to be laid before this dark and gloomy world; and yet I do not suppose that I have succeeded in expressing that deep feeling which I have suffered. O, reader! if the tear starts, if your heart aches within you as you think on my gloomy narrative, pause!—that those tears may swell into a stream;—that your heart may almost burst, to think how common were my sufferings, and that every day brings forth the same story, and say :

"Who is that, forlorn and wasting,
  Wrapped in study and despair?
All the pangs of death she's tasting,
  Sad world, indeed, O, who can bear!

" Once by virtue's fireside dwelling,
  She was blessed with parents' love,
Now, her heart with anguish swelling,
  Finds no rest, like Noah's dove."

I will now give a description, as near as I can, of the situation of the American grave-yard, of the manner in which the dead are buried there, and how much they are exposed in their graves.

The American grave-yard is three miles outside of the walls of the city, (Havanna.) It lays out by the sea-side. This is the place they appropriate for burying the poor Protestants, as they call us. It is about three acres, partly fenced, and partly walled in. The wall in many parts is broken down, and the fence is old and broken. Turkey buzzards, cattle, mules, and wild animals enter it whenever they choose. You may go in there at any time you will, and you will see on the graves, part of the dead bodies, an arm, or a leg, or the face of the dead exposed naked, and the buzzards devouring the bodies. If the body would be laid out in a shroud, some of the natives would come and strip it naked, and leave the body exposed on the earth. The friends, however, or the relations of the deceased, generally cut up the shroud into small pieces, so that it may be of no use to the natives, that they may let it alone. You will find no tomb-stones on the graves. Formerly, when any friend would put a tombstone on the grave of their friend, it would be taken immediately away by some of the natives of the island. I have myself, with some friend, and without Manuel's knowing it, gone out there to see this impious scene. I have counted ten, and sometimes twenty bodies exposed out of the ground for the wild animals to devour. I sometimes asked Manuel, if he did not think it cruel and wicked to have the dead so much exposed to be devoured by the wild animals. He used to reply, " no,—it mattered not where the poor wicked Protestants were laid,"—and he compared us to the dumb beasts, and said, if I died without being christened, and would not become a Catholic, that when I died, my body would also be exposed in the same way ; that he could not bury me ; neither could he have my soul prayed out of Purgatory.

During the last year I was living on the island, there was an American female, who belonged here in New

York, and who had a mother and two sisters living here, who, she said, were Christians. At that time, she was living with a Spanish gentleman; and as she was young, and handsome, she was frequently visited by the Priests. She was sick with the black-vomit, and lived only five days. I saw her a number of times during the time that she was sick. Her constant cry was about her poor mother, and to warn all of her female friends, that would call and see her, and who were living in the same capacity with herself, to leave that life, and the island, and return to their dear parents, and prepare to die. I must die, she said, unprepared. It was the wish of her friend, and some of her favorite friends of the Priests, for her to be christened. They told her that she would be lost; and that they could not bury her, or have her buried in the " *Compassant*,"—(the Catholic grave-yard;) that she would be obliged to be laid in the American grave-yard, for the wild beasts to devour. This awful dread and terror of having her body exposed to the wild animals, (as she had been out to the American grave-yard,) made her consent to be christened in the form of the *Holy Catholic Church*, as they call it. As soon as some of her American female friends heard this, they objected to it, and kept the Priests out of the house until the breath was out of her body. The Priests that belong to St. Domingo Convent, felt very much vexed about it, and threatened to have these American female friends put into Moro Castle, for depriving them of saving that poor soul from going to hell. There were several Priests who met there from different Convents; and they held a consultation upon what should be done. They concluded, in the end, that she should be buried in the Holy Ground, because they had heard her say, that she was willing to be christened; and that if she died without the Priests, it was because her wicked Protestant friends would not let them come.

She was about eighteen years old, and her name was Mary Stewart. She had some property; and, as soon as the breath was out of her body, they began to seize upon her things, and to carry them away.

20

The Catholic grave-yard is very different from the American; for the graves are all covered with beautiful flowers, and it is fenced in with a high stone wall, and the graves all have Crosses at the head of them.

It was during the cholera, in the year 1833, that I made my escape from Manuel, and from the island, when my Priest had left the city with the Marquis M———'s family, the same lady who had hired those robbers to kill me. A great many families left the city during the cholera, all taking their Priests with them, believing their Priests could save them. Before he went into the country, he supplied my wants, and gave me money to make me comfortable. He left an old Alcowater in the house, to remain during his absence. I was assisted to get away by one, whom it might injure to mention his name, who felt very much for my forlorn and lost condition; and through the mercies of the Lord, and the love he had for my poor immortal soul, I am brought to this Christian country, and am placed among Christian friends: and I hope and trust, that I am not only reclaimed in this world, but am in the arms of my dear Saviour.

APPENDIX,

CHAPTER I.

ROMISH PRIESTS.

THIS Narrative treats so largely on the conduct of the Roman Catholic Priests, that the reader is entitled to every degree of information concerning their rank and office, which it is possible in a brief space to bestow.

The Council of Trent, in its twenty-third session, decrees, that " *sacrifice and Priesthood* are so joined by the ordinance of God, that both are found together in every dispensation ;"— "that the Catholic church, having received by divine institution, the holy and visible sacrifice of the Eucharist, (the Mass,) she has a new, and visible, and external Priesthood, in the place of the old; (Mosaic;)—that this Priesthood was instituted by the Lord our Saviour, and that to his Apostles and their successors in the Priesthood, the power was given to consecrate, offer, and minister his body and blood; and also to remit and retain sins."

This is then the peculiar office of a Roman Priest; to wit: *To offer Mass, and also to remit and retain sins.* And the Roman Catholics are taught in the catechism, that the office of the Priest transcends all others in dignity, inasmuch as their power of consecrating the body of the Lord, and remitting sins, is incomprehensible, and unequalled by any power on the earth.

The Priesthood is divided into seven Orders, beginning with the Clerical tonsure, or the shaving of the young student's head, and ascending, gradually, to the rank of Priest. They are called Porter, Reader, Exorcist, Acolyte, Sub-deacon, Deacon, and Priest. The first four of the seven are called *Minor Orders;* the three latter are called *Holy Orders.* The Porter keeps the church door. The Reader reads to the people. The Exorcist receives power over evil spirits, to cast them out. The Acolyte serves the Priests at the altar, by attending the candles in the offering of the Mass. The Sub-deacon prepares the altar-linen, the sacred vessels, the bread and wine, the water to wash the Priest's hands at Mass, and to read the epistle, and assist as a witness, and sees that nothing occurs to disturb the celebration of the Mass. The Deacon waits on the Bishop as the Sub-deacon serves the Priest, and, in an emergency, he may expound the Gospel to the people, but not from an elevated place. The Priest has power to offer sacrifice to God, and to administer the Sacraments of the Romish church.

Ordination, they say, confers grace, and constitutes one of their seven church Sacraments: it impresses a character on the Priest, that never can be destroyed or taken away. Death alone severs a Priest from the obligation of his vows; even the grave receives him in his habits, though he may have been removed from public office on account of scandalous vices. This we have seen illustrated in the Narrative most amply. Neither open concubinage, nor secret murder, was sufficient to take away the office of the Priests of Cuba. They were never laid by, as unfit for duty, while their base indulgences failed to disfigure their countenances, and odiously to deprive them of some one of the features of the face. When the curse of their indulgences breaks uncontrollably out upon their eyes, nose, or mouth, then, in shame, they are laid by, and no longer suffered to consecrate and offer the Romish Mass. In conformity with this imperishable character of the Priest, the great Council of Trent pronounced, "Whoever shall affirm that he who was once a Priest may become a layman again: let him be accursed." Sess. XXIII.

The Bishops are not an Order by themselves, but they are of the Order of Priests, set apart to the high office of overseers and governors of the church, to whom belongs the administration of the rite of ordination: and any man who says "that Orders conferred by them, without the consent or calling of the people, or the secular power, are invalid, let him be accursed." That is, they make Priests whom they will, and whom they will they reject, without giving any account to the people, or taking care to consult those over whom the Priest is placed;

although the Bishop full well knows how to remove an ob-
noxious Priest from one part of the Roman domains to another;
and to replace a notorious offender, by an utter stranger; and
to change the residence of one who is endangering the Roman
credit to a new field, which he enters with all the sanctity of a
man under a solemn vow of chastity, obedience, and poverty,
for the sake of the kingdom of heaven.   Such were Father
Hosa, and Father Panterilla, and Father R——, and others,
who took refuge from Havanna in these United States, or were
ordered hither by the Bishop of Cuba.

The Pope himself, and the Cardinals, and all the multitude
of the lower Hierarchy, are of the Order of Priests, holding the
rank of Bishops, &c. &c.   The Pope is *Bishop of Rome :* and
his Cardinals are nominally Priests and Deacons of Rome,
and its vicinity.

The Council of Trent made no definition of the powers of
the Bishops, probably from a difficulty of discerning readily
between those of the Bishop of Rome, and of the other Bishops.
But, according to the Doctors of Rome, the Bishops are all in
the rank of the Apostles, over whom they place the Bishop of
Rome instead of Peter.   The Scriptures do not furnish an instance of Peter's exercising authority, or even seeking to do it,
over the rest of the Apostles; so far from it, they tell of Paul's
withstanding him publicly to his face, and putting him under
open rebuke, which he bore with meekness, for he was to
blame.   Yet history is full of the feats of authority of the
Bishop of Rome, who is the head of the Roman Priesthood,
the fountain of all grace, and honor, and power, to the Romish
Priests, wherever they are found on the face of the whole earth,
and the object of their homage, whom they swear to obey, when
absent, and in whose presence they fall down and worship.

This is not a sketch of ancient history, or of poetic fancy;
but it is the testimony of modern travelers, taken here from the
classical Tour of Eustace, (Vol. II. 168,) himself a Roman
Catholic, zealous for that faith.   Describing the manner in
which the head of the Roman Priesthood is received, when he
shows himself to the multitude, he says : " The Pontiff appears,
elevated on his chair of state under the middle arch (of St. Peter's.)   Instantly the whole multitude below fall on their knees.
The cannons of St. Angelo, (a neighboring fort) give a general
discharge; while rising slowly from his throne, he lifts his hands
to heaven, stretches forth his arm, and thrice gives his bene

20*

diction, to the crowd, to the city, and to all mankind. A solemn pause follows; another discharge from the fort is heard; the crowd rises, and the pomp gradually disappears." *Cramp's Text Book*, p. 314. How much it would serve the Pope, if he could thunder! Poor man, that he should be beholden to the castle of Angelo for a voice to announce his presence, and the conclusion of his blessing! For the blessing itself no man hears. The Rev. Dr. M'Auley of this city gives me leave to say he stood within ten feet of the Pope this very year, when he came forth to bless some fifty thousand people, and neither could the sound of his voice be heard, nor his lips be discovered to move.

Mr. Eustace adds, that, in the ceremony called the adoration of the Pope, which takes place almost immediately after his election, " he is placed in a chair on the altar of the Cistine chapel, and there receives the homage of the Cardinals. This ceremony is again repeated on the high altar of St. Peter's."— Their Roman altars are nothing to me. A Pope or a slave may alike sit or stand on them ; but to the Romans themselves, it is the most holy place, where the Lord is daily offered up ; and for a Priest to approach it, he must kneel down ; and for a commoner to pass by it, he must kneel down ; because it is the place of the Lord of Hosts ; the holy elements are treasured there. They worship and adore the consecrated elements, in that place ; and in that place they adore the Pope, who "*as (or instead of) God, sitteth in the temple of God, showing himself, that he is God.*" 2 Thess. II.

Candidates for the Priesthood are admitted to the Minor Orders, at the age of fourteen. Sub-deacons must be twenty-two ; Deacons twenty-three ; and Priests twenty-five.* They are educated at public seminaries; the poor gratuitously, the rich at charges. They are required to learn grammar, singing, and other ordinary branches of education; to become versed in Scripture, Ecclesiastical reading, the homilies of the Saints, and the ceremonies of the Sacraments. They must attend Mass every day, Confess and receive the sacrament once a month, under direction of their Confessor. They receive the first tonsure, immediately on their admission to wear the clerical habit ; and, from that time, are gradually initiated into the services of the church.

* By a *dispensation* they can be ordained at any age.—ED.

One of the distinguishing and indelible marks of the Romish Priesthood is the vow of chastity, obedience, and poverty. How it is kept by them in Cuba, the reader very well knows. Their licentiousness is not usually exceeded by their wealth, even when they pursue the steps taken by Father Francisco, and by Father Panterilla, to increase riches. The article of obedience has reference to the duty they owe to their Superiors; and that, they are forced to perform to the letter.

It is not in Cuba alone where the corrupt Priests of the Romish doctrine of celibacy are found. In every part of the world, where it is forbidden to marry, the same licentiousness is said to prevail; and, in the very nature of frail man, it must prevail. Jos Blanco White, whose place as royal chaplain to the king of Spain, gave him opportunity to know, thus speaks of his own observations.

"I cannot think of the wanderings of the friends of my youth, without heart-rending pain. One, now no more, whose talents raised him to one of the highest dignities of the church of Spain, was, for many years, a model of Christian purity. When, by the powerful influence of his mind, and the warmth of his devotion, this man had drawn many into the clerical and religious life, (my youngest sister among the latter,) he sunk at once into the grossest and most daring profligacy. I heard him boast that the night before the solemn procession of *Corpus Christi*, where he appeared nearly at the head of his Chapter, one of *two* children had been born, which his two concubines had brought to light within a few days of each other. Such, more or less, has been the fate of my early friends, whose minds and hearts were much above the common standard of the Spanish Clergy. What, then, need I say of the vulgar crowd of Priests, who, coming, as the Spanish phrase has it, from *coarse swaddling clothes*, and raised by Ordination to a rank of life, for which they have not been prepared, mingle vice and superstition, grossness of feeling, and pride of office, in their character? I have known the best among them, I have heard their Confessions; I have heard the Confessions of persons of both sexes, who fell under the influence of their suggestions and example; and I do declare, that *nothing can be more dangerous to youthful virtue, than their company.*

"I have seen the most promising men of my University, (Salamanca,) obtain country Vicarages with characters unimpeached, and hearts overflowing with hopes of usefulness. A

virtuous wife would have confirmed and strengthened their
purposes; but they were required to live a life of angels in celibacy. They were, however, men, and their duties connected
them with beings of no higher description. Young women
knelt before them in all the intimacy and frankness of Confession. A solitary home made them go abroad in search of
social converse. Love seized them, at length, like madness.
Two, I knew, who died insane; hundreds might be found,
who avoid that fate by a life of settled systematic vice." PRAC-
TICAL AND INTERNAL EVIDENCE AGAINST CATHOLICISM,
Page 132.

Such fruits prove the tree to be corrupt, which produces
them. They are common in Roman catholic countries. The
vulgar crowd of Spanish Priests, named by Mr. White, are introduced to us one by one in the course of this Narrative;
their grossness of feeling, their superstition, their vices, their
pride of office, are all unveiled. The circle of Priests in
which Rosamond moved, contained characters of various
grades; but they were all licentious, cruel, and wanting natural affection, as their vows, together with the ordinary duties
of their office, most certainly make them. They may start in
life pure and innocent; and may cherish ardent hopes of serving the Lord in the ministry. I am willing to think they do;
but it is impossible to continue in this state through a long life
of temptation. The Priest may praise celibacy, and boast of
chastity, and sprinkle Holy Water to frighten away the evil
spirits, and even Cross himself every time an assault is made
on his vows; he may resist the warm kiss of the devout penitent, impressed on his hands, when she has frankly told him,
by herself alone, all that is, or has been, in her heart, and receives absolution and a blessing in return; but in the effort to
maintain his innocence, it is easy to believe that out of a hundred Priests, ninety-eight would sooner or later sink under the
power of temptation, and the other two would go mad.

That word of Manuel's, when he took his habit between his
thumb and finger, and extending it, said; "Rosetta, this habit
does not change our feelings; we have feelings like other
men;" is a true word, whether spoken in New York or Havanna. The vow of the Priest is the same; and the temptations of the Priest are the same, here, as elsewhere; but the
restraints upon the licentiousness of Priests are tenfold greater
here, than in a Roman catholic country. The eye of a jealous

people is upon them, and they are defended from the allurements of their own official duties, by a proper dread of that public reproach, which, in this country, assuredly falls on the wanton lip and leering eye of a professed teacher of morals and of religion.

CHAPTER II.

Reader.—" Where is that Church, against which Christ tells us Satan shall not prevail?

J. B. White.—" Let me answer you by a question, though I fear it will appear to you rather out of the way.—Where is the plough we pray God to speed?

Reader.—" Oh, Sir! we do not mean any particular plough. We only pray God, to prosper and bless the labors of the husbandman.

White.—" Very well.—Now, suppose that God had, in the Scriptures, promised that evil should never prevail against the *plough;* what would you understand by the words?

Reader.—" I believe they would mean that all the crops should never fail at once, so that it would be impossible ever to grow any more grain.

White.—" And what would you think, if a society of farmers, with a rich man at their head, had established themselves at London, and wished to have a monopoly of all the corn on earth, saying to the government; ' You must go to war to defend our rights; for God has said: Evil shall not prevail against the *plough.* And who can be *the plough,* but the head and society of farmers of the county of Middlesex, wherein stands the great city of London, which is the first city of the world?'

Reader.—" I should certainly think they were a set either of madmen or rogues, who wished for their own benefit to levy a tax upon all farmers, wherever they were.

White.—" I will leave you to apply what we have said, to the use which the Pope and his Cardinals have made of Christ's promise to the Church, that Satan should not prevail against his Church.—Church, here, must mean Christianity in general; not Christianity confined to the walls of any town. The meaning, therefore, of the promise must be, that Satan shall never succeed in abolishing the faith in God through Christ;—not that the Pope and Rome must always be right; and much less, that the Pope is the spiritual governor of the world.

" As far as the Roman Church regulates her faith by the Gospel, we believe her to be a true portion of the Universal Church of Christ. But in regard to her inventions, whereby she makes void the power and spirit of the Gospel, we declare her corrupt and heretical; and in proportion to the additions, which out of her own fancy she has made to the Gospel, she has separated herself from that multitude of persons of every age and country, who, being called by the grace of God, to believe in his Son Jesus Christ, have conformed, and do now conform their lives to the obedience of the Gospel, and ground their hopes of salvation on the promises made therein.

"Many suppose the Roman church has reformed; has abandoned its ancient errors, its blind superstitions, its idolatries, its political meddling, its secret works of darkness, its intolerance. But Rome no more admits the doctrine of any salvation out of the pale of her church, now, than in the thirteenth century. She distrusts, and where she *can*, she disfranchises aliens to her faith, now, as much as in the days of *Leo the Tenth.* Her celebration of the Mass is the same; her Convents and Monasteries are the same; her Monks and Nuns are the same; her worship of images, and pictures, and Crosses, is the very same; her Latin services, her exclusion of the Holy Scriptures, her Priestly power, and Papal claims, are the same; not one of them is renounced; and the order of Jesuits, once disbanded, is again organized by Rome. Her private Confessions, her Absolutions, her Indulgences, her doctrine of Purgatory, her vaunting display of robes and habits, her overbearing pride, her Roman yoke, in all its hardships of penance, scourgings, fastings, and fines, are the same now, as they were in the days of Luther. In what is Rome reformed? Are her Priests more pure? Her Nuns more chaste? Her ceremonies less numerous? Her devotions better understood? Her designs less grasping? In what is Rome reformed? She anathematizes all who dissent from her Bishop, with the same curse, and pronounces it in the same spirit, as in the sixteenth century. Because her power is brought low, and nations have learned to break her burdensome yoke, she seems changed; and outwardly she is changed; but the reform is on the outside. It proceeds from no retraction of her principles, her aims, her doctrines, or her practices. They are the same, and will be for ever. The Jews did not adhere to the Mosiac law, and to the traditions of the Elders, more devoutly, than the Roman catholics adhere to the traditions of Rome. Jerusalem

was destroyed: it could not be reformed. The preaching of
John, the miracles and doctrines of the Lord Jesus, the displays
of the Holy Spirit in the lives of the Apostles, failed to reform
the Jews. The destruction of Jerusalem did not reform them.
They retain their errors to this day. And Rome is no nearer
conversion. Rome gives no fairer evidence of a reformation
of heart, than the dispersed of Israel give of loving the name
of Jesus, the Christ crucified. They hate the name, as Rome
hates reform.

"It is written, that Babylon shall be destroyed; and it is admitted by competent judges, and by the proudest Cardinals of
the Papacy, that in the New Testament, Babylon means Rome,
only *heathen* Rome. But the reader knows, that as the worship of images is the mark of a heathen, so Rome is, and has
ever been a heathen city. It may be confidently affirmed of
every century, since the foundations of Rome were laid, that
the inhabitants of Rome, by a majority, were worshipers of
images, were, and are idolators; and the past affords us no encouragement to expect they will ever be any thing else. The
prophet tells how she shall come to an end, and by whose
hand, (*Rev.* 18: 8;) but, while the Lord spares her, we are
bound to labor for their good, to open their eyes, and to convert
their hearts, who are, wherever they reside, Roman citizens,
not now a title of honor, as it was in the Apostolic times; but
a name which expresses Lordship, and the dominion over other
men, and places on the earth.

" While laboring, however, for the conversion of the Romans, it is good to bear in mind what has been already
attempted without success, in order to guide the effort in a
direction likely to be more successful. In the days of the great
Reformation, the nations who adhered to Rome, asked, and
urged, and then demanded a thorough reform of the Papal
church. The French Ambassadors to the Council of Trent,
were particularly instructed to insist on a reform in the church
service, in order to the abolition of all superstitions and useless
ceremonies; the concession of the cup in communion to the lay
members of the church; the administration of the Sacraments
in the common languages, and not in Latin; also the singing
of psalms and other spiritual songs; the reading of the Scripture, and the public prayers and praises, in the common languages instead of the Latin; the reformation of the licentious
lives of the Clergy, and many abuses which had crept into the

Court of Rome, and the church at large, of which they furnished an ample list.

"The Spanish Prelates, in that Council, zealously co-operated with those of France in this work of reform; and it seemed, at one time, as if they would have carried it. The Cardinal Lorraine came into the Council at its twenty-third Session, with thirty-nine French Prelates, and urged the most prompt and energetic measures. He was followed by the Ambassador of France, Du Terrier, who boldly declared, that the Church must be brought back to the standard of the Scriptures, the Canons, and the venerable Councils : ' Unless this is done, Holy Fathers,' (said he,) 'in vain will you inquire whether France is in a state of peace.—We can only answer you, as Jehu answered Joram, when he said : Is there peace, Jehu ? —What peace, (he replied,) so long as the fornications*— ' you know the rest. But unless this is done, in vain will you seek for advice or help from this, or that quarter,'" &c. (Pallavicini, L. 10, C. 3. Sarpi L. 7, S. 3. Le Plote, V. p. 549. *Quoted by Cramp, P. 294.*

Notwithstanding the efforts of the great Reformers, and of the Council, and the spirited efforts that were made by some in the Council, the Sovereign Pontiff, who presided by his legates, overruled the whole. In order that the Decrees and decisions of the Council should be according to his own arbitrary will, he urged every Bishop in Italy to attend it. These, being completely under his control, and mere tools in his hands, were influenced wholly by interested motives. The debates and wrangling of the Council were protracted to twenty-one years. Some were for a general Reformation, but the influence and authority of the Sovereign Pontiff over his legates and partisans, wearied out and bore down all opposition; no Reformation was effected; but, on the contrary, the worst features, and the highest claims of the Romish church received an official stamp, such as had never before characterized the "*Man of Sin.*"

The Council was convened in Nov. 1542, under Pope Paul III., and was continued under Julius III., Marcellus II., Paul IV., and Pius IV.—five Popes—and its Decrees were confirmed and ratified by Pope Pius IV., Jan. 26, 1564.

When the struggle for a Reform was conducted under these

* 2 Kings ix. 22.

favorable auspices for so long a time, without any real success ; and when the Roman Priests have from that day to this hardened themselves in the Roman faith, and in the pride of Roman dominion, I see not the ground on which to build a hope of the present Reform of that usurping power. Its signs and lying wonders, its pretended miracles and Saints, its exactions, oppressions, superstitions, and self-conceit, are increased and multiplied every day; and not one of its burdens are removed.

It remains yet to be cried : " *Alas ! alas !—for in one hour so great riches is come to nought.*" Rev. xviii. 16.

The doctrine of Infallibility is one that forbids the idea, or the possibility of Reform. All Roman catholics believe, that their " *church cannot err in faith, morals, or general discipline :*" and they " believe in all things, according as the Holy catholic church believes." And that church condemns, and curses blackly in the face, all who refuse to receive her doctrines, and to obey her Canons. To Reform such a church is impossible. Her members may be converted and brought away from her; but the supposed Infallible one cannot be Reformed. Her subjects may fall off from her obedience, may reject her yoke; but the destruction of the yoke follows ; and this destruction is the only Reformation that haughty Rome allows. " The first lispings of the infant,—the conclusions of the learned,—the declarations of the noble,—the Priests' instructions,—the Pontiff's Decrees,—re-echo the sound : " *Out of the Roman catholic church there is no salvation !*"*—Of course, Reform cannot be admitted from without; and how shall it spring up within ? The Sovereign Pontiff has the most absolute dominion over the minds and consciences of his dependants. They cannot begin to think of a Reform which does not lead them to think of curtailing his powers ; and that thought, the pretended Vicegerent will much sooner blast with his thunderbolt, than cherish with his blessing. Having it established, that all Christians ought to obey the Roman catholic church, the Pope will see that they do it; and any one who undertakes to Reform that church, will find it alike necessary and impossible to obtain the Pontiff's leave.

* Cramp's Text Book of Popery, p. 47.

CHAPTER III.

THE VIRGIN MARY.

THE Virgin Mary is so frequently mentioned in this Narrative, and holds a place so prominent in the affections and devotions of Roman catholics, that the following notice of her worship may prove acceptable to the reader.

The blessed Virgin is placed at the very head of the list of Roman catholic Saints. Her common titles of honor are: " The Queen of heaven ;" " The Mother of Mercies ;" " The Mother of God." Five days of the year are set apart to her service, as solemn festivals of praise.

1. The day of her conception, which is celebrated Dec. 8.

2. The day of her birth, which is celebrated Sept. 8.

3. The day of the annunciation by the angel that she should have a son, and call his name Jesus, which is celebrated March 25.

4. The day of her purification according to the Mosaic law, Feb. 2.

5. The day of her pretended assumption to the skies, which is celebrated Aug. 15. For the Romans believe she was taken up to heaven.

I do not recollect another Saint in the calendar, to whom Rome has appropriated more than one day in the year; but even this preference of the Virgin, in honor, falls far below the proportion of the respect paid her by presents, and prayers, and offerings of devotion in every form. What Hume relates of her altars in England, is true of her altars in all the dominions of the Bishop of Rome at this day; and is seen verified in this Narrative. The pirate-robber who would propitiate the favor of heaven, crowned the image of the Virgin with a coronet of pure gold, while the rest of the Saints were, probably, treated only to silver coins; and when Poncheetee would gain her estate in Spain by the aid of the Saints and of Father Francisco, her devotions were paid at the shrine of the Virgin; and when Rosamond was ready to sink under her trials, she, too, learned of the Roman Priests, to cast herself at the feet of the Virgin, and pour out her sorrows there. thought of going to the throne of grace, and, in of her soul, of seeking for rest in the Lord; but she fell before the supposed Mother of Mercies, and worshiped at the image of Mary. So the image of the Virgin leads the van of the Roman catholic processions, and every where receives the first and last honors of the devout Papist.

When Father Manuel Canto would have Rosamond make sure of good luck in gambling, he charged her to bear the Virgin on her heart, and to pray to her unceasingly for good fortune through the day; and when the Italian banditti. excused themselves to an English traveler for the necessity of living by robbery, they drew from their bosoms a picture of the Virgin and child, set in silver, saying: "We know we are likely to die a violent death; but in our hour of need, we have these," (touching their muskets,) "to struggle for our lives with, and *this*," (kissing the picture of the Virgin,) " *to make our death easy.*"   *Graham's East of Rome, pp.* 155, 161.

Some of the prayers offered to her in the Roman catholic Breviary, or prayer-book, as translated by a Roman catholic Priest, will show the estimate in which she is held by the highest authorities of the Roman church:

" O holy Mary! succor the miserable; help the faint-hearted; comfort the afflicted; pray for the people; intercede for the Clergy; make supplication for the devout female sex; let all be sensible of thy help, who celebrate thy holy commemoration;"—" Grant, we beseech thee, O Lord God, that we, thy servants, may enjoy perpetual health of mind and body; and, by the glorious intercession of Blessed Mary, ever Virgin, may be delivered from present sorrows, and come to eternal joy, through our Lord Jesus Christ."

The concluding expression "through our Lord Jesus Christ," is a form, which the Romans keep up; but which here is plainly obsolete and empty, because the substance is contained in the words previous, " *by the glorious intercession of Blessed Mary, ever Virgin.*"   And certain it is, that the Roman catholic, who is sure of her favor and intercession, feels no need of any other.

The word " *ever Virgin*" expresses an article of universal faith among the Roman catholics; and, at the same time, furnishes the Priests with one good and sufficient reason, for them, to deny the reading of the Testament to the people. Every reader of the Scriptures must know, that our blessed Lord was the *first* born of the Virgin, and that he had brethren and sisters according to the flesh, born of Joseph and Mary, —so, that this article of universal credence now among the Romans, is a delusion of the apostacy; therefore, to conceal this, and other of their falsehoods, the Holy Scriptures are denied to the laity; for the Clergy find their account lie in holding fast the traditions of the Fathers, let what will become of the divine commandments.

She is hailed in the ROMAN CATHOLIC PRAYER-BOOK, by forty-four different titles of glory, with an aspiration, "Pray for us;" accompanying each. Among them are the following:

Holy Mary!
Queen of heaven!
Virgin most powerfu.
Ark of the covenant!
Gate of heaven! }*Pray for us!*
Refuge of sinners!
Queen of angels!
Queen of all saints!

While the pastors hail her in this manner, and the people respond, "Pray for us;" and while the Prayer-book glorifies her above all Saints, the people regard her as easier of access, and more willing to save, than God; the people worship her more freely and commonly than the only living and true God, who forbids the worship of images, and who will not give his praise to another. The manner in which the people regard her, is described in a Roman catholic school-book, as follows: "She is most powerful with God, to obtain from him all that she shall ask of him. She is all goodness in regard to us, by applying to God for us. Being Mother of God, he cannot refuse her request; and, being our mother, she cannot deny her intercession when we have recourse to her." *See Cramp's Text book of Popery, p.* 357.

The Roman mode of worship practically excludes the thought of God, and removes all dependance on Christ, as the intercessor and Saviour; it makes the Saints all and in all; and the Virgin the Queen of Saints, and the Queen of heaven; and this is the Antichrist, "*that denieth the Father and the Son.*" 1 John 2: 22.

One doctrine concerning the Virgin Mary has caused the

21*

Roman church no small controversy for the last six hundred years. Polemics have reasoned, and enthusiasts have waxed warm, on opposite sides, until the Roman Mother has found it exceedingly difficult, at times, to restrain the anger of her children. She has never settled the point in controversy, by an authentic Decree, though she has favored those who maintain the immaculate conception of the Virgin Mary, until the great body of the Romans take it for a matter settled.

This controversy shook the great Council of Trent, until, to avoid a schism, the Council decreed, that it would not decide the question in dispute, but leave it open, as the Jews did that relating to John's baptism: *Whence is it : of heaven or of men ?*

Those who hold the immaculate conception, maintain that the Virgin Mary was conceived in the womb of her mother, with the same purity that is attributed to Christ's conception. The festival in honor of this pretended fact, commenced in the 12th century. (*Mosheim, Chap. 12, Part 2, Chap. 3, Sect.* 19.) The Dominicans and Franciscans took opposite sides, and the Popes were often compelled to interfere for the purpose of restraining their animosity. *Sixtus* IV., in the years 1477, and 1483, enacted, that Indulgences should be granted to those who devoutly commemorate the wonderful conception of the Virgin, to the same extent as were enjoyed on *Corpus Christi* day ; and that the disputants should refrain from reviling and condemning each other, as the church had not decided the matter.

Nothing being gained by holding the better opinion, the worse grew and increased with the confidence that those who honored the Virgin would be honored by her. Rome kept the festival of the supposed conception day, and thus strengthened the Franciscans, without condemning their opponents.

When the question of original sin was settled in the Council of Trent, it was admitted by all, that Adam's sin was transmitted to all his posterity, only that the Franciscans would except the blessed Virgin, and the Dominicans refused. Of the Pope's legates, De Monte favored the immaculateness ; Santa Croce opposed it ; and Cardinal Pole gave no opinion. In this situation of the matter, the Council agreed to pass it without a decision, declaring, " that it is not its design to include in this Decree, which treats of original sin, the blessed and immaculate Virgin Mary."

But in the seventeenth century, the kingdom of Spain was

convulsed with factions growing out of this dispute, to such a degree, that solemn embassies were sent to Rome, to bring the dispute to an end by an edict of the Pope. After the most earnest entreaties, all that the court of Spain could procure of the Pope, was, a declaration, that the opinion of the Franciscans had a high degree of probability on its side, and forbidding the Dominicans to oppose it in a public manner. But this was, in the Delphic spirit, accompanied with another declaration, prohibiting the Franciscans from treating as erroneous the opinion of the Dominicans. The *immaculates* interpreted this in their favor, and celebrated it with public rejoicings on both sides of the Atlantic. An Order was instituted in honor of the supposed event, and a law was enacted, requiring a declaration upon oath, of a firm belief in the doctrine of the immaculate conception, from every individual previous to his taking a Degree in any of the Universities, or being admitted into any civil or religious corporations, which abound in Spain. The same oath is administered even to mechanics, upon their being made free to work at their trade. *Doblado's Letters from Spain, p.* 24, 25, quoted in Cramp's Text Book of Popery, p. 75.

The Spaniards are remarkably zealous for the Virgin. They honor her at all times. The common courtesies of life are not exchanged without reverently mentioning her name. "When you enter a house," says a respectable traveler, "unless you wish to be considered as impious, you must begin with these words: 'Ave. *Maria purissima!*' 'Hail, spotless Virgin!' to which you will certainly receive this answer, '*sin peccado concebida,*' 'conceived without sin!'" *Bourgoing's modern state of Spain, Vol.* 2, *p.* 276, *quoted by Cramp, p.* 75.

In 1708, Pope Clement XI., appointed the festival in honor of the immaculate conception, to be annually celebrated throughout the Roman church. But the Dominicans still hold out. They deny the obligation of this edict upon them ; and they are suffered, without molestation, to refuse any part in the celebration. *Mosheim's 17th century, Sect.* 2, *Part* 1, *Chap.* 1, *Sect.* 48. Bellarmine says, the immaculate conception is piously believed by the greater part of the church. *De Culter Sanct. L.* 111, *C.* 16. That was probably true, when he wrote, above two hundred years ago; and it is certainly true now; for, in all respects, the tendency of the doctrines and practices of Rome is toward corruption, from age to age.

There is said to be no service in the Roman catholic church

so impressive, as the evening service, or "*Ave Maria*," to the blessed Virgin. They teach, that it is "none other than that chanted in heaven by the Saints, around the throne of the Almighty, and called the sweet communion of "All Saints." *Six Months in a Convent, p. 75.* Having described the ceremony, as it is performed in Venice, with the organ, the assembled multitude, the tinkling bell, the silent devotion to the Virgin on the bended knee, when every head bows in adoration, and not a whisper disturbs the spirit of supplication; in a minute or two, the bell tinkles again, and the whole congregation rise, as one man: one says, "I witnessed this scene several times, and never without a universal degree of emotion." It was equally impossible not to honor the feeling of devotion, and not to condemn the Roman doctrine, which teaches the supplicants to address their prayers to the imaginary "*Queen of Heaven.*" *Gilly's Tour through Piedmont.*

CHAPTER IV.

PURGATORY.

CONSTANT reference is had in this Narrative to the influence on Roman catholics, of their doctrine of Purgatory. It is one of the great fountains of their power to get wealth, and will pay for a few moments' attention.

The following is an extract of the Decree of the Council of Trent, setting forth the doctrine. "Since the Catholic Church, instructed by the Holy Spirit, through the Sacred Writings, and the ancient traditions of the Fathers, hath thought, in Holy Councils, and, lastly, in this Œcumenical Council, that there is a Purgatory, and that the souls detained there are assisted by the suffrages (that is, by the Masses, alms, prayers, and works of charity) of the faithful, but, especially, by the acceptable sacrifice of the Mass; this Holy Council commands all Bishops diligently to endeavor, that the wholesome doctrine of Purgatory, delivered to us by Venerable Fathers, and Holy Councils, be believed and held by Christ's faithful, and every where taught and preached."

They learn the doctrine not "through the Sacred Writings." No mention is made of such a place in the books of Divine Revelation. They learn it through the "traditions of the Fathers," and teach it to their children for holy truth "*teaching things which they ought not, for filthy lucre's sake*." *Tit.* 1, 11.

But where it is, and what it is, the Council no more tell us, than the Bible, only the Council speak of it, as a place of distress, in which the souls of the deceased are confined for a season, on their way toward heaven, out of which they are helped to escape by the suffrages, or offerings of the living. Cardinal Bellarmine is more particular. He tells us it is "a place, in which, after death, the souls of those persons are purified, who were not fully cleansed on earth, in order that they may be prepared for heaven, wherein nothing shall enter that defileth." De Purgatorio, L. 1, C. 1, 2d Maccabees 12, 43–46, and Tobit 4, 18, are quoted to prove the doctrine, and also the fast of the men of Gilead, for the death of Saul; and of David for the death of Abner, and many like passages of Scrip ture he wrests to the support of the Roman doctrine of Purgatory.

Purgatory they suppose to be in the centre of the earth, one of the four compartments of the infernal regions. The first of these is the abode of the hopeless; the second is Purgatory; the third is the place of unbaptized infants; the fourth is *Limbo;* where the pious dead tarried before the resurrection of the Lord. That is empty now, for the Lord took them with him to glory, and Purgatory will be empty hereafter. The punishment of the place is by fire, horrible, and enduring.

The Priests paint, in the most vivid colors, the pains of this place, to which every pious Roman catholic, unless he dies a rare Saint, inevitably is subject. The Priests also teach, that the duration of the pains of the deceased believer, may be shortened by the kind offices of the living, more *" especially,"* as the Council of Trent says, " *by* the acceptable sacrifice of the Mass," which only a Priest can offer, and which, in Roman catholic countries, he will not offer, without his fees for the service in hand; so that the proverb is sure, " *No penny, no Pater-noster.*" They have prayers for every condition with the Mass; one, to be offered at the moment of death; others, at stated intervals after death; and, again, at the anniversary of the decease. On " *All Souls'-day,*" extraordinary Masses are celebrated for their universal benefit. A small fee paid to the Priest, enables one, at any time, to arrange with him, to appropriate a part of the benefit of the service to the relief of the relative or friend, for whose soul he is concerned.

The extent to which this corruption is carried almost removes our indignation, by the excitement of our mirth. In Italy and Spain, travelers are continually solicited, by dependants on the churches and Convents, for contributions in aid of the poor souls in Purgatory; and contributions are made in favor of the unknown and friendless sufferers in the flames, who have no one to remember their painful condition. The Pope has granted for Spain, and confined the grant to Spaniards, eight or ten days in the year, when every Spaniard, by kneeling at five different altars, and there praying for the extirpation of heresy, is entitled to send a species of " *habeas animam,*" or writ, to take the soul of any one he pleases out of Purgatory. The name of the person intended to be drawn. should, for fear of a mistake, be mentioned in the prayers. And then, if it should happen, that he is out already, or confined within the walls where the Pope's writ of *habeas corpus* is not supposed to run, they are taught to add other names, and conclude with addressing it finally to the relief of *the most worthy and disconsolate.* Thus they make sure of a reward for their pains, by the rescue of some one from the flames of Purgatory. These privileged days are announced to the public, by a printed notice, placed over the basin of Holy Water, at the entrance of the church. The words written are plain and peremptory: "*Hoy se saca anima,*" literally, "*this is a soul-drawing day.*" *Doblado's Letters from Spain, p.* 169, *quoted in Cramp's Text Book, p.* 339.

In "THE LONDON ROMAN CATHOLIC DIRECTORY," may be found, in plain English, the appointed days, when every Roman catholic is empowered by the Pope, to free one soul from the pains of Purgatory, by means of a Plenary Indulgence. These Indulgences are, by the king of Spain, bought, wholesale, of the Pope, together with (I believe) the exclusive right of retailing them in the Spanish dominions. The monopoly, or sale, is a great source of revenue to the crown of Spain.

The Romish doctrine of Purgatory, is stated thus by Joseph Blanco White: "They believe that there is a place very like hell, where such souls as die, having received absolution of their sins, are made to undergo a certain degree of punishment; like criminals, pardoned on the gallows, but subjected to hard labor in the state's prison for a certain time. In the pagan, and Roman doctrine, an idea is inculcated, that pain, and bodily suffering, have the power of pleasing God. This notion gave birth to that of Purgatory, and it is the same notion which induces devout, and sincere Roman catholics, almost to kill themselves with self-inflicted sufferings, by stripes, and floggings, and fasts, and penances of every kind, to make them feel *holy.*"

"The poor souls think the heavenly account has a credit side, in which every suffering they voluntarily endure in the flesh for their sins, will be entered up; and, at death, will be subtracted from the debtor side. The balance, if against them, they must work out in Purgatory, at a dreadful advance of penalty and interest, for their presumption and delay; while, if the balance should fortunately be in their favor, they are admitted to glory at once; and the overplus of their merits, goes into the treasury account of the Saints, for the benefit of others, who will pay the Pope to obtain it. This treasury account is the fund, on which the Pope draws for the Indulgences he sells. The young reader will think I am jesting; but in sober earnestness, this is the doctrine and practice of Rome at the present day. Pope Leo the Tenth adds the merits of Christ to the Pope's fund. 'The Roman Pontiff may,' he says, 'for reasonable causes, grant Indulgences out of the superabundant merits of Christ and the Saints, to the faithful, as well for the living as for the dead;' and, in thus dispensing the treasure of the merits of Jesus Christ, and the Saints, he either confers the Indulgence by the method of absolution, or transfers it by the method of suffrage." *Cramp's Text Book, p.* 340.

The Council of Trent passed a Decree, " so that," as they say, " the gift of Holy Indulgences may be dispensed to the faithful in a pious, holy, and incorrupt manner." *Sess. xxv.*

The whole benefit of these Indulgences arises out of the doctrine of Purgatory; and is applicable to the state of the souls in that place of confinement. They are granted, and sold at the rate of so many days in Purgatory. *One day's indulgence* means, that the purchaser shall have for his service or cash, one day taken off from the time of his sentence to Purgatory; " two hundred days' Indulgence," entitles him to a deduction of two hundred days from the time of his sentence; and when we learn, that, for every kiss impressed on the great black Cross in the coliseum at Rome, two hundred days Indulgence are allowed, every one fortunate enough to reach it, would seem easily to kiss away the pains of Purgatory. Of this, however, the poor Roman catholic may not be too sure, for the pains of Purgatory run to the utmost verge of time; and that is a period remote in the calendar of Rome: for the Pope sells at no very exorbitant rate, ten, twenty, and even thirty thousand years' indulgence. Rogues of the Roman faith have it, therefore, in their power, for a very reasonable consideration, to carry the Pope's writ of Indulgence with them, to an extent that flatters them with the hope of escape shortly from the scorching fires to the blissful pains of the world to come.

" Incalculable treasures have flowed into the lap of the Roman catholic Clergy, for which they have to thank the doctrine of Purgatory. The Pope knew his interests too well, not to tack the doctrines of Transubstantiation, and the Mass, on that of souls in Purgatory. If a Mass, he said, is a repetition of the great sacrifice on the Cross, and it is in the power of the

Priest to apply the benefit of it to any one, by naming that one in the select consecrating prayer, then, by sending such a relief to a soul in Purgatory, that soul has the greatest possible chance of being set free from the burning flames, and entering at once into heaven. Who, that believes this doctrine, will spare his pocket, when he thinks his dearest relations are asking the aid of a Mass, to escape out of the burning furnace! Accordingly, you will find, that no Roman catholic who can afford it, omits to pay as many Priests as possible, to say Masses for his deceased relations and friends, and that the poor of that persuasion both in England and Ireland, establish clubs, for the purpose of collecting a fund, out of which a certain number of Masses are to be purchased for each member when he dies. Their accounts are regularly kept, and if any poor member dies, without having paid up his subscription, he is allowed to be tormented to the full amount in the other world, where the difference between rich and poor, according to these doctrines, is much greater than in this life. A rich man may sin away, and settle the account with Masses; but the poor man must be a beggar even at the gates of heaven, and for his want of money to buy Masses and Indulgences, he must stay out his full time in the fires of Purgatory. If a man, for instance, has been guilty of the most horrid crimes, murder, adultery, and piracy, during a long life, but, on the gallows he repents of them with full Confessions to the Priest, and receives Absolution of the Roman, his soul goes to Purgatory. There he might be for millions of years, but if you procure him a Plenary Indulgence from the Pope, or, if he obtained one for himself, before his death, all the merits he wanted, are given him, and he flies directly to heaven." PRESERVATIVE AGAINST POPERY, by J. B. White. "Spaniards! ascend to heaven,"— is said to have been the last words of the Roman Priest, to the pirates hung at Boston, this Spring. They had probably devoted money enough out of their plunder, to provide themselves beforehand, every one, with a Plenary Indulgence; and then, by the Absolution of the Priest, they might, according to the doctrine of Rome, ascend directly to heaven.

The Romans are offended, when their Pope is charged with giving permission to sin, to those who are able to pay well for it. The Pope does not so word his Indulgences; but their effect is to permit sin; for when a criminal has bought a Plenary Indulgence, or one hundred thousand years to be deducted

22

from his sentence in the fires of Purgatory, at a certain price, he will be tempted to think he can sin with impunity, at least, for a few days.   Mr. Eustace, himself, a Roman catholic, asks, in view of the notoriously depraved state of the public morals in Italy, whether it may not be ascribed to "the corruptions of the national religion; to the facility of Absolution; and to the easy purchase of Indulgences?" *Classical Tour, Vol.* 3, *p.* 131. The modern traveller may answer, who saw a man at Tivoli, that had stabbed his brother to death, had been to Rome, bought his pardon of the church, and received a written protection from a Cardinal, in consequence of which he was walking about unconcernedly, "a second Cain, whose life was sacred." *Graham's three months East of Rome, p.* 34, quoted in Cramp's Text Book, p. 345.

CHAPTER V.

Roman Pride, Tradition, Confession.

IN the course of this Narrative, enough has already been presented of the peculiarities of Romanism, to make the reader astonished at the delusion of the millions who trust in the Infallibility of the Roman Church, and to create in him a desire to know more about the grounds of their confidence. It will aid the understanding of the Narrative, to know what are the doctrines of Rome upon the topics brought to view in its pages. With the aid of the Rev. JOSEPH BLANCO WHITE, a native of Seville in Spain, and formerly Chaplain to the king of Spain, but now an Episcopal minister of England, I will spread out some of the doctrines of Rome.

Differences are made more manifest by a striking contrast. Take the following from Mr. White, under the parable of two governors.

The people of two neighbouring islands, which acknowledged the authority of the same sovereign, received each a governor from the Metropolis. One of the governors presented himself with his commission in one hand, and with the book of the Laws in the other. "Gentlemen," said he, "my name is Protestant Church. Here is the commission which authorizes me to govern you according to these laws. You have every one a copy in your possession. If ever any of you should think that I am stepping beyond my powers, or governing against the laws, he may examine the point for himself, and consult his friends about it; and if, after all, he feels inclined not to be under me any longer, I will not at all molest him in his removal to the neighbouring island, or elsewhere, carrying away every thing that belongs to him."

The other governor pursued quite a different course. He appeared with all the pomp and display of a great king. He gave out that his name was Holy Roman; and that he had authority from the sovereign to rule all nations, and not only govern according to the book of the laws, but to make new statutes, at his will and pleasure. At the same time, he forbade the possessing and reading of the book of the laws, and charged his officers everywhere to search out, and punish with severe penalties, all those who should possess or read any copy of the laws, without his, or his officers' leave; which leave he only granted to those, who would buy the copy at a great price, having his interpretation along with the laws. Some of his people presented him a petition, saying, "they were perfectly willing to obey any one commissioned by their sovereign; but still they conceived themselves entitled to possess and read the laws of the country; and that, if the sovereign had given their respected governor authority to make additional laws at his will, they would obey them too, provided he would publish, or exhibit, an authentic copy of his commission for this high trust."

The Roman governor was wroth; and answered the petitioners with a voice roaring with fury, that his commission was not written with ink, but was sealed with sovereign power; and that those who scrupled it, should feel its withering touch. The petitioners murmured. "Take these fellows," said the governor, "and let them die by fire." While his servants executed his mandate, some of the citizens attempted to escape from the island; but, at every port, and creek, troops were stationed, who arrested the fugitives, and put them to death without mercy, or confined them in dungeons, until they would take an oath to obey the commands of governor Roman Catholic Church, as reverently as the book of the laws. And, let me tell you, there was among the laws which he added to the statute book, not one but what gave him, or his officers, an increase of wealth and power.

The tyrant governor will not be questioned. He wishes to be thought *Infallible,* and to be believed on his bare word, and he puts to a most cruel death, not only those who resist his will, but those who would escape from him by flight.

The Protestant Clergy declare, that they have no authority but what the Scriptures give, and they submit all their doctrine, and their lives, to be tried by the book of the laws. The Roman Clergy, on the other hand, claim all power, and refuse to submit their doctrine, or their lives, to be tried by any man, except themselves; by any standard, except of their own making. How manifestly are the enormities detailed by Rosamond, the fruits of this irresponsible and exorbitant power!

I have thus far copied almost word for word from Mr. White's third dialogue, "PRESERVATIVE AGAINST POPERY."

and shall continue to do so, while it continues to interest the reader of this Narrative.

The Roman Church grounds its claims on its own authority, and supports its authority with confiscation, fire, and sword. Its fear of the Bible is wonderful. If the Scriptures were favorable to the claims of the Roman Clergy, they would not object to their free circulation. But having introduced many things into the church, which are forbidden in the Bible, they are constrained to keep the Sacred Word under the shadow of their interpretations, lest its pure light should confound their traditions, and images, and false gods.

In every article which Rome, by tradition, attempts to add to the pure gospel, one may plainly see she is striving after wealth and power. The Romans declare that the Scriptures alone are not sufficient for salvation, but that there is a word of God handed down by *hearsay*, which governs the sense of the *written* word. By this *hearsay*, they assure the world that the Scripture must be explained; so that, if the BIBLE says *white*, and the tradition or HEARSAY, says *black*, a Roman Catholic is bound to say that *white* means *black* in God's written Word.

To enable them to distinguish the true from the false *hearsays*, they pretend to a perpetual inspiration in the authorities of their church; but the existence of this miracle in a community by a great majority composed of men like the Roman priests of Cuba, cannot obtain the least credit.

The council of Trent demand that the Old and New Testament, together with the traditions pertaining to faith and morals, and preserved by a continual succession in the Catholic church, shall be received and observed with equal respect and affection. These traditions are words said to have been spoken by the Lord, or dictated by the Holy Spirit; and whoever knowingly despises these traditions is accursed by the Council. See its sess. 4.

Having thus established the validity of their traditions, they proceed, with the Scribes and Pharisees of old, to make void the law of God by their *hearsays*. They introduce, at this open door, every strange doctrine of Rome, Transubstantiation, Purgatory, Confession, images, relics, &c. But I will confine attention, principally, at this time, to that doctrine of Confession, by which Father Manuel Canto took advantage of Don Zobrisco's child Mariettee; and by which many a

22*

Roman priest, in every clime, is enabled to defile the innocent, in the fold of the father and husband, and under the clothing of religion.

In the first place, all Romans pay their Priests a superstitious veneration. A Priest, even when raised to that office from the lowest of the people, is entitled to have his hands kissed with the greatest reverence by every one, male and female, high and low, even by a prince of his Communion. Children are taught devoutly to press their innocent lips upon those hands into which, as they are told, the very Saviour of mankind, who is in heaven, comes down daily: (that is, in the performance of the Mass.) The laws of Roman Catholic countries are, with regard to Priests, made according to the spirit of these extravagant notions. A Priest cannot be tried in Spain by the judges of the land for even the most horrible crimes. "Murders of the most shocking kind have often been perpetrated by Priests in my country," (says J. Blanco White,) "but I do not recollect an instance of their being put to death, except when the murdered person was also a Priest. I knew the sister of a young lady who was stabbed to the heart at the door of the church, where the murderer, who was also her Confessor, had, a few minutes before, given her Absolution. He stabbed her in the presence of her mother, to prevent the young lady's marriage, which was to have taken place that day. This monster was allowed to live, because he was a Priest;" and his judges were Roman Catholic Priests.

What, but the most profound veneration, and servile fear, of the Roman Clergy, could secure them impunity of this kind? The same spirit actuates Priests and people in Cuba, and in Italy, and in Ireland, and in North America. The equality of man with man in this country is maintained by the laws, and titles of nobility are forbidden by the Constitution of the United States; yet the power of the Roman Priests to disperse some mobs, far exceeds that of the officers of the law; and the humble reverence of the Priests for their Roman Bishops, transcends the authority of the American Constitution. In the intercourse of private life the Roman Bishops are styled "My Lord!" and they receive the salutations of their humble followers kneeling or falling before them. For this the Roman Clergy are indebted to tradition, without which pretended source of divine revelation, it would be impossible to persuade whole nations, that a Priest can, at any time, turn a wafer into the Son of God, and can search the hearts of the people, to curse them in their sins, or to absolve them from the penalty of their transgressions.

Whoever has a man's conscience in his keeping, must have the whole man in his power. This is so well known even in Roman Catholic countries, that, when there was a kind of parliament in Arragon, they made a law to prevent the king from choosing his own Priest or Confessor; and the right of electing him was reserved to the representatives of the people, called *Cortes.*

But the bold usurpations of Rome leave her subjects neither understanding nor will, where her interests require them to become blind tools of her own.* She maintains that it is the perfection of faith to believe whatever doctrines she holds, without hesitation or reservation, whether they appear to be true or false: and, indeed, if they *appear* to be false, the greater is the merit of believing them *implicitly.* And she maintains that it is the very height of human perfection, to put the conscience wholly into the keeping of the Priests. Not a single pious book of common reputation in the Roman church, can be found, which does not make unlimited obedience to a Confessor the safest, and most perfect way, to salvation; and, in the same proportion as a Roman Catholic has a will and understanding of his own in religious matters, in that same proportion he acts against the duties enjoined by his religious profession.

The Roman church makes the Confession of every sin, by *thought, word, and deed,* necessary to receive Absolution from a Priest; and teaches, that without Absolution on earth, where it is possible to obtain it, there can be no remission in heaven. The most sincere repentance is not sufficient to save a Roman sinner, without Confession to a Priest, and the Priest's Absolution, if it is possible to apply to a Priest. The Council of Trent teach that all sins committed before baptism are cancelled by baptism; and that sins after baptism are blotted out by Confession to the Priest, and his Absolution pronounced. If sins are knowingly concealed, they are not forgiven. The fainting soul that refuses to open his wound to the surgeon, can not expect it to be healed. The penitent is, therefore, re-

---

* "A *religieuse* should never have a will of her own." Lady Sup. of the Charlestown Nunnery, in "Six Months in a Convent,"—p. 46.

quired to search his recollection diligently, and to explore all the corners and hiding-places of his heart, for the sins he has committed; and to Confess them to a Priest, that he may have forgiveness with God at the hands of the Priest.

On the other hand, they assert, that, even imperfect repentance, which they call *attrition*, will save a sinner, who Confesses, and receives Absolution.

The evident object of doctrines so inconsistent with the letter and spirit of the Scriptures, is, no doubt, that of making the Priesthood absolute masters of the people's consciences. Every Roman Catholic is bound, under pain of excommunication, to Confess, at least once a year; and thus the Priests become intrusted with the secrets of all hearts in the great congregation. They enforce their authority, by impressing the penitents with the belief, that any one sin of the heart knowingly concealed from the Priest through a sense of shame, will make the Absolution pronounced on them a sacrilege, and a mortal sin. The effects of this bondage, the reluctance which young people especially have to overcome, and the frequency of their making up their mind to garble Confession, in spite of their belief, that by silence they increase the number and guilt of their sins, are evils which none but a Roman Priest can be perfectly acquainted with.

The paltry plea of Roman Catholic writers, that Confession is a check upon men's consciences, causing them to restore their ill-gotten wealth, deserves only indignation, as a barefaced attempt to bribe men's love of money to the support of Romanism. In a case where the main interests of religion and morality are concerned, it is an insult to hold up the chance of recovering stolen money through the hands of a Priest, as if to draw away public attention from the monstrous evils, which the reader has seen, and has yet to see, springing out of the Roman doctrine of Confession. Restitution is no more probable among Roman Catholics, than among any other denomination of Christians. It is less probable. For every Protestant firmly believes in the necessity of restitution in order to obtain the divine forgiveness; and he is in no danger of anticipating pardon, without restitution, which the Roman catholic is, owing to the dependance which Romans place on the power of the mysterious words, "*Ego te absolvo*, &c.," used by the Priest in pronouncing Absolution. Having heard the words, the Roman, in the faith that he has received the full pardon, is in no little danger of neglecting the conditions on which it is pronounced. He may, in the joy of his deliverance from the penalty of theft, forget to restore the stolen articles.

The Protestant who earnestly and sincerely wishes the divine pardon, knows that he cannot obtain it, without equally earnest efforts to make restitution; but when the Roman Catholic has assured his Confessor that he will try his best to indemnify those he has wronged, the words of Absolution are, to him, a sort of charm, that removes the guilt at once, and, consequently, relieves his uneasiness about restitution.

One of the greatest evils of Confession is, that it has changed the genuine repentance preached in the Gospel,—that conversion and change of life, which is the only true external sign of the remission of sins through Christ, into a ceremony, which silences remorse at the slight expense of a little sorrow for past offences. As the day of Confession approaches, (which, for the greatest part, is hardly once a year,) the Roman Catholic grows restless, uneasy, and gloomy. He mistakes the shame of a disgusting disclosure, for sincere repentance of his sinful actions. At length, he goes through the disagreeable task, and feels relieved. The old score is cancelled; and he may run into a new spiritual debt, with lighter heart. "This I know," says Mr. White, (to whom the reader is indebted for all that is most valuable in this chapter,) "this I know from my own experience, both as Confessor and as penitent. In the same characters, and from the same experience, I can assure you that the practice of Confession is extremely injurious to the purity of mind enjoined in the Scriptures." Filthy communication is inseparable from the Confessional. The Priest, in the discharge of the duty enjoined upon him by his church, is bound to pry out, and listen to the most abominable descriptions of all manner of sins. He must inquire into every circumstance of the most profligate course of life. Men and women, the young and the old, married and single, the rude and the gentle, are all bound to describe to the Confessor the most secret actions and thoughts, which are either sinful in themselves, or may be so from accidental circumstances.

Consider the danger to which the Priests themselves are exposed; a danger that becomes every day more overwhelming to the poor soul of the Priest, as the filthy communications he has before received are working their natural corruption of his good manners, and correct habits; a danger so imminent,

that the Popes have, on two occasions, been obliged to issue
the most severe edicts against those Priests who openly attempt
the seduction of their female penitents.   I will not, however,
press this subject, because it cannot be done with sufficient
delicacy.

No invention of the Roman church equals this of Confession,
as regards the power it gives the Priesthood.   One of the greatest hinderances to the establishment of a free and rational form
of government in Roman Catholic countries, in Italy, Austria,
and Spanish America, lies in the opposition which free and
equal laws meet with, from the Priests in the Confessional;
and the greatest danger to a free government arises from the
same source; for a Priest can promote even treason with
safety, in the secrecy which protects the Confessor's office.

It is astonishing that the Roman church could persuade the
nations to submit to a power so revolting and dangerous, as
the Priests wield in the Confessional; and it is a question how
far it should be tolerated, and how far restrained, by the laws
of this land of civil and of religious liberty, a land that in prof-
fering freedom to all, does not indulge any with leave to tram-
ple on the neck of a fellow-creature, even a Priest on the neck
of a freeman, in the name of Rome.   The time has come when
the people of the United States are called on to look Rome and
her cohorts in the face; and to establish some bounds to the
deluge of filthy and impious customs, which are pouring into
the country from the territories of the Pope.   The errors of
Rome did not grow up in one night, nor did the power of her
Bishop overtop the kings of the earth in one day.   Hers has
ever been a keen-eyed policy, reaching far into futurity, and
gathering into her fatal grasp the liberties of all nations.   Her
aim is fixed on the subjugation of this country to her imperial
sway, and though the time of conquest must be remote, her
plan is to make it sure in its day.

The man of power in this world, that pretends to be infallible, must be by nature intolerant, so soon as his infallibility becomes predominant.   The infallible man, when he has the
power, will compel other men to conform to his infallible example, and to believe his infallible opinions, and to bow before
his infallible will and pleasure.   Such a one is growing up,
and daily strengthening itself in these free states: such a one is
the Roman church that is now gentle as a candidate for public

favor; and yet, in its nature, is oppressive as the Roman Priest in the Confessional.

The enormous power of searching the hearts and of forgiving the sins of the people grew up imperceptibly in the hands of the Priesthood, together with the whole system of the Roman religion. It was the practice in the primitive Church, to exclude scandalous persons from public worship, until they confessed their misconduct before the whole congregation. This mode of discipline became burdensome at length, and it was left by the congregation with the pastors to receive the confessions of the scandalous, and to restore the truly penitent to the rights of a worshiper. In the growing ignorance and corruption of aftertimes, the people began to believe that this act of external reconciliation with the congregation was a real absolution of the moral guilt of the sin; and the church of Rome, with that perpetual watchfulness, by which she has never omitted an opportunity of increasing her power, foisted upon the Christian world what Romans call the Sacrament of Penance, obliging her members, as they wish for the Lord's gracious pardon of their manifold sins, to Confess them every one to a Roman Priest.

CHAPTER V.

SUPERSTITION.

White. Before I proceed, I must ask you whether you have a clear idea of superstition?

Reader. I believe I have a tolerable good notion of it.

White. Superstition consists in credulity, hopes and fears about invisible and supernatural things, on slight and fanciful grounds. We call that man superstitious, who is ready to believe any idle story of ghosts and witches; who nails a horse-shoe upon the ship or barn to keep off bad luck, and dreads evil consequences from stepping out of doors the first time in the morning with his left foot first. Rome encourages this state of mind, though not these very things.

Every church may be compared to a great school of religious instruction. I will present you a pupil of the Roman school, and draw the picture from various Roman catholics whom I have intimately known.

Imagine my Romanist friend retiring to his bed at night. The walls of the room are covered with pictures of all sizes. Upon a table there is a wooden or brass figure of our Saviour nailed to the Cross, with two wax candles, ready to be lighted, at each side. Our Romanist carefully locks, lights up the candles, kneels before the Cross, and beats his breast with his clenched right hand, till it rings again in a hollow sound. It is probably a Friday, a day of penance: the good man looks pale and weak. I know the reason—he has made but one meal on that day, and that on fish; had he tasted meat, he feels assured he should have subjected his soul to the pains of hell. But the mortifications of the day are not over. He unlocks a small cupboard, and takes out a scull, which he kisses, and places upon the table at the foot of the Crucifix. He then strips off his clothes, and with a scourge, composed of small twisted ropes hardened with wax, lays stoutly to the right and left, till his bare skin is ready to burst with accumulated blood. The discipline, as it is called, being over, he mutters several prayers, turning to every picture in the room. He then rises to go to bed; but before he ventures into it, he puts his finger into a little cup which hangs at a short distance over his pillow, and sprinkles with the fluid it contains, the bed and the room in various directions, and finally moistens his forehead in the form of a Cross. The cup, you must know, contains Holy Water—water in which a Priest has put some salt, making over it the sign of the Cross several times, and saying some prayers, which the church of Rome has inserted for this purpose in the Mass-book.

The use of that water, as our Roman Catholic has been taught to believe, is to prevent the devil from approaching the places and things which have been recently sprinkled with it; and he does not feel himself safe in his bed without the precaution which I have described. The Holy Water has, besides, an internal and spiritual power of washing away venial sins; those light sins, I mean, which, according to the Romanist, if unrepented, or unwashed away by Holy Water, or the sign of the Cross made by the hand of a Bishop, or some other five or six methods, which I will not trouble you with, will keep the venial sinner in Purgatory for a certain time.

The operations of the devout Roman Catholic are probably not yet done. On the other side of the Holy Water cup, there hangs a frame, holding a large cake of wax, with figures raised by a mould, not unlike a large butter-pat. It is an Agnus Dei, blest by the Pope, which is not to be had except it can be imported from Rome. I believe the wax is kneaded with some earth from the place where the supposed bones of the martyrs are dug up. Whoever possesses one of those spiritual treasures, enjoys the benefit of a great number of indulgences; for, each kiss impressed on the wax, gives him the whole value of fifty or one hundred days employed in doing penance and good works; the amount of which is to be struck off the debt which he has to pay in Purgatory.

I should not wonder if our good man, before laying himself to sleep, were to feel about his neck, for his Rosary or Beads. Perhaps he has one of particular value, and like that which I was made to wear next my skin, when a boy. A Priest had brought it from Rome, where it had been made, if we believe the certificates, of bits of the very stones with which the first martyr, Stephen, was put to death.

Being satisfied that the Rosary hangs still on his neck, he arranges its companion, the Scapulary, formed of two square

23

pieces of the stuff which is exclusively worn by some religious order. By means of the Scapulary, he is assured either that the Virgin Mary will not allow him to remain in Purgatory beyond the Saturday next to the day of his death; or, he is made partaker of all the penances and good works performed by the Religious of the Order to which the Scapulary belongs.

At last, having said a prayer to the Angel, who, he believes, keeps a constant guard over him, the devout Romanist composes himself to sleep, touching his forehead, his breast, and the two shoulders, to form the figure of a Cross ✛. The prayer and ceremonies of the morning are not unlike those of the night. Armed with the sprinkling of Holy Water, he proceeds to Mass; if it happens to be one of the privileged days, in which souls may be delivered out of Purgatory, you will see him saying a certain number of prayers at different altars. He will repeat the Rosary in honor of the Virgin Mary, dropping through his fingers either fifty-five or seventy-seven beads, which are strung in the form of a necklace. There may be a blessing with the *Sacrament*, which the good Catholic will not lose, for the sake of the Plenary Indulgence which the Pope grants to such as are present. On that occasion you would see him kneeling and beating his breast, while the Priest, in a splendid cloak of silk and gold, in the midst of lighted candles, and the smoke of frankincense, makes the sign of the Cross with a consecrated wafer, enclosed between two pieces of glass set in gold.

It would, indeed, be an endless task, were I to enumerate all the methods and contrivances of this kind, recommended by the church of Rome to all her members, and practised by all who are not careless of their spiritual concerns. These are facts which no honest Roman Catholic will venture to deny. I therefore ask, whether, since Revelation is the only means we have of distinguishing between religion and superstition, I ask whether the whole system of the church of Rome, for the attainment of Christian virtue, is not a chain of superstitious practices, calculated to accustom the mind to imaginary fear, and to fly to the church for fanciful remedies? St. Paul had a prophetic eye on this adulterated Christianity, when he cautioned the Colossians, saying: "*Let no man, therefore, judge you in meat or in drink, or in respect of a holy-day. Let no man beguile you of your reward in a voluntary humility, and worshiping of angels, intruding into those things which he hath not seen, vainly puffed up by his fleshly mind, and not holding the head from which all the body by joints and bands, having nourishment ministered, and knit together, increaseth with the increase of God. Wherefore, if ye be dead with Christ from the rudiments of the world, why, as though living in the world, are ye subject to ordinances, (touch not, taste not, handle not, which all are to perish with the using,) after the commandments and doctrines of men? Which things have indeed a show of wisdom in will-worship and humility, and neglecting of the body."* Col. ii.

I cannot conceive a more perfect resemblance than that which exists between the picture of a devout Romanist, and the *will-worship* described in this passage. Observe the distinction of days, the prohibition of certain meats, the worshiping of angels, the numerous ordinances, the mortification and neglect of the body, and most of all, the losing hold of the head, Christ, and substituting a constant endeavour to *increase,* spiritually, by *fleshly,* that is, external means, instead of fortifying, by a simple and spiritual worship, the *bands and joints,* through which alone the Christian can have nourishment, *and increase with the increase of God.*

Reader. I confess that the likeness is very striking. But I wish to know if all will-worship of the Romanists is fully recommended by their church.

White. It is, and in the most solemn and powerful manner. You have only to look into the devotionals which are used among the Romanists, and you will find their Bishops encouraging this kind of religious discipline in the most unqualified terms. I could read to you passages innumerable, confirming and recommending more *fleshly ordinances* than ever the Jews observed: and this, too, in English Roman catholic books, which, for fear of censure on the part of the Protestants, are generally more shy of disclosing the whole system of their church, than those published abroad. But what settles the point at once, and shows, that it is the church of Rome, and not any private individual, that adulterates the character and temper of Christian virtue, I have only to refer you to their Common Prayer-book, which they call the *Breviary.* Now, that is a book not only published and confirmed by three Popes, but which they oblige their whole Clergy to read daily, for at least an hour and a half. Such, indeed, is the importance which the church of Rome attaches to that book, that she d clares any Clergyman or Monk who omits, even less than an eighth part of the appointed daily reading, guilty of sin worthy of hell,—a mortal sin, which deprives man of the grace of God. The *Breviary* contains Psalms and Collects, and lives of Saints, for every day of the year. Those lives are given as examples of what the church of Rome declares to be Christian perfection, and her members are, of course, urged to imitate them as far as it may possibly be in every one's power. Now, I can assure you, having been for many years forced to read the *Breviary* daily, that there is not one instance of a Saint whose worship is not grounded by the church of Rome, mainly upon the most extravagant practice of external ceremonies, and the most shocking use of their imaginary virtue of Penance.

Reader. What do they mean by penance?

White. The voluntary infliction of pain on themselves, to expiate their sins.

Reader. Do they not believe in the atonement of Christ?

White. They believe that the atonement is enough to save them from Hell, but not from a temporal punishment of sin.

Reader. But have they not *Plenary Indulgences* to satisfy for that temporal punishment?

White. So they believe; but the truth is, that they cannot understand themselves upon the subject of penance and Indulgences. Penance, however, the Roman church recommends even at the expense of depraving the sense of the Gospel in their translations. As there is nothing in the New Testament which can make self-inflicted pain a Christian virtue, the Romanists, wanting a text to support their practices, have rendered the third verse of the 13th Chapter of Luke, "*unless ye be* PENITENT, *ye shall all perish,*" Yet, this was not enough for their purpose; and, as the same sentence is repeated in the 5th verse, there they slipt in the word PENANCE. Their translation of that verse is, "*unless ye shall* DO PENANCE, *you shall all alike perish.*" By the use of this word they make their laity believe, that both Confession, which they call *penance,* and all the bodily mortification which go among them by the same name, are commanded by Christ.

Reader. That, Sir, I look upon as very unfair.

White. And the more so, my friend, as in the original Gospel, the word used by the inspired writer is the same in both verses, and cannot by any possibility mean any thing but a *change of the mind*, which we properly express by the word *repent.*

Reader. What, Sir, is the origin of their attachment to bodily mortification?

White. A mean estimate of the atonement of Christ; and the example of some fanatics, whom, at an early period of the corruptions of Christianity, Rome declared to be Saints and patterns of Evangelical virtue. The Monks, who took them for their models, gained an unbounded influence in the church; and, both by the practice of some enthusiasts among them, and by the stories of miracles which they reported as being the reward of their bodily mortification, confirmed the opinion of the great merit of penance among the laity. Here, also, the mutual aid of the doctrines invented by Rome, contributed to increase the error; for as the Popes teach that the *Indulgences* which they grant are taken from the treasure of merits collected by the Saints, it is the interest of those who expect to escape from Purgatory by the aid of Indulgences, that the treasure of penances be well stocked; and they greatly enjoy the accounts of wonderful mortifications which their church gives them in her Prayer-book. You know that Saint Patrick is one of the most favorite Saints among the Irish Roman catholics, as having been the first who introduced Christianity into their Island. The church of Rome gives the following account of his daily religious practices; holding him up, of course, as a pattern, which if few can fully copy, every one will be more perfect as he endeavours to imitate:—The *Breviary* tells the Roman Catholic, that when their patron Saint was a slave, having his master's cattle under his care, he used to rise before daylight, under the snows and rains of winter, to begin his usual task of praying *one hundred times* in the day, and again *one hundred times* in the night. When he was made a Bishop, we are told that he repeated every day the one hundred and fifty Psalms of the Psaltery, with a collection of canticles and hymns, and two hundred collects besides. He made it also a daily duty to kneel three hundred times, and to make the sign of the Cross with his hand eight hundred times a day. In the night he recited one hundred Psalms, and knelt two hundred times,—passed one third of it up to his chin in cold water, repeating fifty Psalms more, and then rested for two or three hours on a stone pavement.

23*

Reader. I cannot believe it possible for a man to perform what you have said, unless he have the strength and velocity of a steam engine. That account must be false.

White. I will not enter into the question of its probability; all I have to do with, is the principle which it inculcates, and proposes to the Roman catholics. External ceremonies, and a course of self-murdering practices, are proposed by the church of Rome, in nine out of ten lives of her Saints, as objects of imitation. In the same spirit, St. Catherine of Siena is represented as so addicted to the practice of fasting, that heaven, to indulge her in the performance of that pretended virtue, kept her by miracle, without food, from Ash-Wednesday till Whit-Sunday. (So the *Breviary* proclaims before the face of the world.) That is, 94 days, from the fourth of March to the seventh of June.

Reader. How far does the church of Rome recommend the infliction of pain, as penance?

White. To an excess that destroys every year many well-meaning and ardent persons, especially young women of that Communion.* These deluded creatures read the lives of Saints set forth by their church, and there they find many females who are said to have arrived at great perfection by living like St. Elizabeth of Portugal, one half the year on bread and water; besides the constant use of scourging their bodies, sleeping on the naked ground, wearing bandages with points that run into the flesh, plunging into freezing water, and ten thousand other methods of gradually destroying life. But when a young, tender, and ardent mind, is taught that God is pleased by voluntary suffering, and reads that the church of Rome has made Saints of those who have died by penances, every thing which falls short of actual self-murder, will assume the appearance of moderation.

The church of Rome, in her *Breviary*, commends Saint Theresa, because " *her ardor in punishing the body was so vehement as to make her use hair shirts, chains, nettles, scourges, and even roll herself among thorns, regardless of a diseased constitution.*" These are the words of the Breviary: from

---

* "Sister Mary Magdalene was in a consumption. She had entered the Convent nine months before in perfect health, and was now worn out with austerities." She died soon after. " *Six Months in a Convent,*" p. 105.

So many were the victims that died under the austerities of the Monastic Rules in Kentucky, that the friends and relations of these self-murdering devotees, had to remonstrate with the Superior of the Order; who, at length, in consequence of their repeated solicitations and complaints, relaxed the severity of the discipline.—Ed.

which the enthusiastic Roman catholic properly infers, that to disregard a diseased constitution, and hasten death, is a virtue. That such is the effect of the Popes' lives of the Saints, is clear from what the *Breviary* relates of another female Saint, called Rose of Lima. She, it is said in the Roman catholic Prayer-book, "from a desire to imitate St. Catherine," wore, day and night, three folds of an iron chain round her waist, a belt set with small needles, and an iron crown armed inside with points, all next the skin. She made to herself a bed of the unpolished trunks of trees, and filled up the chinks with pieces of broken pottery. The *Breviary* adds, that she did all this in spite of her "tortures from sickness," and was therefore frequently visited by Saints, angels, and even by our Saviour from heaven.

Reader. But, do Roman catholics really believe in those visits?

White. A sincere Roman catholic cannot disbelieve what his own church so constantly teaches, without entertaining strange suspicions against the veracity of the organ and ground of his faith. Nothing can be more positively asserted, than these supernatural wonders; nothing more frequently repeated, than the thousands of miracles contained in the *Breviary.* If, therefore, a Roman Catholic believes them all, or the greatest part, he must be credulous like a child; if he disbelieves them all, or the greatest part, he must look on the Popes and the church of Rome, either as a set of rogues, or downright fools.

Were I to translate the stories of Saints from the *Breviary,* you would imagine I was amusing you with tales of goblins and fairies. You would hear of three different Saints who have sailed on their cloaks, as if on board a ship, carrying sometimes several Monks with them. In that manner we are assured by the Pope, that Saint Francis de Paula crossed the straits of Sicily; Saint Raymond de Pennafort, from Majorca to Barcelona; and Saint Hyacinth, a large river of Poland, swollen by a flood. You would hear of a Saint Frances of Rome, who would stand for a long time in a river without being wet; and who used to quench her thirst with grapes produced by miracle, in the heart of winter. You would find a Saint Peter of Alcantara, who was provided with a roof of snow, under which he might pass the night, and who made his staff grow into a fig-tree!

What man of common sense would remain in the church of England, if our Prayer-book had it, as a most certain fact, that

Westminster Abbey had been built at Paris, in France, and
that some hundred years ago, it had taken a flight to the French
coast, opposite to Dover: and having rested a few years, had,
in a second flight, placed itself where it now stands?

Reader. Has the *Breviary* any story like this?

White. Perfectly like it. It relates that the house in which
the Virgin Mary lived in the land of Judea, was carried through
the air, by angels, to the Coast of Dalmatia, and from thence
to Loretto, in the Pope's dominions, where it is worth millions
to the Popish Clergy; such is the number of Pilgrims that go
to visit it, and the large and valuable presents which for many
centuries have been sent by Roman catholic Princes and No-
blemen to ornament it.

Reader. There is so much falsehood in the face of that
story, that I would not believe any thing in the shape of a Miracle from the same channel.

White. Yet there are Roman catholics, who, rather than
give way to the Protestants, will endanger the credit of the
whole Gospel, by asserting that he who will not believe in the
miracles which are reported on the authority of the church of
Rome, has no reason to receive those of the Gospel. Were we
to believe the Roman catholic Prayer-book, there is scarcely a
Saint, who did not begin to work miracles from its birth: nay,
we are told of St. Bridget, that she saved her mother from
drowning, being as yet in the womb!

The bells used to ring of their own accord when Saints were
born, as happened with St. John *a Deo*, St. Peter Celestinus,
and many others; a swarm of bees built a honey-comb in the
hands of St. Ambrose, St. Peter Nolascus, St. Isadore, and several other Saintly babes, while in their cradles. Another baby
Saint had her face changed into a Rose, from which her name
was given her. These holy children often speak before they
are five months old, as was the case with St. Philip Beniti, who,
at that age, scolded his mother for not giving alms to some
begging Friars. All these wonders, and ten thousand others,
still more absurd, are asserted in the Prayer-book of the church
of Rome.

Reader. I cannot help thinking, that though the church of
Rome is not the best school for Christian instruction, it must
afford a mine of amusement to its followers. Her ceremonies,
her miracles, her relics, must afford an agreeable variety to
those who have never doubted her creed.

White. Ah, my friend! nothing can be more deceitful than the appearance of that church. There is more misery produced by her laws and institutions, than I can possibly describe, though I have drunk her cup of bitterness to the dregs. In the first place, a sincere mind, which is made to depend for the hope of salvation, on any thing but faith and unbounded trust in the Saviour, can never enjoy that Christian peace, " *which passeth all understanding.*" I have known some of the most conscientious Roman catholics, which that church can boast of; my own mother and sisters were among them. I have been a Confessor not a few years, and heard the true state of mind of the most religious Nuns, and such as were looked upon as living Saints, by all the inhabitants of my town. From this intimate knowledge of their state, I do assure you, that they are, for the greatest part, so full of doubts about their salvation, as not unfrequently to be driven to madness.* In their great anxiety to accumulate *merits*, (for they are taught that their penances and religious practices are deserving of reward in heaven,) they involve themselves in a maze of external performances. Then comes the fear of sin, in the very things which they undertake under the notion of pleasing God; and, as they believe their works are to be weighed and valued in strict justice, the sincerity of their hearts cannot help discovering, not only that they are nothing worth, but that sin is often mixed with their performance. In this state, they are never impressed with the idea, that " *the blood of Christ cleanseth from all sin*," whenever the sinner, with a lively faith, receives him as his only Saviour. They are not taught that good works are the fruit of true faith; but that they bear a true share with Christ in the work of our salvation. They are thus forced, by their doctrines, to look to themselves for the hope of heaven; and what can be the consequence, but the most agonizing fear ? With the view of heaven and hell perpetually before their eyes, and a strong belief, that the obtaining of the one, and the avoiding of the other, depends on the performance of a multitude of self-imposed duties, as complicated, and more difficult than those of the ceremonial law of the Jews; what can be the result, but distracting anxiety? In his progress through the stormy sea of life, the Romanist clings with one hand to Christ and to

---

* This I confirm, and my knowledge of the fact is derived from the same source as that of Joseph Blanco White ; and that is, from Confession.—Ed.

the Saints, and depends on the strength of the other to break the waves. He looks, (as man always does, in cases of great danger,) not to the stronger, but to the weaker ground of his dependance for safety. Fear constantly predominates in his heart. "Mind your swimming hand," say his Priests; "ply it stoutly, or Christ will allow you to sink!" "*Repent; and believe on the Lord Jesus Christ, and ye shall be saved,*" is the language of the Bible. We *must change our mind,* (for that is what repentance means,) from the pursuit of righteousness, and bring forth fruit meet for repentance, placing our whole trust in Christ, in order to become justified with God. But the Roman catholic believes, that his good works are, in part, at least, the ground of his justification, and he is anxious to increase it, by the performance of numerous external ordinances, and especially by the endurance of self-inflicted misery, all which fails to satisfy the conscience, fails to compose the troubled heart to rest.

CHAPTER VI.

THE APOSTACY—IMAGES.

Our Lord, in discoursing with his disciples of the sign of his coming, and of the end of the world, cautions them, that "*Many false prophets shall rise, and deceive many.*" *Matt.* xxiv. 11. By prophets, ministers are intended, or preachers. He had already taught them how they might know them "*by their fruits,*" on two different occasions, *Matt.* vii. 15; and *Matt.* xii. 33.

The blessed Peter, and the beloved John likewise, forewarn us of the same thing. "*There shall be false teachers among you, who privily shall bring in damnable heresies, even denying the Lord that bought them.*" 2 *Pet.* ii. 1. "*This is that spirit of Antichrist, whereof ye have heard that it should come.*" 1 *John* iv. 3.

But Paul is more particular. In the 2d Thess. 2d chapter, he speaks of the "*falling away,*" which shall unfold itself gradually, and come forth in the form of *the Man of Sin, the Son of Perdition, whom the Lord shall consume with the spirit of his mouth, and destroy with the brightness of his coming.* In other places he speaks of the same thing. 1 *Tim.* iv. 1; *and* 2 *Tim.* iii. 1.

The book of Revelation exhibits the same fact in the delineation of *Babylon the Great,* its seat, its power, its character, and its fall. And the learned Roman catholics admit, that the Babylon of the Revelation is Rome, but they say it is manifestly Pagan Rome, and not Christian Rome, that is intended by the prophecy. (*Eus. His. L.* 2. *c.* 14. *Bar. An. Vol.* 1. 380. *Bellarmine.*)

It is essential to the *apostacy* intended, that it should occur in the Church; for it is impossible to "*fall away*" from ground, on which the falling body did not once stand. And, moreover, Paul says expressly, that the man of sin shall sit in the temple, or house of God, 2 *Thess.* ii. 4; and that the house of God is the church. 1 *Tim.* iii. 15. So, likewise, it is essential to *false* prophets and teachers, that they should come in the form and profession of Gospel ministers. "*By their fruits ye shall know them.*"

The fruits of the Roman prophets and teachers, are plainly exhibited in these papers; but lest some should think it impossible that sensible and learned men, professing godliness, and resting their eternal hopes on the Gospel and its promises, should worship images of wood and stone, and fall into the snares of the great Adversary, to do his works of darkness, as these pages show, I have thought good to examine some of the doctrines of Rome in connexion with the practices of those who teach them, as narrated here; among which, that of image worship, or idolatry, is one of the most conspicuous.

Idolatry in the church is the most barefaced apostacy. Romans themselves admit it. How, therefore, do they pretend to be the true church, and yet bow down before, and lift up their eyes and their voice unto, a graven image? Charity forbids that we should believe them guilty of it, so long as the evidence in the case does not compel our belief; and having been so long time one, who accounted this charge of idolatry against the Romans to be the offspring more of bitter prejudice, and settled hatred, than of immutable truth, I am willing to meet the reader with abundance of facts, to enable him to judge for himself of the apostacy of Rome from the Christian faith in the matter of worshiping idols.

No evidence of the use of images in the churches, or in connexion with Christian worship, is found earlier than the time of Constantine. Paul openly rebuked the Athenians for thinking that "*the Godhead is like unto gold, or silver, or stone, graven by art, or man's device?*" *Acts* xvii. 29; and the silversmith who made shrines at Ephesus, caused no small excitement against the Apostle, because he brought contempt upon images, not excepting that of the Great Diana, "*whom Asia, and all the world worshipeth.*" *Acts* xix. 27.

The Apostle does not charge the Athenians with the folly of thinking the gold, or silver, or graven image, was God; but in the *likeness* of God: nor do Demetrius and the craftsmen say, that all Asia and the world worshiped the *image*, but Diana, whom the image represented. Yet the Romans think it no sin to reverence and kneel before the images, because they know that the silver Crucifix is not the Christ, and the painted and carved wood, or graven stone, is not the Virgin Mary; and because they only paid their adorations to the heavenly inhabitant, through the visible representation on canvass, wood, and stone.

The Athenians and the Ephesians could have equally well defended their worship from the attacks of the Apostle by the same argument now in common use among Roman catholics. The worshipers of Juggernaut now, and of Dagon in the times of Samuel, could equally well explain the difference between the God they worshiped, and the image, *before which* they worshiped him.

The ancient Romans were devout in this way. The Scipios, the Ciceros, and the Fabii of old Rome, feared the heathen gods, and the retributions of the world of spirits: these gods, however, were in heaven, were spirits of the air, and not the images, before which they worshiped the gods. The Greeks undoubtedly worshiped the supposed heavenly inhabitants, and feared the thunder-bearing Jupiter; but they paid their vows, like the modern Romans, before images of gold, silver, or stone, graven by art, or man's device, in the likeness of the godhead which they adored.

It appears throughout this Narrative, (as it is, also, well known to all travellers in Popish countries,) that the Roman catholics have their images, and do worship before them; and they call the wood or stone by the name of the person it is meant to represent, as if that person were present in the place of the picture, or graven or molten image. Such a habit have they, and have those who learn of them, that they speak of the image of Peter, as Peter; and of the image of Mary, as the virgin herself; insomuch that in this very Narrative, one of the corrections to be made, was, the insertion of the "*image of,*" before the name of the image: as for example, the Narrative read according to the language of Roman catholics, "candles burning under our Saviour and the Virgin Mary;" which, as afterward corrected by her, reads, candles burning under *the image representing* our Saviour and the Virgin Mary. So "they carried our Saviour and the Virgin Mary;"—that is, they carried canvass, wood, or stone, representing the Lord of glory and the blessed Virgin. But Roman catholics uniformly call the images ST. MARY, ST. PAUL, ST. MICHAEL, our SAVIOUR, &c. &c. It is almost incredible that such a thing exists in the present enlightened age of the world, and among professors of the Christian religion; but they are common in the Roman church, and are universal in Roman countries. They may be

24

traced to their source, in the church, about the time of the Diocletian persecution, and the triumph of Constantine which
closely followed it.

It strikes the reader of the Bible with wonder, that Israel
should have enticed Aaron to make for them a calf to worship,
even while Moses in the mount received the Tables of the
Law, written with the finger of God; and that Solomon should
have turned from the temple which he had built, and from JE-
HOVAH, whom he had invoked in the dedication, and whose
glory, by a divine manifestation, filled the house, to worship
"*Ashtoreth, the goddess of the Zidonians,*" and "*Milcom, the
abomination of the Ammonites,*" and "*Chemosh of Moab, and
Molech.*" 1 *Kings,* xi. 5—8. It fills the mind with astonish-
ment, that while the Jews experienced so much of the divine
favor, they should have apostatized from God, and have made
to themselves images; that they should not have considered
nor understood enough to say of the wood : "*I have burned
part of it in the fire, yea, also I have baked bread upon the coals
thereof, I have roasted flesh, and eaten it ; and shall I make
the residue thereof an abomination ? Shall I fall down to the
stock of a tree.*" *Isa.* xliv. 19. They were given into the hands
of ancient Babylon for their idolatry; and it may be for the
same reason that the church of the Gentiles has been given
into the hands of modern Babylon. It is amazing, but not
more strange, that the modern church should fall into idolatry,
than that the ancient church should apostatize. The sin of
idolatry was the ruin of Jerusalem, and the same sin has long
overhung the church of Rome with threatening clouds of
swift destruction.

The introduction of images into the sanctuary of our Lord
Jesus Christ, is so contradictory to the plain terms of Holy
Writ, and yet so common, that one can hardly believe the customs of the Roman catholic church. They deny the worship of
images, but their actions give a flat denial to their words. To
explain this state of things, we look earnestly into the origin
and history of the practice of image worship in the church.

Neither the Apostles, nor any writers of the Church after
them, make mention of images in the churches, until the 4th
century. *Minutius Felix,* about the year 211, published a
dialogue of a Christian and Pagan, disputing about the relative
value of their different modes of faith and worship. The Pagan
demands of the Christians : " cur nullas aras habent templa nulla

nulla nota simulacra?" (Why they have no altars, no temples, no celebrated statues?) That which to the Pagan was a reproach, was glory to the Christian; but it is *not* the glory of modern Rome: she has altars, and temples, and statues enough, to satisfy any Pagan of ancient or modern times. *See Baronius' Annals*, vol. 2. p. 238.

This Baronius is the Annalist of Rome, and without hesitation his statements are received by the Roman catholics, as those of Robertson are by Scotchmen. The first color of an image in the church that he takes notice of, is a picture of a man carrying a sheep on his back, representing on the glass communion cup, the Shepherd's recovery of his hundredth sheep, lost in the mountains. (See the parable, Luke xv.) This is mentioned by Tertullian, *De Pud. cap.* x. *Bar. vol.* 2. *p.* 349. Of these cups, "numbers were found in the ancient cemetery of Priscilla, Via Salaria, Rome, opened in 1578." Bar. 1. 529.

Supposing the fact were, as Baronius states; the figure on a consecrated cup used in the Sacrament, is a very different thing from an image set out by itself; and the use of the cup is legitimate, whatever image may be on it; while worshiping before an image is forbidden, whatever its form may be. But the story is improbable.

The next mention of the introduction of images made by the historian of the Roman church, is in connexion with the name of Gregory Thaumaturgus, *St. Gregory, the miracle worker,* who lived in the middle of the third century. Gregory was a Bishop of Great Armenia, in Asia. During the 7th or Decian persecution, A. D. 250, he saved his life by flight. On his return after the persecution, he instituted games and festivals in honor of the recent martyrs, and in imitation of the Pagan games, at the tomb of the celebrated dead. Virgil's description of the games at the tomb of Anchises is of this sort. Gregory Nyssen, who lived within a hundred years of Gregory Thaumaturgus, celebrated the memory of the great man in an oration, from which Baronius furnishes the following extract. Bar. Vol. I. p. 372.

" He returned again to the city; and passing through, and searching all the country around, he instituted a supplement, and as it were, a corollary of love to the Holy Deity, (additamentum, et quasi corollarium studii, erga numen divinum instituebat,) everywhere requiring the people to assemble in the name of those who had struggled for the faith; (during the late persecution,) and to celebrate festal days, and solemn rites, (to their memory;) and when different men in different places, had brought forth the bodies of the martyrs, the assembled throngs rejoiced on the anniversary, keeping holydays in honor of the martyrs. And when he had observed how the simple and illiterate multitude persisted in the mistaken respect for images, in order that he might by all means perfect in them what is most excellent; to wit, that, forsaking vain superstitions, they should turn unto God, he permitted them, in honor of the holy martyrs, to make merry, solace themselves, and riot with joy: (permisit eis, ut in memoriam sanctorum martyrum, sese exhilirarent et oblectarent, atque in laetitiam effunderetur.)*

Euthimius, in Panopol. Pars. 3. Tit. 20. quoted by Baronius, says: This Gregory Thaumaturgus, first of all, ordered the wooden Crosses placed by him in certain places, to be worshiped, (adorari;) and that the people should flee to them, as to a sacred refuge. The Saintly acts recorded of the same Gregory, say: "With lighted lamps and candles, he removed the bodies of the martyrs, and placed each one of them honorably by itself; and he ordered the sign of the Lord's passion, the Cross of Christ, to be worshiped in each of these places." And again: "The martyr here also set up the Cross, and bade the multitude assiduously engaged there, and flocking to that place with prompt and ready desire of heart, to offer worship by the adoration of the Cross." Bar. Vol. 3. p. 67. A. D. 311. Sec. 23.

This Euthimius lived in the 12th century; (Lempriere;) and the acts of Gregory are a forgery; yet these are the authority of Baronius for the first worship of the Cross. In forging a story, the great object of desire is, to support the point at issue by a probable statement of pretended facts; and the forger of this story would not have laid the scene of the first worship of the Cross in Armenia, if he could have mustered courage, to lay it in Jerusalem, or Rome; and he would not have dated it A. D. 311, had he dared to have insulted the memory of the

---

* Nyssen does not say that Thaumaturgus gave way to this prejudice "of the simple and illiterate multitude," so far as to allow them holy images as well as holy days, and feasts and games, in honor of the martyrs, although his words imply as much. And here is the first introduction into practice, of *the doctrine of intention.* The doctrine itself was not generally taught, until the order of Jesuits arose; but Thaumaturgus acted upon it. The worship of heathen images, and the keeping of heathen feasts in honor of the dead, were plainly unchristian acts; but Thaumaturgus altered the *intention of the mind,* so as to worship images of the saints, and to keep the feasts of the martyrs in the church, without the sin of idolatry.

Apostles and Christians of the first three centuries, with charging this idolatry of the Cross upon them. Neither the impudence of Euthimius, nor of the forger of the Acts of the Martyrs, attained a sufficient height, to pretend a case of the worship of the Cross, which the historian of the Roman church has deigned to notice, until the 4th century.

In introducing his quotation respecting Gregory Thaumaturgus from Gregory Nyssen, the Roman catholic historian exclaims; "Sed quid!"—But why?—Is it not lawful, to transfer *to pious uses*, the things after their being consecrated by a Holy Rite, which things are impiously used among the pagans in superstitious worship, in order that Christ may be honored of all, even by a high contempt of the devil, in the very way he delights to be worshiped ?"—Oh, what a wonder, that the learned historian of the Roman church, who himself received on one occasion, thirty-one votes out of the seventy for Pope, should think, by the devil's delights, to honour the Saints and their King!

Theodoretus, an Asiatic Bishop, who died about A. D. 460, (Lempriere,) is the next witness introduced by Baronius, to prove the contiguity and fitness of image worship. In his Evang. Verit. Lib. 8. de Mart. Theodoretus treats of the Pagan holydays, piously and devoutly transferred to the service of the Roman catholic church, in honor of the martyrs, and says: "The materials of the overthrown Pagan temples, being rebuilt in temples and altars of the martyrs, are consecrated (to the use of the Church.) The Lord brought his own dead Saints into the temples, in place of your gods, and these, indeed, empty and stript of glory he sent away. And this honor he gave his martyrs: instead of feasts of Pan, of Jupiter, and of Bacchus, that is, solemnities in honor of Jove and of father Bacchus, solemn rites are to be performed with a feast, in honor of Peter, Paul, Thomas, Sergius, Marcellus, Leontius, Antoninus, Mauritius, and other holy martyrs. Instead of the ancient pomp, low obscenity, and immodesty, chaste, pure, and temperate feasts are held, not stained with wine, nor corrupt with wantonness; not filled with laughter, but resounding with cheerful songs, and solemn with hearing sacred discourses." *Bar. vol.* 1. *p.* 588. *and vol.* 1, *p.* 373. This Theodoretus was once deposed from his Bishopric, but whether for teaching idolatry, does not appear. He is certainly explicit and probable in his statement, that the *Saints' holydays* and altars were modestly substituted in place of those of the heathen gods.

24*

some extent, at least, in Asia, so early as the 4th century. It is a very natural account of the origin of the monstrous practice of image worship in the Roman church, and since it is furnished by the learned and most renowned of the historians in that church, it is to be hoped that the Roman catholics will take heed to it.

Baronius reasons upon the statement of Theodoretus in this manner. So Paul seems by very extraordinary prudence, to transfer the altar at Athens, dedicated to the unknown god, to the service of the true God. Again, he did not forbid to eat meat offered to idols, unless a weak brother should be offended at it; "but the superstitious worship of idols having been a long time wholly extinct, and when all occasion of offence seems to have at the same time ceased, why is it not lawful to use any of them, especially when, not by private habit, but by the common custom of the whole Church, some customs common with Pagans are in use, (in the Church.") He then enumerates the dresses of the Roman Priests, and a number of customs, common to the ancient and to the modern Romans, to Pagan and to Christian Rome. *Bar. vol.* 1. *p.* 373. So he admits and justifies idolatry, or image worship.

Eusebius, the historian of the era of Constantine, is also quoted in defence of the use of images in the church. The quotation is an account of the images of our Lord, and of the woman who was healed of her issue of blood, by the touching of the hem of his garment; and exhibits a painful specimen of the credulity and idolatry of the 4th century. Eusebius was a celebrated Bishop, as well as historian. He says, he himself saw the images, (or statues as he calls them,) at Cesarea Philippi; that they were made of brass, and represented the woman supplicating, and the Lord extending his hand towards her. "At his feet," says Eusebius, (meaning the feet of the image representing the Lord,) "grows a certain foreign and unusual herb, which, when it has grown high enough to touch the hem of his brazen garment, has the virtue and medical power of healing every kind of disease. This statue, they say, is a likeness of Jesus, which remains to our times, and journeying to that city, we saw it with our own eyes. *Nor is it wonderful that those gentiles, who were blessed by the Saviour, when he dwelt among men, did make images of him, seeing that we esteem the pictures of Peter and Paul, the Apostles, and even of Christ himself, expressed and preserved in paint-*

ings, with a variety of colors: and that, moreover, as is very likely, because our ancestors, approaching as nearly as possible to the imitation of heathen customs, used in this manner to place before them in honor, those who had been, as it were, their deliverers,—that is, those who had brought them any salvation or relief." Bar. An. A. D. 31. Sec. 75.

This is very plain. Eusebius saw these images; and he and other Bishops esteemed the pictures of Christ and his Apostles; and this custom of esteeming the pictures was adopted by their ancestors from a natural propensity, to come as near as possible to the heathen customs. The urgent reason he does not name, but doubtless it was to save themselves in times of severe persecution, by showing to the persecutors, that though they bowed not to images and statues of the heathen gods, they kept and reverenced the pictures of the Lord and his Saints. No ingenuity can devise a more natural way than this, for the gradual introduction of image worship into the bosom of the church, through her pastors and Bishops, who were the first to be smitten in persecution, and also the first to betray their flocks by the introduction of Pagan customs into the spiritual worship of the Christian Church.

But observe, as evidence of the credulity of that age, that this eminent Bishop believed the story of the divine herb, and its miraculous powers of healing; and observe, as evidence of the ignorance of the age, that this Bishop and learned historian knew so little of the Gospel, that he does not mark, nor does Baronius, the discrepance between the pretended images of the healing, and the fact of the healing. The woman with the issue of blood was healed, not by the Lord extending his hand to her supplication; but by extending her hand in faith, to touch the hem of his garment. Again, she was not a gentile, which the account of Eusebius implies, but a Jewess, as the Scripture implies; and her healing took place, not at, or near Cesarea Philippi, but near Capernaum. The Syrophenician woman was a gentile, and the healing which she sought was much nearer to Cesarea Philippi, in a gentile land; but then that healing was not performed on the woman, nor was it of an issue of blood; it was for her daughter that she obtained the Lord's mercy, and because the daughter was vexed with a devil. The whole story, therefore, sets out in the plainest manner, the credulity, and ignorance, and strange tendency to idolatry, of the great Bishop Eusebius; all which the Roman historian swallows without hesitation, and with a high relish. He makes much of the images of brass, seen by Eusebius, and of the pictures of the Lord and his Apostles, referring to them triumphantly in proof of the contiguity of image worship. I hope the reader will not think lightly of this Baronius, for he is the most eminent historian of the Roman religion, and his statements and opinions are of the greatest weight among all Roman Catholics.

But of this Eusebius, one of the members of the Tyrian Synod, Potamon the Great, Bishop of Heraclea in Egypt, said some hard things to his face. Bishop Eusebius presided in the Synod. Potamon was a member, and addressed the president thus: " Do tell me, were not you and I in prison together during the persecution? I, indeed, lost an eye for maintaining the truth; but you seem to have escaped without any corporal injury; nor have you any testimonial to show of your fidelity; but living, you stand without the loss of a member. How did you escape from prison, unless you promised the persecutors, that you would do that which is base? Eusebius rose in anger, and dismissed the assembly." (*Epiphanius*, quoted by *Bar. vol.* 2. *p.* 762.)

Baronius, and every other historian admits, it is not easy to show that images were used in the Church, before the reign of Constantine; and the reasons which he assigns, are, that the Emperor Diocletian, who preceded Constantine, *ordered them all to be destroyed!*

Much has been said and written of the 10th, and last persecution of the Christians by Diocletian, and of all the persecutions by the Roman Emperors; but who has, at any time, heard before, that the Pagan and persecuting emperors ever destroyed *images?* They worshiped images, and they loved those, who, like them, worshiped images, and they destroyed only the Christians, who, of all men, alone, refused to bow to an idol, made of wood or stone. Diocletian never persecuted idolators, nor destroyed images. No Pagan on record, ever persecuted another for image worship, or destroyed the images of others. Pagans reverence each other's gods. Conquering nations, especially Rome, adopted the gods of the subject nations; and Rome set up an image to the name of Jesus, among her host of deities in the Senate Chamber. It is wholly new under the sun, that the idolators of Rome, or of any other country, have destroyed the images of the gods of other people; and that the persecution of Diocletian was poured out upon the *images* of the church, utterly to destroy them, is a Jesuit's fiction, contrary to the plain testimony of all ancient history.

It is asserted, however, by Baronius, and admitted, that Constantine made many silver images of the Lord, and of his Apostles, of John Baptist, and the Angels, and a multitude of others. Writers of every age and name, may be quoted to prove the Emperor Constantine's use of images in Christian worship: and this most publicly, and often. He came to the throne a Pagan, he was crowned with Pagan rites by Pagans, he married a Pagan, the daughter of the persecuting Emperor, Maximilian, and he lived surrounded by Pagans, administering the government of Rome by a Pagan senate, and he died, and was buried with the usual *apotheosis,* * or deification, of a Pagan emperor of Rome. His own statues were everywhere worshiped by the loyal Pagans, and equal honors were paid by him to statues representing the KING OF KINGS. He tolerated Christianity; but the medals, and adulatory poems and history of those times, show, that *Constantine also worshiped the heathen gods, attributed publicly his prosperity to their favor, and gave them, by name, the honor.* See *Baronius, A. D.* 307. 14.

This is a new light, in which to view the first Christian emperor; and it shall be the work of a few moments to show clearly, it is the true light.

Baronius had access to authorities on this point, probably equal to those possessed by any other historian. He had a strong predilection to prove and maintain the Christianity of Constantine, and any thing which he admits, may be readily taken, to prove the emperor's idolatry.

---

* The apotheosis was done thus for the emperors of Rome. Being dead, the body was laid in the tomb, like that of a common mortal, and the whole city went into mourning. A *Statue* or image of the deceased, however, was laid, as if sick, on a couch in the palace. The Senate sat on the left in black, and the ladies, in white, on the right hand of the sick image, mourning all the day for seven days; during which physicians came daily, and, on examination, pronounced the image getting worse. In the end of the days, it was dead, and nobles bore it on their shoulders to the old Forum, where their sons on one side, and their daughters on the other, sang elegies in memory of the deceased.

Thence they removed the image to the Campus Martius, where a square mass of timber was laid t ,, for the occasion, like a hut, filled with combustibles, and overspread with gold-cloth, and paintings. Beneath this frame is another, and within that another, to the last and the least, in which the image was placed on its couch, and covered with every sort of aromatic, until all the compartments were filled. Then they rode in a circle around the pile. The successor to the empire first applied a torch to the pile, or frame; others imitated him. The flames seize the combustibles, and burst out: at the same time an eagle is let loose from an inner window, which is thought to bear the dead emperor's soul to heaven, to a seat among the gods. From that time he was worshiped as a god, and had sacrifices, altars, temples, and priests, decreed to his service by the Senate of Rome. *Bar. An. vol.* 2. *p.* 311.

It is not necessary to say that in proving his idolatry, his claims to Christianity must fall to the ground with those of Rome.

Reader.—"But do you think to show, at this late day, that Constantine the Great was not a Christian?"

I answer, that I will show indisputably what he was, and then you may say, whether he was a Christian or not. Probably the emperor will appear to have been a politician first, and a Christian, when that did not interfere with his royal sway, and the stability of his throne.

When Constantine came to the throne of his father Constantius, the empire was governed by four emperors. Maximinian. whose daughter Constantine married, had Asia, or the East; Licinius had Illyricum; Maxentius had Italy and Africa, and Constantine had the West, or Gaul, Spain, and Britain. At that time they were *all* Pagans; and, except Constantine, they were also persecutors. In the year 312, Constantine, by agreement with Licinius, marched against Maxentius, and suddenly overthrew him in battle. He attributed his success to a dream, in which he saw a Cross in the heavens with this motto: "*In hoc signo vincas.*"

This has been told with as many variations, as accompany the air of a fashionable strain of music. He adopted what is called a Cross for his banner; and his soldiers fought under it like the favored of heaven; but his banner came no nearer to a Cross, than the emperor did to Christianity. The form is found impressed on many coins of his. According to Baronius, Constantine's name appears with it only in this form. And this is a Cross, but not the likeness of that on which the Son of Man submissively laid down his life at the word of a Roman governor.

The conqueror gave a decided advantage to the persecuted Christians of Italy and Africa. But Rome and her Senate were pagan. So were the other emperors. Constantine could not, if he would, prevent the usual demonstrations of heathen joy for his success. He joined in those demonstrations. He was particularly attentive to the feelings and prejudices of the Romans. He triumphed in the usual heathen form of the Ro man emperors. The arch that was erected to celebrate his victory, was decorated with the usual emblems of Paganism. The Senate erected a statue to the god "*paulo ante Italiæ scutum et corona, a short time before the glory and defence of Italy."* Baronius says this was an image of our Saviour; *" Romæ non ignotam effigiem, an image not unknown at Rome,* which image the emperor Alexander had set up among his household gods. [He reigned at Rome, A. D. 235.] Nor could the Senate, on that account, appear to depart from the customary worship, by erecting a statue to Christ, seeing that Alexander had not departed from it, when he placed this image among the other images of the gods, in the place where he daily went for prayer." *Bar.* A. D. 312. *Sec.* 69. Alexander Severus had statues of Abraham and of Christ in the gallery of his gods. *Milman's Hist. of Jews, B.* 19.

These things belong not to the character of an humble Christian; nor to Christianity. The emperor, at this time, made no profession of Christianity. He was a Pagan, who yet favored Christians, and doubtless respected their faith. He was *Pontifex Maximus,* or Pagan high-priest of Rome, and exercised the powers appertaining to that office, in which office he was followed by his Christian successors on the imperial throne, for more than fifty years, until Gratian was crowned. Gratian first refused this heathen title and pagan office. But the authority of the Pontifex Maximus was important in the government of the Pagan Senate and city of Rome, for by it the emperor could prohibit the voting of the people in the elections, if he found the results likely to displease him: by it he could at any moment interrupt the proceedings of the Senate, could stop the execution of their decrees, could force the consuls to resign, and could make a war depend on his single will.

Indeed, this pontifical power of the Roman emperor is the parent stock into which the Papal power was ingrafted; and the Bishop of Rome has taken for his model, the Pontifex Maximus of Pagan Rome.

Political considerations might seem to justify Constantine in continuing this office, and to justify his successors after him; but it is manifest that the union of this Pagan office, and its necessary duties, with the profession of Christianity in the person of the emperors, for sixty years, must have opened the flood-gates of Pagan superstition into the bosom of the church. And this was by no means the only gate by which those superstitions were commended to the courtiers, and dependants of the emperors, at whose will and pleasure all the officers of the empire held their honors.

After subduing Maxentius, Constantine, A. D. 313, settled the government of Rome, and met Licinius in conference at Medislanum, and gave that Pagan his sister in marriage. They issued a joint decree, restoring to Christians liberty of conscience, and the restoration of the property of which they had been robbed. They also induced Maximinus in the East, to suspend the persecution which had commenced under Diocletian, and to allow Christians, in his dominions, to live in peace.

The first act of Constantine's life, in which he ventured to offend Paganism in favor of Christianity, appears to have been his neglect, A. D. 313, of the public games got up with great brilliancy in honor of the emperor and of the gods. To the great disappointment of the Romans, Constantine refused to attend.

Maximinus was a proud heathen. He claimed to be, and, in some respects, he was, the greatest of the three emperors. His pride and indolence together, betrayed him into a war with his neighbor Licinius, who beat him, and ruled over the East in his stead.

Licinius soon grew wearied of Christians in his prosperity; for he also had vices which they reproved. A mutual jealousy sprang up between him and Constantine, which was aggravated by their different religions. Constantine identified his interests with Christianity; and Licinius, his with Paganism. At length they armed, and fought with all their hosts and strength, in the name of their gods, for universal empire. Before joining battle, Licinius called his officers around him, in a grove, lighted with wax candles, and filled with images of the heathen gods, and there he put the question of their being the true gods, on the result of the battle and of the war, as that result might be determined by the courage of his army, and the favor of his gods; and he proclaimed to them, that if Constantine should be victorious, the new and strange god, whom Constantine worshiped, must be acknowledged to be supreme. They engaged. After contending all day, Licinius withdrew from the field. Constantine followed him into Thrace. They fought as before, Constantine having the advantage with great cost. By his own account, he owed the victory to the banner of his Cross, which inspired his soldiers with such courage, that wherever it came, they prevailed: and he, observing this, sent the banner to the place where the battle was the sorest, having fifty chosen men, whose sole care it was to defend the banner. Once the standard-bearer was slain, and a great cry arose, as if the ark was in danger, and the Pagan triumphed: and the Adversary did triumph, while Christians learned to shed human blood in behalf of the Prince of Peace and his Cross.

The emperors made peace, Licinius yielding Illirium, and retaining the remainder of his dominions, and his veneration for the heathen gods.

The next year saw the contest renewed, and Licinius defeated both by sea and land, receiving his life from the clemency of Constantine; and yet strangled by his own hand, or another's, shortly after.

Now possessed of universal empire, nothing withstood the will of Constantine but the ministers of the church, and chief of these, the Bishop of Rome. *Sozomenus,* an historian of that age, says: "Having subdued the whole empire, Constantine no longer concealed his natural temper, but indulging his passion, he did all things at will. He used the *sacred* rites of his ancestors, not so much in honor, as of necessity."

Sozomenus was a Pagan, and the rites which he calls *sacred,* were the pagan rites. These Constantine restored a year or two after the fall of Licinius, so far as to reinstate the public soothsayers, in order to please the Romans, who dearly loved their Pagan ceremonies, and confided in the gods of images. *Bar. An. A. D.* 320. *Sec.* 23. This favor toward the heathen discouraged the Christians, and subjected them to the taunts of the Pagans, who wished to make them join in the performance of the public sacrifices. The Bishop of Rome, Silvester, fled for his life, and concealed himself from the wrath of the emperor, which he had excited by opposition to Constantine's edicts in favor of the heathen worship.

The emperor, having offended the Pagans by his preference of Christians, and the Christians, by his temporizing with sin, and expelling the Bishop, next fell out with the heir of his throne, Crispus, his eldest son, and then with his wife, Fausta, both of whom he put to death, on slight grounds. By this time he was ready to recall the Bishop, and leave Rome. Rome could not endure two Cesars, one of the church, and one of the state. Constantine withdrew, and built the city of Constantinople. Here he ruled the empire without the restraints of the Roman Bishop; and the Roman Bishop ruled in the church with constantly increasing authority.

25

From this time the power of the Roman empire wanes, and the power of the Roman church waxes strong; but so slow was the revolution of power, that it was three hundred years yet before the Roman Bishop shook off the authority of the emperor, and before he, who withheld the Man of Sin in Paul's time, was taken quite away. (2 *Thess.* ii. 6 and 7.)

The occasion of his removal from the government of Rome was the publication of his edict against images, and image worship. The emperor saw that the church had fallen into idolatry, and with an earnest desire to correct the evil, he ordered the idols everywhere to be destroyed. The Bishop of Rome rebelled, on the ground, that the worship of images was a matter of church jurisdiction with which the emperor had no right to intermeddle; and, that custom and convenience, warranted their use in the churches, so that it was a sacrilege worthy of endless death, to enter the churches and destroy the images. The Bishop, therefore, hugged the idols, excommunicated the emperor, gradually shook off the yoke of the empire, from A. D. 725, to 750; and, by the year of our Lord 800, he is said to have put that triple crown on his own head, which he still wears to the end; a crown significant of the three domains of earth, which had fallen under his sway; and also of the sway he wields in and over the realms of heaven, earth, and hell; to bind and loose, to open and shut, to curse and to bless whomsoever he will, for time and eternity.

"The church of Rome has so closely copied the idolatrous superstitions of the Pagans, that all persons, not blinded by fanatic zeal for Rome, are struck with the great similarity. Their lighted candles, their frankincense, their images that came down from heaven, some of their ceremonies of the Mass, and many forms of their private worship, are just the same, as formed a part of the service done formerly to the idols of the heathen. Even the Pagan manner of acknowledging the pretended miracles by hanging up in the temples little figures of wax, or pictures representing the part of the body, which is supposed to have been supernaturally healed, or the accident from which the person escaped, is constantly practised wherever the Priests of Rome direct their flock, without fearing a laugh from their Protestant neighbors." J. B. White.

There is not a disease, not an evil, for which the Pope has not a *labeled* Saint, and his image; not a country of Christendom, nor an art, nor a calling in life, that has not its patron

Saint. Instead of the ancient deities, Jupiter, Apollo, Mars, Venus, Diana, and others, Rome now furnishes statues of the Virgin Mary, Peter, Paul, John, and others. Instead of the old household deities, the Roman catholic worships his guardian angel, and the Saint whose name he bears. And instead of the old local divinities, the Pope furnishes new ones, to preside over every department of nature's works, and to protect every part of the earth and of its inhabitants. St. Anthony, the Abbot, secures from fire; St. Anthony of Padua secures from water; St. Barbara, from the lightning; St. Blas, defends the throat; St. Lucia, the eyes; St. Polonia, the teeth; and, the Virgin Mary, they worship above all.

Her images are the most common. To her the prayer daily ascends. As the reader has seen it in this Narrative, so it will be found in all Roman countries; the sheet-anchor of a Roman's hope is grounded on the favor and protection of the Virgin.

Every day of the year has its Saint, with his image, and altar; and the Council of Trent command their images to be had, and retained, especially in the churches, and due honor and veneration rendered to them. The honor with which they are regarded, is referred to the Saints who are represented by them; " so that we adore Christ, and venerate the Saints, whose likenesses these images bear *when we kiss them; and uncover our heads, and prostrate ourselves, before them.*" (*Council of Trent, Sess.* 25.)

" What forbids," exclaims the historian of the Roman church, " what forbids the conversion of the profane rites to a sacred use, now they are sanctified by the word of God? Were not the holy vessels of the altar, by divine command, cast of Egyptian gold and silver? That many Pagan superstitions have been properly converted to Christian worship, by the example of many, and by the authority of the Fathers, has been demonstrated.—Who can justly complain, because the things formerly offered to idols, are now offered to the martyrs' (images?) What wonder, I say, if the most holy Bishops have converted to the worship of the true God, the customs, formed by the Pagans, from which it seems impossible to separate them, although they have become Christians." *Baronius, Vol.* 1. *p.* 599.

This reasoning shows Romanism in the light of Boodhism in Ceylon; (See the Missionary Herald, Sept. 1833;) and the historian of Rome might truly say: " When Messiah came, no place would receive him.   Potent as his worship became, and deeply rooted as his system has grown up, his Roman followers found idolatry too strong for them to overcome.   They, therefore, craftily intwined it with their own rites, and admitted images, angels, and Saints, to a part of the worship due to God alone; and, however the Messiah may be the object of veneration to a numerous and powerful Priesthood, it admits of a reasonable doubt, whether the great majority of Romans are not still the devoted followers of idolatry, image worship, and *demonolatry.*"   They have disregarded the command : " *Thou shalt not make unto thee any graven image, or the likeness of any thing in heaven, earth, or sea ; thou shalt not bow down to them, nor worship them ;*" but by the example of many, and the authority of the Fathers, they have made the command of no effect.   They have not regarded the fate of idolatrous Samaria ; nor have they feared to multiply images, and altars, and Priests, at a rate that would have overwhelmed the worshipers of Baal with shame; but firm on the rock Peter, and covered with the shield of conceited infallibility, they have fulfilled the Scriptures; and have brought the time near, which they have ripened the world for, when the earth shall be visited with those judgments which accompany the coming of the Son of·man, in his kingdom, to destroy Antichrist, and bring in everlasting righteousness.

Then will that reign come, for which we pray : " *thy kingdom come ;*" then will be fulfilled to Peter that word : " *I will give unto thee the keys of the kingdom of heaven,*" (Matt. xvi. 19 ;) then will Paul receive the " *crown of righteousness, which the Lord, the righteous judge, shall give me at that day ; and not to me only, but unto all them also that love his appearing,*" (2 Tim. iv. 8 ;) and then shall the twelve Apostles know, and understand this word : " *Verily, I say unto you,* (that ye which have followed me in the regeneration,) *when the Son of man shall sit in the throne of his glory, ye also shall sit upon twelve thrones, judging the twelve tribes of Israel.*"   (Matt. xix. 28.)

THE END.

LEAVITT, LORD & CO.

PUBLISHERS AND BOOKSELLERS,

No. 180 BROADWAY.

NEW-YORK.

JONATHAN LEAVITT,
CHARLES AUSTIN LORD,
WILLIAM ROBINSON.

A constant supply of all Books needed in a Theological, Classical and Primary Education. Also,

BIBLES of all the different kinds, from PLAIN and POLY-GLOTT 32mo., to BAGSTER'S elegant FOLIO, London Edition. All the BIBLICAL COMMENTARIES, in common use; A variety of HYMN BOOKS.

SCHOOL BOOKS, in every variety and quantity, at the *lowest Pearl-street prices.* Country merchants and all wanting books, are requested to call before purchasing elsewhere.

MISCELLANEOUS WORKS. An assortment of a Religious and Moral Character; with BIOGRAPHIES, MEMOIRS, TRAVELS, &c. &c.

NEW AMERICAN PUBLICATIONS on every subject of interest, regularly received.

Among many Valuable Works Published by L. L. & Co. are the following :

CALMET'S DICTIONARY OF THE BIBLE REVISED, with large additions. By Prof. ROBINSON. With maps and plates. Royal 8vo. sheep.

Also, AN ABRIDGMENT for young persons, with maps. 12mo. sheep,

"A sufficient testimony to the excellency of this great Dictionary of the Bible is, that it has been translated into the Latin, Dutch, Italian, and Spanish languages. This book is one which, to those who are studying the Bible, *it will be expensive* not *to purchase.*"—*Spirit of Pilgrims.*

COMMENTARY ON THE BOOK OF PSALMS. No. 1, Ps. 1—3. [To be published in periodical numbers.] By GEO. BUSH, Professor of Hebrew and Oriental Literature, in the New-York City University. 1834. No. 2 in Press.

As the several Psalms have no special connection with each other, and each of the numbers may be considered complete on the portion it embraces, a periodical issue was thought preferable to a delay of two or three years in publishing the entire work. The numbers will be publish ed at intervals of about three months, at 50 cents a number, and will extend to ten or twelve.

SCOTT'S FAMILY BIBLE. 6 Vols. 8vo. sheep.

RECOMMENDATIONS OF BARNES' NOTES.

From Abbott's Religious Magazine.

We have previously, in a brief notice, recommended to our readers Barnes' Notes on the Gospels. But a more extended acquaintance with that work has very much increased our sense of its value. We never have opened any commentary on the Gospels, which has afforded us so much satisfaction. Without intending, in the least degree, to disparage the many valuable commentaries which now aid the Christian in the study of the Bible, we cannot refrain from expressing our gratitude to the Author, for the interesting and profitable instructions he has given us.— The volumes are characterized by the following merits.

1. The spirit which imbues them is highly devotional. It is a devotion founded on knowledge. It is a zeal guided by discretion.
2. The notes are eminently intellectual. Apparent difficulties are fairly met. They are either explained, or the want of a fully satisfactory explanation admitted. There is none of that slipping by a knot which is too common in many commentaries.
3. The notes are written in language definite, pointed and forcible. There is no interminable flow of lazy words. Every word is active and does its work well. There are no fanciful expositions. There are no tedious display of learning.

There may be passages in which we should differ from the writer in some of the minor shades of meaning. There may be sometimes an unguarded expression which has escaped our notice. We have not scrutinized the volumes with the eye of a critic. But we have used them in our private reading. We have used them in our family. And we have invariably read them with profit and delight.

We have just opened the book to select some passage as an illustration of the spirit of the work. The Parable of the rich man and Lazarus now lies before us. The notes explanatory of the meaning of the parables, are full and to the point. The following are the inferences, which Mr. Barnes deduces.

"From this impressive and instructive parable, we may learn,
"1. That the souls of men do not die with their bodies.
"2. That the souls of men are *conscious* after death; that they do not sleep, as some have supposed, till the morning of the resurrection.
"3. That the righteous are taken to a place of happiness immediately at death, and the wicked consigned to misery.
"4. That wealth does not secure us from death.

"How vain are riches to secure
Their haughty owners from the grave.

"The rich, the beautiful, the gay, as well as the poor, go down to the grave. All their pomp and apparel; all their honors, their palaces and their gold cannot save them. Death can as easily find his way into the mansions of the rich as into the cottages of the poor, and the rich shall turn to the same corruption, and soon, like the poor, be undistinguished from common dust, and be unknown.
"5. We should not envy the condition of the rich.

"On slippery rocks I see them stand,
And fiery billows roll below.

"6. We should strive for a better inheritance, than can be possessed in this life.

"'Now I esteem their mirth and wine,
Too dear to purchase with my blood,
Lord 'tis enough that *thou* art mine,
My life, my portion, and my God.'"

"7. The sufferings of the wicked in hell will be indiscribably great. Think what is represented by *torment*, by burning flame, by insupportable thirst, by that state when a single drop of water would afford relief. Remember that all this is but a representation of the pains of the damned, and that this will have no relief, day nor night, but will continue from

2

RECOMMENDATIONS OF BARNES' NOTES.

year to year, and age to age, and without any end, and you have a faint view of the sufferings of those who are in hell.

"8. There is a place of suffering beyond the grave, a hell. If there is not, then this parable has no meaning. It is impossible to make anything of it unless it is designed to teach that.

"9. There will never be any escape from those gloomy regions. There is a gulf fixed—*fixed*, not moveable. Nor can any of the damned beat a pathway across this gulf, to the world of holiness.

"10. We see the amazing folly of those, who suppose there may be an *end* to the sufferings of the wicked, and who on that supposition seem willing to go down to hell to suffer a long time, rather than go at once to heaven. If man were to suffer but a thousand years, or even *one* year, why should he be so foolish as to choose that suffering, rather than go at once to heaven, and be happy at once when he dies?

"11. God gives us warning sufficient to prepare for death. He has sent his word, his servants, his son; he warns us by his Spirit and his providence, by the entreaties of our friends, and by the death of sinners. He offers us heaven, and he threatens hell. If all this will not move sinners, what *would* do it? There is nothing that would.

"12. God will give us nothing farther to warn us. No dead man will come to life, to tell us what he has seen. If he did, we would not believe him. Religion appeals to man, not by ghosts and frightful apparitions. It appeals to their reason, their conscience, their hopes, and their fears.— It sets life and death soberly before men, and if they will not choose the former they must die. If you will not hear the Son of God, and the truth of the Scriptures, there is nothing which you will or can hear; you will never be persuaded, and never will escape the place of torment."

If we have any influence with our readers. we would recommend them to buy these volumes. There is hardly any Christian in the land, who will not find them an invaluable treasure.

Extract of a Letter from a distinguished Divine of New England.

It (Barnes' Notes) supplies an important and much needed desideratum in the means of Sabbath School and Bible Class instruction.

Without descending to minute criticism, or attempting a display of learning, it embraces a wide range of general reading, and brings out the results of an extended and careful investigation of the most important sources of Biblical knowledge.

The style of the work is as it should be, plain, simple, direct; often vigorous and striking; always serious and earnest.

It abounds in fine analyses of thought and trains of argument, admirably adapted to aid Sabbath School Teachers in their responsible duties: often too, very useful to Ministers when called suddenly to prepare for religious meetings, and always helpful in conducting the exercises of a Bible Class.

Without vouching for the correctness of every explanation and sentiment contained in the Notes, its author appears to have succeeded very happily in expressing the mind of the Holy Spirit as revealed in those parts of the New Testament which he has undertaken to explain.

The theology taught in these volumes, drawn as it is from the pure fountain of truth, is eminently common sense and practical.

It has little to do with theory or speculation.

The author appears not to be unduly wedded to any particular school or system of theology, but to have a mind trained to habits of independent thinking, readily submissive to the teachings of inspiration, but indisposed to call any man master, or to set up anything in opposition to the plain testimony of the Bible.

We would here say, once for all, we consider Barnes' Notes the best commentary for families we have seen.—*N. E. Spectator.*

RECOMMENDATIONS OF BARNES' NOTES.

If the degree of popular favor with which a work of biblical instruction is received by an intelligent Christian community be a just criterion of its value, the volumes which the Rev. Mr. Barnes is giving the Church are entitled to a high place in the scale of merit.—*N. Y. Evangelist.*

From Review of the Gospels in Biblical Repertory.

We have only to say further, by way of introduction, that we admire the practical wisdom evinced by Mr. Barnes in selecting means by which to act upon the public mind, as well as his self-denying diligence in laboring to supply the grand defect of our religious education. Masterly exposition, in a popular form, is the great desideratum of the Christian public.

The Notes are always readable, and almost always to the point. Nothing appears to have been said for the sake of saying something. This is right. It is the only principle on which our books of popular instruction can be written with success. Its practical value is evinced by the extensive circulation of the work before us, as well as by the absence of that heaviness and langour, which inevitably follow from a verbose style, or the want of a definite object.

Mr. Barnes' explanations are in general brief and clear, comprising the fruit of very diligent research.

We have been much pleased with his condensed synopsis of the usual arguments on some disputed points, as well as with his satisfactory solution of objections.

But Mr. Barnes' has not been satisfied with merely explaining the language of the text. He has taken pains to add those illustrations which verbal exposition, in the strict sense cannot furnish. The book is rich in archæological information. All that could well be gathered from the common works on biblical antiquities, is wrought into the Notes upon those passages which need such elucidation.

In general we admire the skill with which he sheds the light of archæology and history upon the text of scripture, and especially the power of compression which enables him to crowd a mass of knowledge into a narrow space without obscurity.

While the explanation of the text is the primary object kept in view throughout these notes, religious edification is by no means slighted. Mr. Barnes' devotional and practical remarks bear a due proportion to the whole.

From what we have said it follows of course, that the work before us has uncommon merit. Correct explanation, felicitous illustration, and impressive application, are the characteristic attributes of a successful commentary. Though nothing can be added in the way of commendation which is not involved in something said already, there are two detached points which deserve perhaps to be distinctly stated. We are glad to see that Mr. Barnes not only shuns the controversial mode of exposition, but often uses expressions on certain disputed subjects, which in their obvious sense, convey sound doctrine in its strictest form. What variety of meaning these expressions may admit of, or are likely to convey, we do not know; but we are sure that in their simple obvious meaning they are strongly Calvanistic in the good old sense.

The other point to which we have alluded is Mr. Barnes' frankness and decision in condemning fanatical extravagance and inculcating Christian prudence.

With respect to Mr. Barnes' style we have little to say beyond a general commendation. The pains which he has wisely taken to be brief, have compelled him to write well.

THE SOCIAL FIRE-SIDE LIBRARY.

FIRE-SIDE SERIES. A series of 18mo volumes, (of a popular and practical character,) of original and select works prepared expressly for it, illustrating the religious and moral duties of life, family duties and responsibilities, especially those of parents to children, and children to parents, &c. The plan, in a word, includes all those subjects which may afford useful interesting family reading. Several volumes, embellished with steel engravings, are already published, others are in press, from the pens of Rev. Messrs. H. Hooker, T. H. Gallaudet, (late Principal of the American Asylum for the Deaf and Dumb,) Jacob Abbott, (author of the Young Christian,) and others, equally distinguished for their success in writing for children. These volumes consist of 250 pages, retail at 50 cents, and are sold singly or in sets, as preferred.

Vol. I.—FIRE-SIDE PIETY.
Vol. II.—THE MOTHER'S FRIEND.
Vol. III.—CHINA AND THE ENGLISH.
Vol. IV.—REAL DIALOGUES ON THE EVIDENCES OF CHRISTIANITY.

JUVENILE SERIES.—A new series of small volumes, designed for the moral and religious improvement of children, has just been commenced.

Vol. I.—WAY FOR A CHILD TO BE SAVED.
Vol. II.—EVERY DAY DUTY.

CHILD'S BOOK on the Sabbath. By Rev. H. HOOKER. Giving in an intelligent but interesting style an account of the institution of the Sabbath, its change, design, means of observance, &c. &c.

BIBLE STORIES for children. By Rev. T. H. GALLAUDET.

CHILD AT HOME, or the principles of Filial Duty familiarly illustrated. By J. S. C. ABBOTT.

With many other valuable and interesting books suitable for children and youth, and for Sabbath School Libraries.,

THE EVERY DAY CHRISTIAN. By Rev. T. H. GALLAUDET.

MOTHER AT HOME, or principles of Maternal Duty familiarly illustrated. By J. S. C. ABBOTT.

FAMILY AT HOME, or familiar illustrations of the various Domestic Duties. By G. D. ABBOTT.

PIKE'S GUIDE TO YOUNG DISCIPLES.

PIKE'S RELIGIOUS AND ETERNAL LIFE, or Irreligion and Perpetual Ruin.

DAILY DUTIES. By A Married Lady. 12mo.

PAYSON'S FAMILY SERMONS. Sermons for Christian Families, by EDWARD PAYSON, D. D. 18mo.

EVENING EXERCISES for the Closet, for every day in the year. By WM. JAY. Stereotype edition. The superior excellence of this work is universally admitted. Several thousand copies have already been circulated.

PORTER'S RHETORICAL READER, 16th edition.

PORTER'S ANALYSIS OF THE PRINCIPLES OF RHETORICAL DELIVERY.

STONE'S CHILD'S READER, on a new and popular plan. 18mo.

MEMOIRS OF HARLAN PAGE.

BIOGRAPHIES OF DR. PAYSON, MRS. HUNTINGTON, BURDER, HALYBURTON, J. B. TAYLOR, &c.

MEMOIR OF Mrs. MIRON WINSLOW, late Missionary to India. By her husband, Rev. MIRON WINSLOW. In a neat 12mo. with a Portrait.

WILBERFORCE'S PRACTICAL VIEW OF CHRISTIANITY, with an Introductory Essay, by the Rev. DANIEL WILSON, D. D. 18mo. new edition, with a steel portrait.

DR. PAYSON'S SELECT THOUGHTS. 32mo.

THE RELIGIOUS OFFERING. Here the religious portion of the reading community are presented with a book, that will carry to their children and friends, in as attractive a form as possible, those great truths that relate to man as a moral, responsible, and religious being.

POLYMICRIAN TESTAMENT. 32mo. This Testament contains a very copious selection of *really* parallel passages, being, with *some additions*, the same as are found in the English Polyglot. It has the various readings in a centre column, and short explanatory notes, that will be acceptable to a numerous class of readers—besides 5 maps illustrative of the holy theatre of Christ's and his apostles' labors. This *multum in parvo* book is ornamented by a page exhibiting specimens of 48 *different* languages.

BARNES' "SCRIPTURAL ARGUMENT OF EPISCOPACY" EXAMINED. 18mo.

BUTLER'S ANALOGY OF RELIGION, with an Essay by Rev. A. BARNES. Stereotype edition. 12mo.

ELEMENTS OF MENTAL AND MORAL SCIENCE, designed to exhibit the Original Susceptibilities of the Mind, and the Rules by which the Rectitude of any of its states of feeling should be judged. By GEORGE PAYNE, D. D. *Second* American edition, in one volume, 12mo.

ZINZENDORFF, A NEW ORIGINAL POEM, by Mrs. SIGOURNEY, with minor Poems. In a neat 12mo. volume.

LECTURES ON REVIVALS OF RELIGION. By Rev. C. G. FINNEY, of Chatham-street Chapel, New-York. 1 vol. 12mo.

FOREIGN CONSPIRACY AGAINST THE UNITED STATES. By "BRUTUS." 2d. edition.

JUDGE JAY ON COLONIZATION AND ANTI-SLAVERY. 12mo. 2d. edition.

BIOGRAPHIA LITERARIA, or Sketches of my Literary Life and Opinions. By S. T. COLERIDGE. New edition. 8vo.

NATURAL HISTORY OF ENTHUSIASM, 4th edition.

SATURDAY EVENING. By the same author. 4th edition. 12mo.

FANATICISM. By the same author.

POLITICAL DESPOTISM. By the same. Just Published.

HEBREW GRAMMAR. By GEO. BUSH, Professor of Oriental Languages in the New-York University.

MOTHER'S PRIMER, to teach a child its letters, and how to read. By Rev. T. H. GALLAUDET.

LEAVITT, LORD & CO.'S LIST

of some of the more important

STANDARD WORKS,

On various subjects, which may always be obtained at the lowest prices.

---

1. COMMENTARIES

On the whole Scriptures.

SCOTT, in 6 volumes or 3.   FAMILY COMMENTARY, 1 volume.
HENRY, in 6 volumes or 3.   COMPREHENSIVE do.
CLARKE, in 6 volumes or 3.   MANT & D'OYLEY, 2 volumes.
GILL, 9 volumes 4to.

On the New Testament.

BARNES' NOTES ON THE GOSPELS, in 2 volumes.
Do.   do.   ACTS, in 1 volume.
Do.   do.   ROMANS, in 1 volume.
BURKITT ON THE NEW TESTAMENT.
DODDRIDGE'S PARAPHRASE, &c. in 1 volume.
MACKNIGHT ON THE EPISTLES, in 1 volume.
STUART ON THE HEBREWS, in 1 volume.
Do.   ON THE ROMANS, in 1 volume.
BLOOMFIELD'S CRITICAL DIGEST, in 8 volumes.

German Authors.

CALVIN,   HEGSTENBERG,   NEANDER,
DE WETTE,   HUG,   ROSENMUELLER,
EICHORN,   KUINOEL,   TITTMANN,
FLATT,   KOPP,   THOLUCK.
GESENIUS,   LUCKE.

---

2. THEOLOGY AND DIVINITY.

The Complete Works of

BARROW, 7 vols.   FOSTER.   LIGHTFOOT, 13 vols.
BAXTER, 23 vols.   FULLER, 2 vols.   MASON, 4 vols.
BERKELEY, 3 vols.   GURNALL, 4 vols.   NEWTON, (Bp.) 1 vol.
BEVERIDGE, 10 vols.   HENRY, 1 vol.   NEWTON, (J.) 2 vols.
BICKERSTETH, 1 vol.   HERVEY, 6 vols.   OWEN, 21 vols.
BUTLER, (Bp.) 1 vol. HOOKER.   PALEY, 6 vols.
BUNYAN, 1 vol,   HORNE, (Bp.) 1 vol.   SECKER, 6 vols.
CAMPBELL, 3 vols,   HORNE, (T. H.) 4 vols. SMITH, (J. P.) 4 vols.
CALMET, 1 vol.   HALL, (Bp.) 2 vols.   SHERLOCK, 5 vols.
DICK, 4 vols.   HALL, (Robt.) 3 vols. SIMEON, 21 vols.
DODDRIDGE, 1 vol.   HORSELEY, 1 vol.   TAYLOR, (Jer.) 5 vols
DWIGHT, 4 vols.   HOWE, (Jno.) 1 vol.   TOPLADY, 6 vols.
EDWARDS, 10 vols.   JAHN, 1 vol.   WARBURTON.
ERSKINE.   JAY, (Wm.) 3 vols.   WARDLAW.
FABER.   LARDNER, 10 vols.   WATTS.
FLAVEL, 6 vols.   LEIGHTON, 1 vol.

3. ETHICS, MORALS, ELOQUENCE, &c.

ABERCROMBIE,	COLERIDGE,	LOCKE,
ALISON,	COMBE,	PAINE,
BACON,	DEWAR,	REID,
BROWN,	DEGERANDO,	SPURZHEIM,
BURKE,	DYMOND,	STEWART,
BURTON,	GOOD,	WAYLAND

---

4. HISTORY.

UNITED STATES.—*Bancroft's*, 5 vols.—*Grahame's*, 2 vols.—*Holmes's*, 2 vols.—*Pitkin*, 2 vols. 8vo.—*Ramsay*, 3 vols.—*Willard's*, 1 vol.

ENGLAND.—*Goldsmith.—Hume, Smollett, & Miller*, 4 vols.—*Hallam*, 3 vols.—*Lingard*, 12 vols.—*Mackintosh*, 1 vol. 8vo.

SCOTLAND.—*Scott*, 2 vols.—*Robertson*, 1 vol.

EUROPE, (MODERN.)—*Russell & Jones*, 3 vols.—*Robertson's Charles V.—Heeren's Polit. System*, 2 vols.—*Crowe's France*, 3 vols.—*Sismondi's Italy*, 1 vol.—*Grattan's Netherlands*, 1 vol.—*Fletcher's Poland*, 1 vol.—*Mills's Chivalry and Crusades*, 4 vols.—*Venetian History*, 2 vols.—*Florence*, 2 vols.

ANCIENT, (UNIVERSAL.)—*Rollin*, 2 vols., 4 vols. or 8 vols.—*Heeren*, 1 vol.

GREECE.—*Gillies'*, 1 vol.—*Frost*, 1 vol.—*Heeren*, 1 vol.—*Mitford*, 8 vols.

ROME.—*Ferguson*, 1 vol.—*Hooke*, 3 vols.—*Livy*, (by Baker,) 2 vols.—*Tacitus*, 1 vol.—*Gibbon's Decline and Fall*, 1 vol. or 4 vols.

AFRICA.—*Heeren*, 2 vols.—ASIA.—*Heeren*, 3 vols.

EGYPT.—*Russell*, 18mo.—PALESTINE.—*Russell*, 18mo.

THE JEWS.—*Millman*, 3 vols.

UNIVERSAL.—*Frost*, 1 vol.—*Muller*, 4 vols.—*Robbins*, 1 vol.—*Tytler*, 1 vol.—*Whelpley*, 1 vol.

ECCLESIASTICAL.—*Goodrich*, (Elements,) 12mo.
Marsh, do. 12mo.
Milner, with continuation, 1 vol. 8vo.
Mosheim, do. 3 vols. or 2 vols.
Waddington, do. 1 vol.
Burnet's Reformation in England, 4 vols.
Eusebius's Ecc. Hist. First Six Centuries, 1 vol.
Scott's Lutheran Reformation, 2 vols. 18mo.
Smedley's Reformed Religion in France.
Winslow's Sketch of Missions, 12mo.
History of Popery, 12mo. *Of the Inquisition*, 12mo.

5. BIOGRAPHY.

LNDER THE GREAT, 18mo.
:R, (Rev. R.) 2 vols. 8vo.
LRIUS, 12mo.
'ARTE, various.
l,   do.
l,   do.
:R, (Rev. Geo.) 12mo.
', (Sebas.) 8vo.
LES THE FIRST, 2 vols.
LEMAGNE, 18mo.
TMAS, (Rev. J. S.) 18mo.
:E, (Adam,) 12mo.
JN, (De Witt,) 4to.
RN, (Z.) 12mo.
IDGE, (S. T.) 8vo.
IBUS, (C.) 2 vols. 8vo.
4ER, (Archb.) 2 vols. 18mo.
VELL, (Oliver,) 2 vols. 18mo.
t, (Baron,) 12mo.
.E SOVEREIGNS, 2 vols. 16mo.
RICK THE GREAT, 2 vols. 18mo.
iE IV., 18mo.
LM, (Isabella,) 12mo.
LM, (Mary Jane,) 12mo.
(Rev. Robt.) 18mo.
TON, (Alex.) 8vo.
., (Bp.) 2 vols. 8vo.
', (Patrick,) 8vo.
Rowland,) 12mo.
RD, (John,) 18mo.
S, 2 vols. 18mo.
iohn,) 2 vols. 8vo.
ON, (Dr.) 2 vols. 8vo.
N, (Mrs.) 18mo.
HINE, (Empress,) 18mo.

LAFAYETTE, 2 vols. 18mo.
LEO THE TENTH, 4 vols. 8vo.
LORENZO DE MEDICI, 2 vols. 8vo
MARY QUEEN OF SCOTS, 2 vols. 18mo.
MARTYN, (Henry,) 12mo.
MARION, (Gen.) 12mo.
MILTON, (John,) 12mo.
MOHAMMED, (by Bush,) 18mo.
MORE, (Hannah,) 2 vols. 12mo.
MORRIS, (Governeur,) 3 vols. 8vo.
NAVIGATORS, (early,) 18mo.
NELSON, (Lord,) 18mo.
NEWTON, (Sir Isaac,) 18mo.
NEY, (Marshal,) 12mo.
PAGE, (Harlan,) 18mo.
PAINTERS AND SCULPTORS, 3 v. 18mo.
PAYSON, (Rev. Dr.) 12mo.
PETER THE GREAT, 18mo.
PLUTARCH'S LIVES, 8vo.
ROSCOE, (Wm.) 2 vols. 12mo.
SCHILLER, (Fred.) 12mo.
SCOTT, (Sir W.)
SIDDONS, (Mrs.) 12mo.
TAYLOR, (J. B.) 12mo.
THORBURN, (Grant,) 12mo.
TRAVELLERS, (celebrated,) 3 vols. 18mo.
WASHINGTON, (George,) 2 vols. 8vo.
WELLINGTON, (Duke of,) 2 vols. 12mo.
WESLEY, (Rev. J.) 12mo.
WICLIF, (John,) 18mo.
WINSLOW, (Mrs. M.) 12mo.
WILLIAMS, (Roger,) 12mo.
WOMEN, (celebrated,) 2 vols. 12mo.
WONDERFUL CHARACTERS, 8vo.

---

6. VOYAGES AND TRAVELS.

l Adventures, &c.
son, in Greece, 12mo.
w, in Malta, &c. 8vo.
, in Europe, 2 vols.
Voyages, 2 vols.
on Columbia River, 8vo.
izes, in Great Britain, 12mo.
t, in New England, 4 vols.
in Polynesia, 4 vols.
ng, round the World, 1 vol.
ff, in China, 1 vol.
ton, in United States, 2 vols.

Henderson, in Iceland, 12mo.
Humboldt, in S. America, &c. 18mo.
Jameson, in Italy and Germany, 2 v.
Kay, in Caffraria, &c. 12mo.
Lander, in Africa, 2 vols.
Modern Traveller, 10 vols.
Morrell, round the World, 8vo.
Pardoe, in Portugal, 2 vols.
Owen, in Africa, 2 vols.
Polar Seas and Regions, 18mo.
Rush's Residence at London, 8vo.
Stewart, in South Seas, 2 vols.

Stewart, in Great Britain, 2 vols.
Visit to Texas.
Walsh, in Brazil, 2 vols.

Wines' Naval Sketches, 2 vols.
Willard's France and Great Britain.

---

7. SCIENCES AND ARTS.

NATURAL PHILOSOPHY.—*Arnott's* Physics, 2 vols.—*Cavallo's* Philos., 1 vol.—Library U. K. Treatise, 2 vols.—*Olmsted,* 2 vols.

CHEMISTRY.—*Brande,* 2 vols. 8vo.—*Eaton,* 12mo.—*Mitchell,* 8vo.—*Porter,* 2 vols. 8vo.—*Silliman,* 2 vols. 8vo.—*Turner,* 12mo.—*Webster,* 8vo.

MEDICINE.—*Bell, Broussais, Brigham, Cloquet, Combe, Cooper, Doane, Dunglisson, Dewees, Eberle, Good, Halsted, Hitchcock, Hooper, Macnish, Magendie, Paris, Richerand, Spurzheim,* &c. &c.

NATURAL HISTORY.—*Buffon,* 5 vols.—*Cuvier,* 4 vols.—*Godman,* 3 vols.—*Goldsmith,* 4 vols.—*Nutall,* (Ornithol.) 2 vols.—*Smellie,* 1 vol.

BOTANY.—*Comstock, Eaton, Lindley, Lincoln, Torrey.*

ARCHITECTURE.—*Benjamin, La Fevre, Nicholson, Shaw.*

---

8. POETRY.

Adams, Aikin, Addison, Baillie, (Joanna,) 1 vol.—*Bloomfield, Bowles, Beattie, Bryant,* 1 vol.—*Burns,* 1 vol.—*Butler, Brooks, Byron, Campbell,* 1 vol.—*Child,* (Mrs.) *Cheever, Coleridge,* 3 vols. *Cowper,* 1 vol.—*Crabbe,* 8 vols.—*Collins, Davidson,* (L. M.) 1 vol.—*Dryden, Falconer, Gay, Gray, Goldsmith, Halleck, Heber, Hemans, Hogg, Hoole, Keats, Mellen,* (Grenville,) *Millman, Milton, Montgomery, Moore, Norton,* (Mrs.) *Percival, Pollok, Pope, Rogers, Shenstone, Somerville, Scott, Southey, Shakspeare, Shelley, Tappan, Thomson, White, Willis, Woodworth, Wordsworth, Young.*

---

9. EDUCATION.

GENERAL TREATISES.—*Abbott, Alcott,* Am. Inst. Lectures, *Babington, Dwight, Edgeworth, Hall, Hamilton, Mitchill, Phelps, Simpson, Taylor, Wood.*

SPELLING BOOKS.—*Cobb, Cummings, Emerson, Parley, Picket, Sears, Webster, Worcester.*

READING BOOKS, (Elementary.)—Am. Pop. Lessons, Child's Instr.
Cobb, No. 1, 2 and 3.—*Colburn, Emerson, Hall, Pierpont,
Putnam.*

———— (Advanced.)—*Angel, Bailey,* (Young Ladies',)
Emerson, (G. B.) *Emerson,* (B. D.) *Pierpont, Porter,
Putnam, Sullivan, Worcester.*

ELOCUTION.—*Barber, Emerson, Lovell, Putnam, Porter, Russell.*

GRAMMAR.—*Brown, Greenleaf, Hall, Ingersoll, Kirkham,
Murray, Parker, Smith, Van Doren, Webster.*

RHETORIC.—*Blair, Jamieson, Mills, Whately.*

LOGIC.—*Hedge, Jamieson, Whately.*

DICTIONARY.—*Cobb, Grimshaw, Walker, Webster.*

GEOGRAPHY.—*Adams, Blake, Beecher, Cummings, Clute,
Fowle, Goodrich,* (3 kinds,) *Hall, Olney, Parley, Willett,
Willard, Woodbridge, Worcester.*

HISTORY.—*Davenport, Goodrich, Grimshaw, Hale, Parley,
Webster,* and *Willard's* UNITED STATES.
Goldsmith, Grimshaw, Pinnock, and *Robbins's* ENGLAND.
Grimshaw's FRANCE.—*Parley's* EUROPE.
Frost, Grimshaw, Peabody, and *Robbins's* GREECE.
Grimshaw, and *Parley's* ROME.—*Parley's* ANCIENT generally.
Frost, Robbins, Tytler, Wells, Whelpley, Worcester's UNIVER.

CHRONOLOGY.—*Blair, Putnam.* MYTHOLOGY.—*Dillaway, Moritz,
Robbins, Tooke.*

NATURAL PHILOSOPHY.—*Blake, Blair, Comstock, Grund, Jones.*

CHEMISTRY.—*Beck, Comstock, Grund, Jones, Lincoln, Turner.*

MINERALOGY.—*Comstock, Shepherd.*

BOTANY.—*Blake, Comstock, Eaton, Lindley, Lincoln, Torrey.*

ASTRONOMY.—*Blake, Burritt, Grund, Guy, Ostrander, Wilbur,
Wilkins.*

ARITHMETIC.—*Adams, Babcock, Cobb, Colburn,* (2,) *Daboll, Davis
Davies, Emerson,* (3,) *Hall, Parker, Smith, Smiley.*

BOOK-KEEPING.—*Bennett, Edwards, Goddard, Marsh, Preston.*

MATHEMATICS.—*Cambridge Course, Day, Hutton, Young.*

ALGEBRA.—*Bonnycastle, Bourdon, Bridge, Colburn, Day,
Davies, Euler, Grund, Ryan, Young.*

GEOMETRY.—*Euclid,* (Playfair, Simpson,) *Grund, Legendre*

MECHANICS.—*Bouchalart, Farrar, Renwick, Young.*

MENSURATION.—*Bonnycastle, Day.*

SURVEYING.—*Davies, Day, Flint.*

CALCULUS.—*Farrar, Ryan, Young.*

CLASSICAL STUDIES.

LATIN GRAMMAR.—*Adams, Patterson, Ross, Ruddimann.*

—— READER.—*Jacobs, Walker.*

—— LEXICON.—*Ainsworth*, 18mo., 8vo., royal 8vo.

—— CLASSICS, (with notes,)—*Cæsar, Cicero, C. Nepos, Erasmus,—Horace, Livy, Ovid, Sallust, Tacitus, Virgil.*—Also, Leipsic and London editions of others.

GREEK GRAMMAR.—*Buttman, Fiske, Goodrich, Valpy.*

—— READER.—*Jacobs.*—LEXICON.—*Donnegan, Groves.*

—— CLASSICS, (with notes.)—*Æschylus, Demosthenes, Herodotus, Homer, Plato, Thucydides, Xenophon,* and Leipsic and London editions of the whole.

FRENCH GRAMMAR.—*Bœuf, Levizac, Perrin, Surrault, Wanostrocht.*

—— LEXICON.—*Boyer, Meadows, Nugent, Wilson.*

—— ELEMENTARY.—*Bolmar, Longfellow, Perrin,* &c.

SPANISH GRAMMAR.—*Cubi, Josse, Sales.*

—— LEXICON.—*Newman.*

ITALIAN GRAMMAR.—*Bachi.*—LEXICON.—*Baretti.*

GERMAN GRAMMAR.—*Bernay, Follen.*—READER.—*Ibid.*

HEBREW GRAMMAR.—*Bush, Frey, Seixas, Stuart, Stowe.*

—— LEXICON.—*Gesenius, Gibbs, Parkhurst, Robinson.*

———

10. MISCELLANIES.

ENCYCLOPÆDIA.—*Americana*, 13 vols.—*Britannica, Edinburgh,* 20 vols.—*Metropolitana,* 3 vols.

FICTION.—*Bulwer, Cooper, Edgeworth, Fielding, Galt, Godwin, Irving, James, Mackenzie, Paulding Porter, Richardson, Sherwood, Simms, Sedgwick, Scott,* &c. &c.

LIBRARIES AND COLLECTIONS.—Harper's Family Library, Theological, Juvenile, Classical, Dramatic.—*Lardner's* Cabinet Cyclopædia,—*Dove's* English Classics, *Constable's* Miscellany, Religious Library, Select do., &c.

———

The above forms part of the *outline* of a new and extensive Catalogue of Books *now to be obtained in the United States,* preparing by Leavitt, Lord, & Co.

Printed in the United States
149181LV00008B/156/A

9 781437 245370